Yardsticks For Failure

IVO GRAHAM

Yardsticks For Failure

ADVENTURES IN FRIENDSHIP AND FLUSTER

HEADLINE

All photos and drawings courtesy of the author except page 13,
credit: Avalon / Channel 4 and page 51, credit: Cinematic Collection,
THE WEINSTEIN COMPANY
Heart mosaic designed by William Andrews

First published in 2025 by Headline Publishing Group Limited

3

Cataloguing in Publication Data is available from the British Library

Hardback ISBN 978 1 0354 1130 6

Typeset in Monotype Sabon by CC Book Production
Printed and bound in Great Britain by Clays Ltd, Elcograf S.p.A.

MIX
Paper | Supporting
responsible forestry
FSC
www.fsc.org
FSC® C104740

Headline's policy is to use papers that are natural, renewable and recyclable
products and made from wood grown in well-managed forests and other
controlled sources. The logging and manufacturing processes are expected
to conform to the environmental regulations of the country of origin.

HEADLINE PUBLISHING GROUP
An Hachette UK Company
Carmelite House
50 Victoria Embankment
London EC4Y 0DZ

The authorised representative in the EEA is Hachette Ireland, 8 Castlecourt
Centre, Dublin 15, D15 XTP3, Ireland (email: info@hbgi.ie)

www.headline.co.uk
www.hachette.co.uk

For Tom, who always wrote things down

In this our first piece, the artist leaves the viewer to decide which of the three characters is beckoning the other(s), but one thing is for sure: books are involved. A literary yet playful tone is immediately established.

Contents

'I wundure were the story will tok use. I do not kno.'
A piercing reflection of the uncertainty we all may feel at this
point in the book, and in life in general, regardless
of the size of our ears.

INTRODUCTION

Caveat Town

And you may ask yourself, how did I get here?
  1990: Ivo is born
  1991: Ivo starts to laugh
  1992: Ivo's sister is born
  1993: Ivo starts to seek attention
  1994: Ivo moves to near Swindon
  1995: Ivo's brother is born
  1996: Ivo starts to make jokes
  1997: Ivo starts to annoy his family
  1998: Ivo goes to boarding school (1)

1999: Ivo starts supporting Swindon Town
2000: Ivo watches first Swindon Town relegation
2001: Ivo moves to Australia for two years
2002: Ivo does first long-distance run
2003: Ivo goes to first music gig (Linkin Park)
2004: Ivo goes to boarding school (2)
2005: Ivo watches first comedy gig (Bill Bailey)
2006: Ivo watches second Swindon Town relegation
2007: Ivo impresses university tutors at interview
2008: Ivo disappoints university tutors by starting stand-up
2009: Ivo wins 'So You Think You're Funny?' competition
2010: Ivo watches first Alex Horne gig (*Odds*)
2011: Ivo watches third Swindon Town relegation
2012: Ivo graduates with no plan
2013: Ivo does first Edinburgh hour
2014: Ivo gets a girlfriend
2015: Ivo moves in with girlfriend
2016: Ivo does first marathon
2017: Ivo watches fourth Swindon Town relegation
2018: Ivo makes a lot of commitments
2019: Ivo's daughter is born
2020: Ivo does a lot of Zoom gigs
2021: Ivo watches fifth Swindon Town relegation
2022: Ivo bids a great man goodbye
2023: Ivo appears on Alex Horne's *Taskmaster*
2024: Ivo writes this book
2025: Ivo's book is published. This is that book. Here we go.

When, in spring 2023, shortly after the first broadcast of *Taskmaster* Series 15, a friendly opportunist called Richard Roper bought me lunch in a Farringdon brasserie and asked if I'd like to write a book, I felt fairly sure that yes, I would. The world did not, and does not, demand this book. If people wanted to read several hundred pages of a posh man shrouding his shortcomings in needlessly long words, Boris Johnson's memoir would be in shops soon enough, and greatly reduced in price not long after. But sure, if my own boarding-school blather had even the most fleeting commercial cachet, then I would be honoured and intrigued to bang out a book's worth of blather by Christmas 2024. Or, as it turned out, by May 2025. Deadlines are not my strong suit.

But what would the blather be *about*? On the one hand, this book has emerged (eventually) in the vague shape that all parties would have most expected it to be, and most liked it to be, from the moment of its first commission: a series of autobiographical essays, a story of a life, my life, my *truth*, and it is nearly all truth, albeit with some elegant and obvious omissions. But it is not a 'life story', 1990–present, even if the timeline overleaf gives you most of the key beats. Quite aside from the ego required, even on commission, to write one's life story at age thirty-four, I'd feel incapable of doing so right now, because not only do I not know how it ends, none of us know how our stories *end*, truthfully I don't even really know where it's going *now*. I am at a crossroads between a lot of different lives.

Though there's sometimes not much evidence of this in my performance, I have been doing stand-up comedy for fifteen years, aka my whole adult life, and for most of those fifteen years I've gone up to spend the month of August at the Edinburgh Fringe. For anyone trying to make a real long-term go of 'this comedy malarkey', as my parents' friends will forever call it, those sleepless Scottish summers swiftly become not just progress reports on one's joke writing and mic technique but also progress reports on one's life. I have pretty much always done stand-up about my life, my domestic situation and its most pressing concerns, since the earliest routines on drinking games and driving lessons with which I entered the Chortle 'Student Comedian of the Year 2009' (first round exit, Kingston heat). For context, but also undeniably for my own self-indulgent pleasure, I have dedicated a chapter later in this book to summarising my Edinburgh shows over the years. You can see the consistency/unoriginality (delete as applicable) of the pattern that is established, how my fearless commitment to truth/shameless lack of imagination (delete as applicable) led to me filling the shows with my personal life, and my personal life expanding to fill them. How long could this pattern last?

In 2019, I became a parent, and my world changed, and then in 2020, there was a pandemic, and everybody's world changed. People were forced to hit pause and take stock, whether they liked it or not. Conveniently enough, I was already doing so. And how lucky I was to be able to spend that time taking stock, rather than, for example, home-schooling teenagers, doing hospital shifts in cut-price PPE, or driving blind down the blurry byways of County Durham. I will try and check these kind of privileges where possible in the book, making the ones I fail to check all the more glaring by comparison.

If you find privilege-checking a bit of a virtuous speed bump in life, well, apologies that you'll have to skirt over it here and there, and perhaps you can try and tempt me to throw off the shackles in a more private environment some other time. Meanwhile, if you find privilege itself disgusting, well, of course I respect that, but I'm afraid you really have been bought, or somehow have bought yourself, one of the worst possible books on that front. This book isn't about my time at Eton 2004–8, or my time at Oxford 2008–12, or my time as a white man (formerly white boy) 1990–present, but all those things do occasionally come up.

So what *does* come up?

Well, parenthood and the pandemic 2019–21 was a hell of a double bill, but they're not so much the subject of this book as the two major things that happened in my life the following year, in 2022.

The first of the two – my being booked for Series 15 of *Taskmaster* – was a significant factor in my getting to write the book at all. If you're not familiar with *Taskmaster*, and I suspect I really am directly addressing just a couple of my parents' friends here, it's a now globally franchised light entertainment show in which contestants are set unusual challenges under timed conditions, with hilariously resourceful or catastrophic results. My results? Mostly catastrophic. Despite this, I am so proud to have taken part in the show, and now to be part of the vast expanded universe of old *Taskmaster* contestants chewing over their contests, desperate to eke out that joyous experience just a little longer. And my experience *was* joyous, even if it was also characterised by pretty constant panic, embarrassment, and so many shots of me with my head in my hands that people on the internet made compilation videos of them. I didn't love watching those videos back. You might be able to picture what I looked like watching them.

The book is called *Yardsticks For Failure* because that is how I described myself (or rather, begged not to be described) at one point on *Taskmaster*. This was not a phrase I had used before, or planned to sneak in deliberately at some point, but one that occurred completely organically from the mental state

I had lathered myself into on the show, where I messed up or was actively disqualified from nearly every task, and came last by a significant distance. A year later, when bouncing potential titles around with Richard, and now his colleague Yvonne at Headline, *Yardsticks For Failure* was a clear favourite. A neck-sprainingly overt nod to the *Taskmaster*-gorging base, sure, but also a very truthful reflection of how I see most of my various performances in life, as blunders against the clock, as noble aims let down by chaotic execution, as books about lateness that themselves end up being late.

I am certainly too quick to embrace this self-deprecating and self-fulfilling prophecy of defeat, and who knows what part of my personal history is most accountable for that. It would be easy to blame the repressed trauma of boarding school – and in my father's day, of course, the yardstick would have been used not just to measure the failures but to punish them – but I think that's an overly convenient diagnosis, and not one I am currently too inclined to explore in a book. Instead, I thought, the story could detail the various professional challenges I was trying to juggle, post-*Taskmaster*, in the hope that whether they came off or didn't, it would make for a merry ride either way. The title came from Frankie Boyle, who had become a very paternal figure to me on the show, with a blend of soothing pride and searing putdowns not unlike that of my actual father. In the last of the ten episodes we filmed in that whirlwind week at Pinewood Studios, Frankie had softened the blow of my latest psychological collapse by suggesting that a yardstick for failure could be my own personal merchandise. And now, in some ways, it is! Thanks, Frankie!

Unfortunately, though the *Taskmaster* records at Pinewood Studios in September 2022 were all set to be the most exciting week of my career, they were quite overshadowed by something that happened earlier that month. I got a call from my best friend on a Monday morning, surprisingly early for a call, I remember thinking to myself, and her voice cracked, like she was playing a trick she hadn't quite committed to, as she told me some devastating news, news that, two years on, we're all still struggling to accept as real. It's the kind of news, and the kind of story, that you have to be careful with, and I have tried to be, because however much it's affecting you, there are other people it affects an immeasurable amount more. In some ways, my reality changed completely that day: in others, it didn't change all that much. I still bumbled off to film *Taskmaster* a fortnight later, and bumbled back to the Fringe a year later, and continued ostensibly to bumble through my already messy life in the same erratic fashion as before. But the legacy of that phone call has informed so many aspects of the last two years, and will continue to inform me and inspire me long into the future. I know that all the other people who got that phone call feel the same, and I am proud to share this journey with them, and this book is largely about that journey, and they were the first people to be sent a copy.

Most of this book is about my family and my friends, the people I love most in the world and to whom I owe so much. I refer to eleven people as a 'best friend': it's a big number, and not a neat number, but these are my best friends, and there were twelve, and now there aren't. The word 'legend' is used more than once: I love the word, and using it to describe the people I love, and I am delighted to play any part in reclaiming it from the clutches of rugby lads, though I love many of those legends too. I've talked round most of the legends' names in this introduction, but I've included most of them for the rest of the book. I checked this with the majority of the legends, and they seemed broadly happy about it, and thinking about how to paint the best picture of my favourite people in some-times just a few words was one of my favourite parts of the process. If you don't want to pause for every one of these sentimental sketches, then do please press on in pursuit of the proper prize: the overarching narrative. If a certain name is going to be coming up a lot in the book, I've tried to telegraph that. If it's a posh name, I haven't changed it: if anything, I was more likely to include it. If multiple people in the book have the same name, I've tried to sidestep or at least acknowledge that. Sure, it would be easier if all the characters had different names, and sure, it would be easier if there were just fewer characters, but, I repeat, you can pause or you can press on! Those are your options! These people mean a hell of a lot to me and I've given this a hell of a lot of thought!

Some of the more unwieldy tangents have, of course, gone into footnotes, which have, undeniably, always been a big part of the 'writing a book' fantasy for me.* Again, you don't have to read them, I mean obviously you don't have to read any of it, just tell Bezos you loved it and chuck it in the bin, but I thought it was worth mentioning up top. One of the Core Principles I decided early on was that the footnotes, long or short, wouldn't all be featured in the audiobook, so if you're consuming this via audiobook, hello, I hope you're enjoying these dulcet tones, just know that (1) I will raise my voice

---

* There's one comedian's book from 2010 that wields an undeniably large influence in this field, so goodness knows what he'll make of this if it crosses his path. But you didn't invent footnotes, Ratko! Don't put this baby in the Corner!

quite aggressively from time to time to make sure people don't use the book to fall asleep, and (2) there are a few slices of detail here and there that you won't get on the audio. I'm not saying that those slices – and all the pictures! – are *immediately* worth pausing to order a physical copy for, but if you do ever press pause at a wilfully ambiguous or offensive statement that you feel sure I ought to have offered a bit more clarification on, why not pop into your local bookshop next time you're passing, wash your hands, dry them, prise the book delicately off the bestsellers shelf, and check if that ambiguity is cleared up in a footnote. And if it isn't, well, you're holding the book now, aren't you? It's probably just as easy to buy it as put it back.

Though he's not the friend to whom this book is dedicated, there's another late great man for whom this introduction chapter is named, a director and dramaturg whose influence has loomed large over British comedy in recent years and will for many yet to come. His name was Adam Brace, and he was a brilliant and boisterous bear of a man whose brilliance and boisterousness I wish I'd pursued so much more than I did. He used to tell me off for spending too much time in 'caveat town' in my shows, and we would laugh and get drunk and resolve that he would help me fix this, and then I got another of those phone calls in April 2023, and now if I ever want to get out of caveat town, he's not going to be there to help me.

If a caveat is 'a warning to consider something before doing anything more', I guess a whole town of them would look like – well, I guess it would look like this book. A marathon of side-quests and shout-outs that should entitle anyone who finishes it to a medal. But that's just it, I'm afraid: I love side-quests, and I love shout-outs, and I love marathons. And if you *have* finished the book, then please do email me to say so at ifinishedyardsticksforfailure@gmail.com, and I'll send you a ten-question quiz about the book's contents, and if you get nine out of ten, I'll send you a medal. I really will. The medals have been made. It was difficult to decide how many to make.

So, to wind up my friend Adam, here's one final caveat, and it is an important one: that while *Yardsticks For Failure* is a pretty full account of the last couple of years of my life, there is one main, indeed *the* main bit of my life, that lurks in the shadows of the story without ever really taking centre stage. Becoming a father in February 2019 was the culmination of my young adult life, of all the domestic leaps and stumbles I'd spent a decade detailing at the Edinburgh Fringe, but it was also the start of a period, still ongoing, which I brush past only semi-jokingly in this book with words like 'freefall' and 'unravelling'. Bits of that story crop up here, but most don't. That story is the most delicate and most unresolved bit of my life, and if I am ever to write a book about it then it needs to be after a fair bit more processing and pondering at my end.

This book is about friendship and family, fluster and failure, running marathons and running clubnights and running late for trains, but it isn't about parenthood, or romantic relationships, or the navigation of the two simultaneously, which goodness some people really do seem to manage better than others. May I say, then, in quite conveniently but quite deliberately the final caveat of this introduction, that I could fill many more books' worth of blather with the adventures I have shared with my daughter over the last few years, and the feelings they have inspired. It is the most obvious truism about parenthood but still one that re-occurs so relentlessly and exhaustingly along the way: that though raising a child can often feel like a pretty brutal yardstick for one's own failures, it is also the key to the kinds of pride and joy that themselves way exceed whatever yardstick of pride or joy you were measuring with back in the simpler times.

My daughter, who will be six by the time this book comes out, is yet to understand the full shambolic scale of my career, but she does now know that Daddy does 'shows' and she's started to request quite insistently that I put her drawings in them. In the murky business of how much of one's child's life to share publicly, how cautious to be even if they've requested it or indeed *especially* if they've requested it, the drawings are my currently preferred compromise. The good news is, I adore my daughter's drawings, and not just because they often occupy her for thirty or forty minutes at a time before the inevitable demand for a snack or a screen. I love the way she draws people, their faces and their clothes and more recently their eyelashes and hairstyles and jewellery. I love the stories the drawings tell, sometimes clear reflections of her recent artistic influences, or domestic concerns, sometimes from a dark recess of her imagination that I cannot hope to understand and that she sure as sugar isn't going to bother explaining to me. Over the last few months in 2024, under the stewardship of Miss Derecourt and Miss Duncombe and the other heroes shaping many more hours of her educational life than I am, she's been learning to write, so now some of the drawings have words too, titles or speech bubbles or just words, massive words with no connection to what's going on in the picture. With a bit of guidance from her, and a fair bit of my own personal prefer-ence, a selection of her recent drawings populate this book, quick blasts of levity and mystery in between the gargantuan prose-dumps of my reality. Edie, if you're reading this one day,

I hope you're happy with the drawings we chose, and I hope you feel I've done justice to them and to you in this damn long paragraph at the end of this damn long introduction. I love you so so much.

That's it. The introduction is over. We're up and running now. The next chapter is all about *Taskmaster*, thank God. Have an energy gel and get stuck in.

CHAPTER 1

Your Time Starts Now

Of the however many people that might have bought this book for a cousin or colleague, I'm flattering myself that as many as 10 per cent had long discussed with said cousin or colleague their hope, even their dream, that Ivo Graham might one day write a book. This would leave just 90 per cent as people who were panicking in Waterstones en route to their cousin's/ colleague's birthday drinks, when this just happened to be the discounted comedy memoir nearest the till. But whether it's destiny or disaster that's brought me to your door, there's a fairly strong chance it all comes back to the ten episodes in

2023 that I spent aboard the late-night-japes-turned-prime-time-juggernaut that is Alex Horne's *Taskmaster*.

May I hammer home some fanboy credentials upfront, please? Though I cannot boast, as LCD Soundsystem's 'Losing My Edge' (more on that song later) might have it, 'that I was there at the first *Taskmaster* live show at Edinburgh 2010', I was already a simpering disciple of Little Alex Horne long before he laid his first golden Greg on the Dave channel in 2015. I was there at *Odds**! I was there at *Monsieur Butterfly*†! I was there when *No More Jockeys* was called *No More Women*‡! I had everything before everyone!

So then *Taskmaster* Series 1 came out in 2015, won by Josh Widdicombe, the curly-haired charmer whose coat-tails I've been riding since we braved the same bearpit of *The Comedy Zone* at the 2010 Fringe.§ If I was on the slow coach to *Taskmaster*, Josh was on the bullet train, and his triumph in the inaugural season, *and* the inaugural Champion of Champions, is his story to tell, not mine. Needless to say, though, I think it's exquisite that he got an actual tattoo of Greg Davies's name on his foot,

---

* Wonderful 2010 show about statistics!

† Wonderful 2014 show about Rube Goldberg!

‡ Once played it with Sophie Duker and our friends Erin and Milly on a road trip to watch a Nick Mohammed show in Cambridge! What a despicably on-brand vignette!

§ By the 2010 Fringe, Josh had already signed with the agent who would change his life and later mine, the quiet powerhouse that is Flo Howard (then Collins) at Off The Kerb. *The Comedy Zone*, like *Taskmaster*, was made by Avalon, its producers generously allowing Josh, an observational wunderkind from a rival agency, to overanalyse Madame Tussauds on their turf for a month, rolling out the same red carpet they would unfurl for him to win the flagship series of their new TV show half a decade later. Keep your friends close and your enemies closer!

that he won the series with a point earned by counting beans on his own, and that when his daughter was born, the *Taskmaster* team sent her a letter (wax sealed, obvs) saying 'Dear Anthea,* have the best life ever, your time starts now.' I think you could trace everything that was immediately so iconic and gorgeous about the show to those three moments alone. And fourteen series later, I'd get to have some moments of my own.

One of the pleasing things about *Taskmaster*'s steady march from digital curio to global superpower, as well as all the lovely *Taskmaster*'s we got to watch along the way, was that it filled aspiring comics with the hope that, should they keep making it indefinitely, most of us would get a go at some point. I just needed to prove my credentials in the field of having an instant breakdown at the slightest provocation. In spring 2021, presented with the simple task of logging into an *Off Menu* live stream from a hotel in Hull and taking a bit more mutually lucrative pod-flak for my love of bananas and yoghurt, I instead revealed the name of my hotel on the stream. This set the Doubletree by Hilton's switchboard ablaze with wind-up callers, and, my spirit broken but still very much live on the internet, I offered a miserable white lie of apology to a very confused receptionist, a white lie which I'm proud to say has since been quoted at me in three different nightclub toilets: 'unfortunately I've been the victim of a prank.' Shortly afterwards, I was invited on *Taskmaster*.

I was giddy with excitement and nerves from my very first introductory meeting with the show's producers, two extremely kind and dedicated men who everyone calls 'The

---

* To respect Josh's privacy, I've not used his daughter's actual name, but the name of a celebrity he fancies.

Andys' because, to be fair, they are both called Andy. I had lots and lots of questions to which their answers were mainly just 'relax and don't overthink it', which only increased my certainty that they must have booked the wrong person by mistake. How could I not overthink it? Filming the show was by all accounts meant to be an utter joyride, and appearing on it seemed to be for most of its participants a life-changing, and in most of the crudest metrics at least, a life-improving venture. But it was also a Huge Deal. The footage from the five days spent doing the tasks,* and then the five days chewing over them at Pinewood Studios, would be watched by more people than probably anything else I'd ever do. This was the big one. Don't balls it up.

Obviously I ballsed it up. Loads and loads of times. Let's rattle through ten of them now.

IVO'S TOP TEN *TASKMASTER* REGRETS

1. Grotesquely overstating the weight of a toilet roll (prize task, episode one)

On a hot afternoon in July 2022, as my final day of task filming was coming to an end, I disembarked a barge, after a majestic river cruise which will *not* be featuring in this regrets list, and, before any end-of-an-era sadness could kick in, was ceremoniously handed one of the great one-page documents of my life. This document listed the ten categories for my 'prize tasks', listed in the usual font on the usual paper with

---

* Five days which I booked in as far apart from each other as the producers allowed, February to July 2022, the longest possible stretching out of the being on *Taskmaster* experience.

the usual seal, for me to mull for two months before revealing my choices in September's studio records. This is the one bit of the process the contestants *can* prep, and so, of course, I failed to do so. Obviously I thought about them constantly: my prize tasks were the mental screensavers of my summer, the thing that my mind would absently wander to while warming the bench at Swindon Supermarine, or dancing to Horse Meat Disco at a Dalmatian rave. But any final decisions were put off and put off until suddenly it was September and there were just a few days to go and I was navigating ten simultaneous maelstroms of indecision and not replying to quite a lot of texts from the producers.

Though we wouldn't know the order the prize tasks would be coming up until the week of the records, the first one I did lock in with producer Andy C happened to be the prize task selected for episode one: 'the most dependable thing that weighs about 1kg'. It didn't take long for me to nominate loo roll* as a dependable thing: I get a pathetic kick in my life from never being out of loo roll, always staying ahead of the game, proactively loading up on the product I am more certain than any other will get used, will be *depended on*. I'm a 'Who Gives A Crap' subscriber now, a sucker for the artful packaging, the environmental conscience, and the fact that, true story, the mother of one of the staff made a joke in 2006 about me having the strong wrists of a single man. Anyway, I

---

* My paternal grandmother, a formidable woman whose storied life does not deserve to be reduced to this vignette alone, once made clear a very strong preference for the word 'loo' rather than 'toilet', and with her voice, and the voice of her pet parrot, still in my mind, that's the word I'll be using for the remainder of this story.

suppose there's a certain neatness to me now having indirectly purchased hundreds of pounds' worth of tissue paper from her daughter.

I lazily, unquestioningly Googled how much a loo roll weighs, and Wikipedia replied immediately: 250 grams. So a four-pack = a kilogram. Perfect. The sweet four. Yeah, it did seem a *bit* heavy, but, uh, excuse me, Wikipedia says it, so it must be true! I don't want to be too much of a fawning Wiki-shill: I know that there are tiers of knowledge and certainty way beyond that which Jimmy Wales and his team are able to provide. It's just that, since my final-year university module on the Socialist Realist literature of the 1920s, I haven't ever needed to know more about a topic than Wikipedia was able to provide. Jimmy might not know all that much about Nikolai Ostrovsky's *How the Steel Was Tempered*, but he knows how much a loo roll weighs! I proposed the sweet four to producer Andy C, and it got a thumbs-up from him. Now as I write this, I wonder if Andy C, or anyone else on the team, knew the mistake I was making. Could they not have intervened? No, no. It's not their job to intervene. Attenborough doesn't intervene.

Anyway, a couple of weeks later I was sat there, on *Taskmaster*, maybe the biggest job I will ever do, and the first sentence out of my mouth had been, through a combination of poshness and panic, so stilted that Greg Davies had already asked if I was OK. I was, in all sorts of ways, not OK, but this was a concern I'd have *loved* not to have had raised until, say, more than five minutes into the first record. Luckily, he then asked me what the most dependable thing that weighs a kilogram is, and so I could pump my confidence back up, with my indisputably excellent loo roll answer. I'd barely said the words 'sweet four', however, than Alex Horne was apologetically, almost pityingly, breaking the news, that a loo roll weighs a hundred grams, so the sweet four would, in fact, weigh less than *half* a kilo. My deep dive into one of the less divisive fields of human research – how much does a fucking loo roll weigh? – had seen me come out quite stupendously off the mark. A whole host of hideous explanations suggested themselves off the back of this: the loo rolls were much heavier at Eton, potentially, private school ply, or perhaps the posh twat's never had to stoop to holding one himself, his anus pampered by a steady rotation of butlers and bidets since birth. Greg didn't say any of this, and nor has anyone online as far as I've been able to scroll, but it was the furiously creative place my head went to immediately, much more creative than when I was actually thinking up the prize tasks in the first place. I had, in one fell swoop, claimed to love loo roll, and then revealed that I was in fact, if not totally unfamiliar with loo roll, then certainly not acquainted enough with its basic weight not to be misled by a glitch – and it must be a glitch – in the Wikipedia mainframe. I was awarded a single point out of five. Of course I was. I needed to bring in a kilo and I was about 600g short. An incredibly dense start to the series, and yet also: nowhere near dense enough.

2. The botched bucket betrayal (live task, episode one)

Having had my dubiously wiped arse handed to me with my prize task, we then proceeded to watch the first three of our pre-recorded tasks back. These, in my case, involved doing a wedding dance to the song 'Dizzy' by The Wonder Stuff (two points out of five), unravelling and then re-ravelling a ball of string (two points out of five), and finally, driving the barge, which to be fair did score me four points, even if I did also quite literally break the barge. The episode was then rounded off with the 'live task' of the five contestants throwing items into buckets in front of the studio audience. This was, in some ways, my dream task: not a sport in which I have any sort of specialist ability but in which I certainly do have a specialist interest, to the extent that I used to have a stand-up routine about what a kick I get throwing things into other things from a distance. And what delightfully *random* projectiles beginning with B we were given to throw! I landed my baby head, didn't quite land my book, then got things back on track with my brush. I was in the lead, with my main competitor being actor and philosopher Kiell Smith-Bynoe.* It was at this point, how-ever, that I chose violence.

One of the central contradictions that keeps my life in such a busy loop of recrimination and regret is the fact that, for someone who broadly wants to be liked and not make a mess, I do make some pretty non-standard decisions in the heat of the moment. Why did I decide to throw my fourth item – the ball – not into my bucket but straight at Kiell's? Yes, it was a fantastic throw, come now, watch it back, in the midst of all those dainty lobs, witness the madman and his laser-guided direct hit. But it was *very* early in the series to be turning on each other: it was day one, we'd barely met, we wouldn't be spitting feathers about banana signs and paper pineapples for a few episodes yet. Come on, Ivo. Kiell is your friend, not your rival. He's never going to be your rival. You're going to come last by such a long way. But you know what, fuck it: get his bucket.

---

* Kiell saying 'once bread has become toast, it can never be bread again' earlier that episode is a strong competitor for my favourite line of the whole series.

The topper, of course, is that even within this baffling lurch to the dark side, there was an entirely on-brand lack of planning. If I'd waited until Kiell had already taken *his* throw, he would have been powerless to avenge the betrayal. Instead, of course, he was still holding his ball, so he could immediately swing round and return fire, which he did successfully, not just undermining the whole cynical point of my treachery but also the impressiveness of my own throw. There's a clip online of the whole incident, slowed down for maximum impact, and my face is so deliciously appalled when Kiell fires back. Another perfect metaphor for Etonians and their attitude to life, delighted to chuck any old pleb* under the bus to advance their own career, but genuinely horrified if their own door is ever darkened by the consequences of their actions.

So episode one ended with a disqualification, my first of eight across the series, and a definite regret, although of what specifically, I'm not sure. Going for Kiell's bucket at all, or merely going for it too soon? *Are you sorry you did it, or are you sorry you got caught?* Who's to say? The day after the first episode was broadcast, as demand swelled in the more *Taskmaster*-focused corners of the internet for me to Explain Myself, I recorded a public statement for Instagram from a lay-by just outside Darlington. My voice wobbled unconvincingly as I tried to double down on the decision, telling Kiell that I wasn't sorry and that I'd do it again if I could. This was fighting talk. But was it true?

---

* I think this is a funny word to use here, but I would also now like to acknowledge that it can cause offence, such as that period about ten years ago where an MP may or may not have said it to a policeman and it was front-page news for what felt like two months. The simpler times!

3. My uncle's glasses (prize task, episode two)

As detailed above, the tantalising full summer's worth of preparation time meant that every even minor failing on a prize task could bruise purply into a top-ten regret, but I'm going to limit myself to just one more of them on this list, and it's this one: my uncle's detachable magnetic glasses.

The brief? 'The thing that makes you feel weird every time you look at it.' And I'm not letting slip any major trade secrets here when I say: you could pick any old crap for this category. It's certainly not 'the thing you carry everywhere but struggle to fit in your bag', an incredibly specific prize task brief which I genuinely resented. For this one, just pick a weird thing, and comically exaggerate the amount of times you have to look at it in your life. Frankie Boyle was romping merrily around his home, pulling fan art off the walls for his prize tasks. That was the kind of fun dad he was on the show. I, his anxiety-ridden son, was, of course, losing my mind.

There are dressing rooms at Pinewood Studios which most contestants for *Taskmaster* and other panel shows will use for little more than just that: dressing. Dressing, texting, maybe a nap, maybe a Nando's. In the week of the *Taskmaster* Series 15 studio records, however, my room became a prize task panic chamber like surely no other contestant's before. In this cauldron of calculation, the adrenaline of the impending record suddenly engaged my brain with my prize tasks in a way that the previous ten weeks of scheduled preparation had failed to do. Andy C and prize task wrangler Luke were suddenly presented with new ideas that I'd failed to mention at any point prior to arriving in the building. For example, even though I was very happy with the Greg face made out of Miniature Heroes that I'd proposed bringing in for 'most heroic thing'*, I then, the day before the episode, remembered the most heroic thing I've actually done in my life: the chilli chilli chicken challenge I completed at a cash-only Chinese restaurant in Oxford in 2012. That night I had got a Polaroid photo of my triumph put on the wall, the winners' wall, so listen, Andy and Luke, if I call up Red Star to explain, and go there to pick up the Polaroid tonight, can I use that on tomorrow's episode instead? I mean, what are you meant to say to that guy? Other than, 'Well, let's discuss it further after you've called the restaurant.'

I was passed between three members of staff at Red Star, none of whom spoke terrific English and none of whom quite managed to get their head round the very clear and logical proposal that I wanted to nip down the M40 that evening and raid their archives for a ten-year-old Polaroid. I was forced to abandon the search, and stick to plan A: the chocolatey Greg-head. A week or so later, I was discussing this particular fool's errand with my beloved uni roommate Matt, a Yorkshire educator and recovering hair gel addict who'd also been at Red Star that spicy night. Matt reminded me that though I had indeed surprised everybody by completing the challenge, ploughing sweatily on to the finish while manlier men mainlined milk around me, I hadn't actually done it in the required half-hour, so had never got a Polaroid on the wall. The thought of driving forty miles to Red Star to look for a ten-year-old photo that never existed is such a hyper-verse of desperation and delusion that it makes me embarrassed even thinking about it now.

Another example? Sure, why not? I'd been quite happy, in my

---

* A huge thanks to TM's Amy Hopewell for helping me on this one, and by helping me, I mean: 'making the whole thing for me'.

manically relieved 'tick it off the list' kind of way, with the silver spoon I'd proposed bringing in for 'luckiest thing', the sort of route-one quip about privilege that I've been leaning on since 2009, most of which come back to things being in my mouth. I hadn't exactly gilded the lily: *Taskmaster* were providing the spoon. I hadn't sought out one of the genuine fancies from the special occasion cutlery drawer back at the Graham hearth, nor gone the extra mile and had my name, or family motto,* engraved onto it, like Steve Pemberton would have done. But, in a series that would be dominated by spoon-based snafus,† this one had a few twists left in the tail. Frankie had expanded the remit of his prize-task art-attack for the previous episode – 'most fun thing to wear on your head that you're not supposed to' – and he'd brought in a graduation cap with a Sylvanian Families Child Catcher scene on it. Of course he had. Utterly random and deliciously dark, sure, that's my dad for you, but deserving of four more points than I got for bringing in a turkey, the turkey on head that brought hilarity to millions in *Friends* and *Mr Bean*? Could I *be* any more unfairly treated?

Well, with a tantalisingly free morning between the recordings of episodes four and five, I decided that I would seek justice, disrespect my TV father, and chase some of that golden inter-episode banter. I would make my own graduation cap,

---

* We don't have a family motto, I really must stress, although there is a 'Graham clan' in Scotland to whom we are distantly related, and as well as its own tartan, the clan does have its own motto, in French weirdly: 'Ne Oublie'. 'Never Forget'. Oh, I've chuckled at the irony of this a few times I can tell you, m'laddie!

† This is one of my favourite words, and my friend Alex Kealy has recently been trying to poach it off me, so I'm going to get it into this book as many times as I can.

festooned entirely with lucky things. So on went the spoon, but also, on went some lucky playing cards,* and on went a figurine of Steve Bruce, the footballer whose detective novels changed my life, and will get their own chapter later on. Bruce never got capped by England, but as crestfallen as he was by that, he might take some relief in being capped by me.

The cap itself was more of an issue. I am, as I reiterated on the show, lucky to have a degree, from one of the fancy dress universities, and I did wear all the graduation gear back in the day, but did I have an actual mortar board at my actual home? Though my London flat is such a moth-eaten memory museum that it's not *inconceivable* that I could lay my hands on one in the back of a cupboard, on this occasion I could not. As such, I spent my breathing-space morning between episode records getting the train into central London and trying to buy or hire a mortar board from a series of gentleman's tailors which either didn't have one or didn't open till later in the day. More heartbreak. Of course, the infinite resources of patience and props at Pinewood mean that the *Taskmaster* team had a mortar board waiting for me when I arrived at the studios, and I could begin the job of accessorising it with the standard accoutrements of silver spoon, playing cards and the Manchester United captain 1992–95. Oh, and a rabbit's

---

* The lucky cards in question were '7 2 off', the hand that became celebrated in my friends' lockdown poker Zooms as being so blessed that you simply *had* to go all in if you had it. I've only since learned, alongside many other things I didn't know about poker while gladly paying Rhys and Radderz £50 a week to sit on a video call with them, that '7 2 off' was picked as the all-in banter hand precisely because it's actually the *worst* possible cards you can have. Ah well! An exceptionally good topper on a loss-making lockdown.

foot, of course! One of the go-to 'lucky things'. What would my rabbit's foot be? Just a couple of Sylvanian family rabbits, what of it? Take that, Frankie! I'm taking your cutesy props and I'm literally dismembering them! Who's the daddy now?

It wasn't actually Frankie's rabbits I was planning to dismember. Those rabbits had been won by Jenny Eclair the previous day. No, I might not have a graduation cap to hand in my home, but I do have a five-year-old, back then a three-year-old, and that means that I have a box under my bed full of generic small gifts that I have either got her and then forgotten about, or speculatively bought for some present in the future. Much like my vast silos of ethical loo roll, this emergency gift box makes me feel proud whenever I encounter it in my home, let alone dip into it. It makes me feel, contrary to the vast evidence on *Taskmaster* and everywhere else, like I am in control, seeing life like a beach ball, with my Sylvanian Family rabbits ready to go for any moment of need. And what a moment of need this was.

I'd never cut off a Sylvanian animal's foot before. Or any foot, for that matter. But this sinister plot was called off before I'd even chosen my weapons, when I opened the Sylvanian Families box in my dressing room to discover, like many a parent in a hurry before me, that I had failed to acknowledge the despicably exploitable grey area between what kids' toys tend to have *on* the box and what kids' toys tend to have *in* the box. Producer Luke had patiently nodded while I explained in a breathless rant that I'd brought a toy rabbit specially to maim for my hat, only to then tip out a Sylvanian Family table and chairs set: the set you *could* seat a couple of rabbits at, sure, as in this picture, but obviously you'd have to buy those separately, wouldn't you, you didn't think they'd be in this box, did you,

you fucking fantasist?! With hindsight, again, it is perhaps for the best that I wasn't chopping up a children's toy in the final minutes before proceeding to set, but it didn't feel like that at the time. When I opened the box and it didn't have a rabbit in it I fell to my knees and let out a howl of genuine anguish that made someone in the corridor knock at the door to ask if I was all right.

Seconds later, Luke was heading down the corridor to Jenny's dressing room, asking if I could have the Sylvanian Families rabbits off the hat she had won in the previous episode. Why did I need them? You don't want to know, Jenny. In the end, the amputation operation was abandoned and the final place on my lucky cap was given to a maneki-neko, the Japanese bobtail cat denoting good fortune. And Japan my country of birth! My whole damn life was on this hat! Alas, my whole damn life came second-last in the task, beaten, most cruelly of all, by Mae Martin's 'lucky glasses', so much cooler and more stylishly accessorised than my lucky cap, featuring amongst said accessories a horse shoe, two four-leaf clovers and . . . two rabbits' feet. Actual fluffy rabbits' feet. Not a Steve Bruce figurine or a Sylvanian table and chair set in sight.

But the biggest prize task regret of all? Well. That was the 'object that makes you feel weird every time you look at it'. The weird thing. Any weird thing. I had been mulling a few unsatisfactory options for this when one evening I was watching *Everything I Know About Love* and saw the main character's dad, a man we are patently designed to like but think uncool, popping his pair of magnetic glasses together to tackle a crossword.* Hey, I thought, my uncle has those glasses!

---

* Member of the cruciferous family of vegetables, begins with a K (8).

Hanging round his neck in a string, two monocles ready to be magnetised at a moment's notice. Despite the fact that I am the sort of literally and spiritually short-sighted person who would massively benefit from having more of his possessions on a string round his neck, I've never been quite able to get on board with my uncle's magnetic reading glasses. But there's a difference between 'never being quite able to get on board' with a thing that I encounter, quite manageably, at most two or three times a year,* and that thing 'making me feel weird every time I look at it'. Still, I suggested it as an option to Andy C, and it got pencilled in, and that pencil turned ever inkier as the days ticked by till the records.

Then I was back in the dressing-room panic-chamber between episodes one and two, in the hour and a half between records, smarting with embarrassment at my chunky loo roll and my Botched Smith-Bynoe Bucket Betrayal. I had to turn this round! I was already a dead man walking! And now I'd brought my own noose! My own detachable magnetic noose! I suddenly remembered that at my parents' house in Wiltshire, my childhood home, nostalgia HQ, a property I should have done a thorough prize-task sweep of at literally any point in the summer, I had on my bedside table a clay model of a human

---

* My encounters with my weirdly bespectacled uncle include, er, his generous invitations to watch Arsenal at the Emirates, where of course I stay loyal in my heart to Swindon, and hum songs about the 1969 League Cup final under my breath, but am also undeniably thrilled to have seen, for example, Jack Wilshere's Goal of the Season-winning pass-mastery against Norwich in 2013, a tiki-taka triumph that I imagine many readers are now already pausing to rewatch on YouTube. I am so chuffed to have seen that goal live, my uncle shouting 'Wow! Wow!' next to me, having been able to see it perfectly, thanks to his detachable magnetic glasses.

head that I made in a pottery class at boarding school in 1999. Like almost every other souvenir of that jauntily traumatic era of my life, I have never thrown this clay head away, despite the fact that it is lacking in any artistry or charm whatsoever. It is a blob the size of a fist with with pin pricks for eyes, a few knife scratches across the top for hair, and a clumsy thumb-hole for a mouth, a mouth that appears to be shrieking in terror. It is genuinely unsettling, has no happy memories attached to it, and yet has been in my childhood bedroom, where I still sleep regularly, for twenty-five years. It was on the bedside table when I lost my virginity in that bed on July 11th 2012.* It is, in other words, almost the definitive 'thing that makes me feel weird every time I look at it'. It had been under my nose the whole time!

Suddenly I was on the phone to my parents, asking if there was any way the shrieking clay head could be transported from Wiltshire to Pinewood in the next hour. My dad wasn't able to drive it, because he wasn't at home. My mum wasn't able to drive it, because she isn't able to drive. There was a brief discussion about whether my mum's carer would be able to bring it, in surely the most egregious diversion from his responsibilities I, or any other disabled person's relative, would have ever commissioned. The thought of asking Nar Singh to do this, or of something happening to my mum while Nar Singh was driving two hours to deliver a schoolboy sculpture to her son, was definitely a queasy enough thought to make me at

---

* The same day as my friend the young Lambert, though we didn't work that out, in quite a random and weird chat, for another ten years. Imagine realising something like that a decade later! A hell of a bond to share with a pal, even if they are four years younger than you.

least hesitate. But I wasn't hesitating for long. We were between records: every second of this process was crucial. I had already asked my mum if the head could be brought down from my bedroom and placed on standby. I cannot claim that the reason this plan did not go ahead is because I thought better of it. The reason the plan did not go ahead was because producer Andy C said that my uncle's glasses were already photographed and legally approved and in the script and it would genuinely cause so much trouble for so many people to change it at this point. And the 'so many people' wasn't even the carer currently putting a clay head in his car. So I stuck with the magnetic glasses. No one really knew what they were or why I found them so weird, Greg made several very legitimate jokes about how shit they were as a prize, and I began mentally drafting quite a long text of apology to my uncle, who didn't even know I'd ever had any issue with his glasses, let alone that I'd decided to randomly open fire on them on TV.

Somehow, I won episode two, which meant that I won the glasses, and I now have my own pair, in my own home, making me feel weird, and quite a lot of other feelings, every time I look at them. And the clay head is still there, too, as disturbing as ever. Both have been drafted into temporary service via my storytelling theatre show *Carousel*, but once that is over, so are they. Maybe I'll auction off the clay head. The mad self-importance and quite stunning nicheness of offering that up to bidders: 'Ivo Graham's most-regretted not-quite-prize task'. But someone will bid £5 for that, and I'd simply love to give that £5 to charity and never have to feel weird looking at it again. Or would I miss it? Of course I'd miss it. I'd probably try and buy it back. Nope, I'm keeping that damn clay head forever.

4. Bingo (task three, episode four)

Every *Taskmaster* task is its own unique flavour of batshit: that's the show's MO. But even by the standards of the hi-jinks I'd come to expect from watching fourteen series at home, I still remember thinking that we came out of the blocks very quickly on day one. On a mild March morning in Chiswick, I emerged from the house to my First Task Ever: a colossal drumkit and the challenge to bounce a ball off as many of its drums as possible with a single throw. It went terribly. I had twenty minutes, spent most of that time moving the kit back and forth across the garden, and managed no more than three successful bounces. I should have just swung the ball instead.* Then I went into the lab, where I was made to write and perform a lecture about the year 1125. More on that later, but needless to say: the lecture was a historical, geographical and presentational binfire. But no time to dwell on that either, because we were straight into the next task, which upped the ante somewhat by incorporating nine mini-tasks in one. Let's play bingo.

Each of these nine mini-tasks worked up a bit of a sweat, whether it was popping bubble wrap, chucking a bin over a gate, or having politeness-cursed phone calls with multiple different family friends called John. The main takeaway from the bingo, however, and the prime pictorial souvenir of my whole time on the show, was being told to sit in the shed and going instead to sit in the caravan. I'm not the first person to have called *Taskmaster* out as essentially a ten-week medical trial for

---

* The studio debate about Mae Martin's elaborate definition of a throw was described by Alex Horne as his 'favourite thing ever', and I'd like to second that. What a thrilling journey through language and meaning!

ADHD, and no single brainfart across the series diagnoses me as brutally and totally as the caravan. Not just going there in error in the first place, but then sitting there for five minutes, blissfully unaware of my mistake until Alex tipped me off on my return. I say 'blissfully': I was sitting there with my head in my hands, as appeared to be my resting state on most occasions on the show. So, just to clarify, in the photos of me sitting in the shed with my head in my hands, that's my emotional state *before* realising I've made the stupidest mistake of the series.

Of course, the very nature of *Taskmaster*, of stand-up comedy, of this lifelong Faustian pact which it is now too late for me to renege on, means that it's often these kinds of errors that I end up cherishing most dear. Of course! They form the backbone of the self-deprecation that has propped up my personality and fig-leafed my privilege for my whole career. Cousin Jasper in *Brideshead Revisited*, a dismally on-brand thing to be quoting from, I know, drops by early in the book to advise the freshman Charles that, degree-wise, 'you want a first or a fourth. Time spent on a good second is time thrown away.' Though that philosophy didn't correspond exactly with my own salad days 2008–12, where even the most wayward comedy dreamer was firmly advised that getting anything below a 2:1 would be a disaster, Jasper's words still play on my mind in all sorts of life situations where glorious defeat seems the next best thing after glorious victory.

But, based on in-the-moment remorse, bingo definitely makes it in. This was day one. I was living at the time with my friends Jack and Caz, the latest in the series of Putney parachutes I was lucky enough to pop open in my general house-hopping freefall of 2019–22, and the third couple who would announce their pregnancy shortly after I moved in with them. Who needs IVF when you've got IVO?* Jack, an endlessly consultable titan of a best friend, who has read and replied to more drafts of this book than anyone but my official editor, had taken the role of 'Ivo's *Taskmaster* prepper' very seriously. We'd had conversations about how I was going to be careful, be strategic, how I wasn't going to forget to check the back of the card. I was going to reflect my love of the show in my preparation for the show. Alas, amongst other delicious inconsistencies across the series, I could not have looked much more simultaneously like a giddy fan of the show *and* someone who'd never watched it before.

I was already thinking, as I arrived on day one, Jack's encouragement still ringing in my ears, that I was now entering my final hours, my final minutes, of 'Schrödinger's *Taskmaster*', an exam paper I was looking at but still not allowed to open, the show soon to shift from a hypothetical reality in which I might thrive, to a real reality in which I might not. And I really did not. The bouncy balls on the drums were a bit of fun. The 1125 lecture wasn't too bad. But by the end of bingo, lunchtime on day one, as I was invited to join the crew in the garden for production manager Sophie's Mr Blobby-themed birthday cake, I had already given up on the thought that I might win series 15 of *Taskmaster*. How could I? I couldn't even tell the difference between a shed and a caravan. I was having a

---

* If you've seen that joke live, many apologies, but I hope you can forgive the repetition. Come on, imagine the moment I realised I had that joke fully formed in my pocket. My house-hopping life 2019–22 was not a straightforward one, but it did give me that joke, and every time I was onstage, closing my 2022 show with it, I did reflect that the pun did go some of the way towards compensating. Shoutout to Lyra, Eliza, Alba and Hector: the ~~IVF~~ IVO generation. May you grow up to have third wheels in your life as reliably fertility-inducing as I was to your parents!

fabulous time, but there was a quiet melancholy in my heart as I tucked into my second slice of Blobby. I wished Sophie a happy birthday, went back to my dressing room, and geed myself up for the afternoon by listening to two of my favourite songs, 'Shed Of Love' by the Housemartins, and 'Chasing Rainbows' by Caravan Seven. Victory was off the table. What's the next best option, Jasper?

5. Trying to salvage too many spoons (task three, episode five)

If we're creating a 'You've Been Grahamed' highlights folder that most efficiently captures the pandemonium of my process, and the many ways in which I frustrate the people who love me, this clip is going right in there alongside the bingo.

On my second day of task filming, in April 2022, I was no longer alone in my dressing room, sharing it not just with Frankie Boyle, the man I've already referred to here multiple times as my father, but also, delicately and delightfully, with his actual children. Frankie-era *Mock the Week* was, needless to say, appointment viewing in the ungentle realm of the C Block common room at Eton, so it was hugely exciting to learn that he was on my *Taskmaster* series, and even more so to open the gate at the start of day two and see him waiting for me as my taskmate. And I'm sure he felt exactly the same when he turned round and saw me, which is why he very *cleverly* offset his deep flattery by failing to acknowledge my existence.

Anyway, the faux frostiness of our first meeting quickly melted over the course of quite literally building a bridge together, and then an exquisitely choreographed 'stage fight' task, featuring Frankie's children wearing masks of my face. Unfortunately, for the next task I was forced to don a mask of my own. This was a deliberately clunky and vision-obscuring headset, patched through to Frankie, who was sat in the lab watching a live feed from the camera on my helmet, and given the unenviable role, but probably still more enviable than mine, of giving high-pitched instructions into my earpiece, to help me find and pick up a series of spoons hidden around the garden. How was I picking them up? With an incredibly strong magnet on a rope, of course! A magnet that I would encounter once more in the series at the pineapple canal, and then again at the Fringe, swung around the Cowgate by its true keeper, poppadom-crushing poet and Task Consultant Tim Key.

I did pretty well on the remotely directed spoon-hunting, and even threw in the parodically deferential bonus ball of replying to Frankie's instructions in a high-pitched voice of my own, despite the fact that it was only Frankie instructed to do so in the task. I wasn't thinking, 'This'll make good telly.' I really did just think it was polite to proceed at the same pitch as my pater. However, as I inched my way blindly around the garden, I did wonder if there was something I was not seeing, in a 'task shortcut' way rather than a 'literally not being able to see anything' way. My housemate Jack had given me another pep talk before I'd come in that day. Check! For! Workarounds! I dreamed of finding one of these workarounds, and making it onto one of those 'These Contestants Really Understood The Assignment' YouTube compilations. I did not make it onto any of these compilations.*

Anyway, here the task was to merely collect as many spoons

---

* At one point I did a pretty nifty loophole shimmy around a pulping wheel, but people didn't really seem to think that was in the spirit of things.

as possible – perhaps some *Mock The Week* avenger wanted to get Frankie to stare into his own reflection in one – so surely I could just bin off the thin spread of garden spoons and just go straight to the kitchen? Right? Right? This occurred to me too late in our allotted time, time which Falsetto Frankie had not warned me was about to elapse, making it a not-ideal moment for me, the Squeaky Blinder, to decide on this bonus mission to the kitchen. I had barely found the cutlery drawer when we were told it was over. Outta time. Didn't make it back to the lab as instructed. The spoons already in my pocket counted for nothing. Disqualification. Nul points.

Again, the nul-ness of the points wouldn't be confirmed by Greg till the studio days in five months. Maybe it hadn't gone as badly as it felt like it did? But it had, of course, gone as badly as it felt like it did. Five months later, we and the Pinewood audience watched it back, and through clever editing and also just the literal reality of what happened, the true epicness of the fail was unfurled. We watched as I entered the house, on Frankie's instruction, clearly able to make it to the lab in time according to the clock on the screen, before, what do you know?, deciding of my own stupid accord to charge into a different room. It couldn't be more painful, or more evocative of the thousands of times in my life I've been late for something because I was trying to fit something else in. And, as the team pointed out on the day, even if I had managed to give the show's insurers a heart attack by diving blindly into a cutlery drawer, the standard kitchen cutlery would not have responded to the magnet. Eton-educated comedian unable to pick up silver spoons. This shit is writing itself.

6. Not doing my required claps during the kitchen task (task three, episode seven)

I was such a fan of the sheer Taskmasterishness of this task: write five ingredients, sure, and a random adjective/nationality/ noun, also fine, and then, what do you know?, I was in the kitchen and suddenly I was cursing every word I had written because of course I then had to use the five ingredients of basil, cumin, garlic, salt and cannellini beans to make the end product of a feisty French duck. So where did that go wrong? Well, where didn't it? I wish I'd managed to make my duck a bit more feisty, somehow, and I'd certainly like to have carried out the task without clutching my head like a chimpanzee whose habitat is under threat (© Boyle), but obviously what's putting this one in the regrets list is the all-but-disqualification for failing to do my forty-two* claps at any point in the four minutes twenty seconds† I was allotted to do the task. How many bloody *Taskmaster* podcasts do I need to listen to? How many pre-show briefings did Jack need to give me? Complete the task! Remember the bit they want you to forget! Make like it's Thursday night in lockdown and do your bloody claps!

7. Putting too many bananas on the jelly (task three, episode eight)

This one can't even be chalked up to the lack of attention span: it was quite simply a dreadful miscalculation when it came to the basic physics of stacking as many things as I could on top of jelly without breaking it. I've enjoyed fact-checking my own failure for this chapter via the fantastically bald episode

---

* Random number selected by me, with a respectful nod to Arthur Dent.
† Random number selected by me, with a respectful nod to Snoop Dogg.

reports on the 'Taskmaster Wikipedia' fan page, so I'll go with their description of this one:

'Ivo decided to encase the jelly with foam bricks before stacking bricks, a chopping board and six bananas on top. As he removed the support bricks, the jelly was crushed by the weight and it broke, so Ivo was disqualified from the task.'

I can't dispute any of that. And in case it isn't clear, if you've not watched the episode, and you've read that report and assumed I was working my way up, banana by banana, before a sudden and unforeseeable collapse in the jelly's core strength somewhere between bananas five and six, disabuse yourself of that narrative immediately. I went straight from zero bananas to six bananas, an escalation that was quite rightly punished by the gelatinous gods. The irony is that my father, as well as his much-podcasted love of Yeo Valley yoghurt, also worships at the wobbly altar of a home-made jelly. Making jellies at home with him was a very happy tradition of my childhood, even though I was often back at boarding school by the time they had set. I have a joint honours in bananas and jelly from one of the most demanding dessert dons in the land. But that all counted for nothing on Taskmaster, where without my support bricks (parents), I too was crushed by the weight, and broke.

8. Drawing the Dutch flag when I meant to draw the French flag (task two, episode nine)

Having to give a lecture on a randomly allocated year from history at a few minutes' notice, especially on a TV show, and on one's first morning of filming, would admittedly stress most people out. Very few of those people, however, would choose to end their lecture, as I did, by presenting a nine-hundred-year summary of their own family tree and concluding it by

shouting, 'Oh no! I'm inbred!' These are genealogical anxieties that should be explored in private, rather than using a
Taskmaster task to get my webbed foot in the door for *Who
Do You Think You Are*? But that, at least, was an attempt at
humour, a classic bit of post-watershed incest bantz. Harder
to justify were the raft of basic factual errors made along the
way. Not getting the king right? Well, that's one thing, but not
getting the French flag right? If you're going to pad out your
lecture on the year 1125 with vague suggestions of Gallic threat,
you've got to get the flag right! I did a languages degree! I lived
in France for six months! Admittedly, I spent more of that
period quoting Arctic Monkeys lyrics with Parisian teenagers
than actually speaking French, but that was genuinely within
my remit as language assistant! Shout-out once more to the
Premières and Terminales of Lycée Jean-Baptiste Say! Vive les
Metz, RIP Erasmus schemes and fuck Brexit!

Speaking of not speaking French, I'd like to offset my flag
snafu* with the all-time great of the genre, the first Girls Aloud
'Greatest Hits' album in 2006. The first draft of that CD's
cover had a Union Jack on, before it was edited, according to
the quite legitimate wishes of Derry's Nadine Coyle, to include
an Irish flag as well. Unfortunately, the latter flag was printed
backwards, meaning that hundreds of thousands of copies hit
HMV's shelves with an entirely unexplained Ivory Coast flag on
the front, and if any blunders in this book slip past the editors,
I do hope they are anywhere near as untouchable as that. To
be a fly on the wall of Universal Music – an ironic label for
sure – when that error was discovered in 2006! Did it cause a
controversy? Did the Girls enjoy any unexpected west African

---

* Just to emphasise again, Alex: this is my word.

commercial boost? Did Cheryl's then-husband Ashley discuss it with his new Ivorian team-mates?* Penny for the thoughts of Salomon Kalou!

9. Not shutting the fuck up (task three, episode nine)

Having already lamented many of my disqualifications, I have now consulted the logs of *Taskmaster* statistician-in-chief Jack Bernhardt to confirm that I was the worst of a wildly (and *controversially*) disqualification-heavy series, and, in fact, the most-disqualified *Taskmaster* contestant of all time.† Yet more damning evidence that posh boys don't think the rules apply to them.

On this task, though, I was so palpably *trying* to obey the rules, and that's why it's more painful than the spoon greed, the forgetting to clap, the collapsing jelly, or any other disqualified disasterclass. This time I really did know what I *had to not do*. This task was both recorded and watched back quite

---

* Fact-checking the Cole chronology of this tangent has been one of the high points of the book-writing process for me, but it is, as with most of my teenage memories, tinged with heartbreak. Quite aside from the stress of the Coles' own uncoupling later down the line, Ashley's road-raging defection to Chelsea in 2006 basically ruined our family holiday because it upset my Arsenal-supporting brother so much. Alas, these motorway mercenaries spare no thought for their heartbroken eleven-year-old fans, weeping into their waterskiing wetsuits at all-inclusive Corsican holiday camps.

† Like the many records for badness broken by Swindon Town in the then 22-team Premier League 1993–94, the stats have to be adjusted for inflation, and to be fair, Joe Wilkinson getting only one less DQ in the six-episode second series has to give him the true crown, especially since his disqualification for touching the red green while throwing a potato remains the most heartbreaking crushing of a dream in the history of *Taskmaster* or indeed any televised games or sport. Hey Joe, sorry they hurt you!

late in the respective processes: filmed on the final day, the last bit of pre-barge business at the paper mill, when I was desperate to go out on a high, and then shown in episode nine, when I was already a goose-shirted laughing stock, and just desperate not to add any more fails to my feature-length blooper reel. The task was to punch ninety-nine holes in some paper without talking to Alex Horne, and Alex was obviously trying to get us to talk to him throughout. But *surely* I could block it out? Wasn't this the emotional and conversational repression that boarding school had programmed me so expensively for? Staying purse-lipped for years while archbishops of Banterbury told me I had updog on my trousers?* This was what the training was for!

In a neat metaphor for quite a lot of my adolescence, I spent the task gritting my teeth in silence while making an almost violently smiley face. I was fairly sure I'd punched the right amount of holes and I was fairly sure I'd stayed on mute. Then I walked out of the paper mill into the sunshine, and my memory of the day up until that point was wiped in the giddy abandon of driving and then crashing the barge. So when the footage was cued in the studio three months later, I wasn't waiting with dread. And the *Taskmaster* team made it worse by showing me successfully completing the task first, before only then calling for the VAR, like the smiling sociopaths they are. A new clip appeared on the screen, and I knew immediately something horrible was about to happen. And here it was.

---

* Do you not know what updog is? Why not ask yourself 'what's updog?' and then let the pained wince of embarrassed realisation curl over your face, a wince I wore most days, 2004–8.

I'm about halfway through the hole-punching and maybe I'm getting complacent. And my friend Alex Horne asks me a question, and I forget, just for a second, that he is not my friend, he is my opponent, a double agent, a bastard whose bank balance balloons with every brave boy he betrays on the box. He asks me a question, and a word or two in response escapes my mouth before I remember the brief and try to swallow them back. But it has happened, and it has happened on camera.

It was agony to watch in the studio. The head back in the hands, the audience groaning in pity, Greg breathing the unsettlingly poetic 'as cruel as it is undeniable', and Father Frankie delivering the devastating, and rather less poetic, KO: 'You just couldn't shut the fuck up, could you?' It was a brutal assessment and one that has been used many times since, by the many people in my life desperate to tie my tongue, to put a word count on the waffle.[*] I would like to think I *can* shut the fuck up. I observe minute's silences, I try not to chat to my friends at concerts, I barely said a single word on *Mock the Week*. But here, I was prattling putty in the paws of Little Alex Horne, who has successfully gaslit far more mentally stable contestants than me over the years, but was hardly having to attend too many evening classes in neurolinguistic programming to upset this particular apple-cart. A disappointed dad, and another DQ.

10. Not shaving my beard (start to finish, episode ten)

Zooming out of individual blunders to focus on my personal grooming is a rogue twist for the tenth and final regret, I'll

---

[*] Shout-out to my editor, Richard Roper! We got it down to 90,000 in the end!

grant, but alongside the prize tasks, one of the other things that *Taskmaster* contestants get comparative aeons of time to stew over in the run-up to the show is their outfit. Needless to say: I love me a good aeon of stew. Since being on the show I've been able to turn up the heat on other people's stews as well, suffocating the excitement out of future contestants with advice that they immediately regret asking for, as I bury them in *Brideshead Revisited* analogies and finger-wagging warnings about the limitations of Wikipedia. And then, of course, the biggest pressure of all: *what* are you going to wear?

It had not escaped me in 2022 that this fundamentally quite nerdy game show, this puzzlers' paradise, had also become a platform for its participants to look low-key, even high-key, iconic. The year before, I'd filmed six episodes of well-intentioned but abysmally-titled travelogue *British as Folk*, and spent most of it getting ribbed by Fern Brady, Darren Harriott and director Marcus 'Penguin' Liversedge for my crypto-bro hoodies and 'winklepicker' Chelsea boots. This missed opportunity to catwalk through the mean streets of Leicester and Treorchy was mitigated by the show's sub-optimal viewing figures, but this would not be the case with *Taskmaster*. Those clips will be your legacy. You don't get a say in the Taskmaster's judgement, but you can decide what to wear to court. And with every series, the collective awareness of this grows, a boiler-suited arms race to represent yourself, and in Phil Wang's case expose yourself, as memorably as possible.

And what visual legacy did I secure for myself? A green jumper from Marks & Spencer. Quite blandly on-brand, in a way, although not as on-brand as the obvious option, which would have been to wear my Eton uniform. Tailcoat, pinstriped trousers, detachable wing collar, and maybe a top hat even though that hasn't been part of the Eton uniform for decades. Print the myth!* I could have sourced a grown-up version of the uniform for *Taskmaster*, not a million miles from the morning suits I cost-ineffectively hire for schoolmates' weddings, or I could have just dug the original out of my parents' loft and squeezed into the top-tier torment of my teenage tails.

The *Taskmaster* producers weren't pushing for this, luckily, and I've never felt too coerced by any panel show paymaster to

---

* Fun fact about twats: though most boys at Eton wore black waistcoats, in keeping with the funereal misery of it all, there was still one loftier echelon of elitist chic. These were the bespoke, design-your-own waistcoats donned by the twenty or so prefects in the Eton Society, aka 'Pop', the roaring rabble of royals and rahs picked by their predecessors to take their place on the poshest pantheon of them all. Does life get any more exclusive, for better or worse (worse), than being eighteen years old, a prefect at Eton, and getting to design your own waistcoat? There's one particularly vintage snap you may have seen, the Prince William Pop generation of 2000, the luscious-locked prince pegged in amongst multiple bankers-to-be and one future Oscar winner, sporting a grin almost as cheeky as his Aston Villa waistcoat. He's just like us! Or at least, just like the other Pop boys repping Wimbledon and Newcastle in the photo, altogether more carefully judged than the goon in a Che Guevara waistcoat, who later told the *Daily Mail* 'I was into art at the time.' William's apparently arbitrary choice of Aston Villa as a quasi-relatable team to support back in the mid-nineties is a source of great fascination to me, an opportunist who has legitimately supported Swindon Town since I was a kid, but certainly relished it a bit more since being given public platforms to shout-out the Red Army and offset my own blue-bloodnedness en route. There's a certain full-circle poetry of the teenage Wills cementing this choice with a waistcoat, itself the iconic style choice of Villa-captain-turned-England-manager Gareth Southgate twenty years later, and however sincere his intentions, he's certainly done a much better job of committing to the bit than David Cameron ever did.

lean on my schooling any more than I am comfortable with, especially when you never really know how it will go down. The figurine of my thirteen-year-old self in my fresh new tails that I brought to *Cats Does Countdown* in 2019* yielded very little laughter on the show, although it did attain a new lease of life as a curry spork on the train afterwards. Every spring I need multiple nudges to reply to emails about what this year's Fringe show is going to be called, and every time my agent Flo suggests that we could just call it 'Eton Mess', especially given that every year the shows do end up being largely about (a) going to Eton and (b) being a mess. There is definitely a parallel universe where that is the title of this book.

But it's become a point of no return now, stubbornness-wise, and I think tails on *Taskmaster* would have been quite the privilege-based pivot. The Marks & Spencer jumper wasn't hugely exciting, admittedly (he says, having dug it out again for this book's front cover), but I thought the preppy vigour of wearing shorts would stake some sort of claim to individuality. Plus the yellow socks, which any of my old school chums watching would *of course* recognise as a nod to my turn as Malvolio in the 2004 Shakespeare Reading Prize. A cheeky *Twelfth Night* throwback, a little Fabergé Easter egg for Hugo and Tristram to enjoy. I'll have you know I won that Shakespeare Reading Prize in 2004, and were the book tokens worth the bullying? They always were.

As well as my task outfit, I had ten more bites at the

---

* And that's not a TV prop, that's a figurine that actually existed, a souvenir from the photoshoot that my parents evidently felt worth spending another £5 on in 2004, and has been in their bedroom since, making them feel weird every time they look at it.

sartorial apple for the studio records six months later. For those, I sought out the most intricately patterned vintage shirts I could,* ramping up the loudness of my threads to drown out the meek whimpers of my actual performance. As the finale approached, with my last place in the series all but confirmed, I was desperate to go out with a bang, not a whimper, on this wild ride to which I would not be returning in Champion of Champions. In autumn 2022, I was spending a lot of very happy time thinking about *Taskmaster* Series 9, where the five contestants all wore black tie for episode ten, an end-of-series treat for wearers and watchers alike. My constant suggestions that our gang should coordinate clothing for our own episode ten were a heavy subplot of our five days filming at Pinewood, along with my attempts to bin off half my prize tasks, and work out how serious Frankie was being with his own suggestion for the finale: that we all drop acid before the cameras started rolling. Serious or not, Frankie didn't get his trip, although it is still my great and sincere hope that we can cross some kind of hallucinogenic Rubicon together when gaps in our respective tour schedules allow. However, we were, if nothing else, psyche-delic adjacent, after it was decided that the most appropriate, and visually pleasing, nod to the loose sixties theme of the series would be to dress up in *Sgt. Pepper* suits. The Fab Five.

After my own unsuccessful attempts to make inroads with an east London costume hire, the job was passed to Patrick

---

* The bird-bedecked Simon Carter shirt that I wore to impress Richard Ayoade on *Cats Does Countdown* in 2019 has since been replaced, I'm pleased to say, by a constant rotating cast of second-hand threads, most of the *Taskmaster* cuts picked for me by an unpaid stylist called Giuseppe, but most since, for better or worse, picked by me alone. I am contributing to many of the world's environmental ills but fast fashion is rarely one of them!

Jack in the show's wardrobe department, a can-do king who, not for the last time, took my flight of fancy dress and made it flesh. Forty-eight hours after the initial suggestion, the Lonely Hearts Club Band took to the studio for the final time, suited and booted and accessorised to the max, giggling as we took our selfies in the wings, then catwalking out in triumph and sitting ourselves down for an hour-long recording in which the costumes were barely referenced once. It was perfect, and it didn't even matter that Frankie hadn't got hold of any of Lucy's sky diamonds. I'll have the photo of us in those outfits on my fridge forever. It was a triumph. So why the hell is it in the regret list?

I should have shaved my beard.

That's it.

Is that laughable to you as a regret? Is it the sort of thing you might regret once, briefly, or not at all? Well, guess what: I regret it every time I see the photo: so every time I use my fridge.

I'd never experimented with a beard until lockdown one, when other aspects of my life streamlined into worryingly healthy patterns and my main nod to the apocalypse swirling outside the gilded cage was to let my facial hair grow out for the first time ever and not shave until restrictions eased. Steady on, Adam Hills!* Truthfully, March–July 2020 wasn't long enough

---

* Hills's legendary insistence on growing and dyeing his hair and beard is one of the most ingeniously unproduceable running themes of *The Last Leg*, a show I once appeared on with a home-made sculpture called the 'Fetaverse', sticking it to Zuckerberg with my satirical tower of cheese. Unfortunately, the Fetaverse got quite badly squashed on the way to set, and I still owe a really quite massive apology to the Brockley-based creative agency who helped me make it.

to get anywhere near Greek Orthodox levels of wildness: it really just meant a man who'd never had a beard, now having a medium-sized beard for a bit. Lockdown, eh? What were we like?! But two years later, on *Taskmaster*, with facial hair now an option in my life, I made the conscious decision to be fresh of face for the tasks, and then re-bearded for the studio. Schoolboy in shorts to daddy in disco pants! What a glow-up! But it didn't occur to me till we were literally walking to set for episode 10 that there was one historic halfway house still on the table: that my phoney Beatlemania would have been truly enhanced by a beardless 'tache,* the ultimate tribute to Paul McCartney, who I'd had the humbling and only occasionally boring privilege of watching live at Glastonbury earlier that summer. I even asked floor manager Kay if it was still possible to run back upstairs and ask Chrissy in make-up for even the quickest of introductions to the one and only Billy Shears. Kay, one of the most patient people I have ever met, very gently said that no, we were literal seconds from recording. It's too late to shave your beard, Ivo. It didn't matter at all, but I was livid with myself, and the photo's on my fridge, and I'll still be livid about it when I'm sixty-four.

Our agonisingly near-perfect psychedelic drip put a lovely gloss on a shambolic final episode, where I made a balloon animal with hands caked in Vaseline, sang a horribly unmelodic lullaby while wearing a dog-lead, and got an arguably quite

---

* Having failed to reach for the razor on the one occasion where it really made sense, I'm still yet to ever roll the dice on the BT (Beardless 'Tache). It's just quite a statement in 2024, even if there are some swashbuckling ambassadors for the look. BT sporters such as Old Wang, who, as we've established, is not afraid to make these kinds of statements on television.

underwhelming final disqualification of the series for not being able to convince Greg that I wasn't standing in a bucket of ice. But there was one last stare into the abyss that would give a name to the episode* and, two years later, give a name to this book. In a task where we had to fill up a pint glass with water from the furthest distance, I'd come agonisingly close to doing so from the other side of the garden, using a, by my standards, very elegant contraption of bricks and string. I had only filled up three-quarters of the glass, so received zero points, the same score as Kiell, who failed to fill his glass despite being given the use of a hose. When Alex implied, not for the first time, that the other contestants should be embarrassed to have stooped to my level, that was the final straw.

'Please stop using me as a yardstick for failure,' I pleaded through my factually inaccurate beard. People laughed. I came last. And here we are.

---

* My fourth episode title, more than anyone else that series! Do I get a trophy for that? No.

The theme of uncertainty persists and deepens.
Here, the reader is invited not just to find their own answer,
but to complete their own question. Art is an open door.

CHAPTER 2

The Master

From the props I brought with me (or nearly brought with me) from my childhood home, to the thirty-one years' worth of character defects which would be broadcast in high definition to the world, wrapping on *Taskmaster* in September 2022 felt like the culmination of many different stories of my life and career. I'm now so very proud and so very sad to recount another of those stories, a feat of eccentricity and dedication which would have done any *Taskmaster* contestant proud, a decade-long story which also culminated in September 2022.

In November 2012, a few months into my post-university

adulthood living in London and trying (and back then in particular, mostly failing) to be a stand-up comedian, I accepted a cinema invitation on one of many 'nights off' to watch *The Master*, the new Paul Thomas Anderson about a troubled veteran (Joaquin Phoenix) falling in with a charismatic cult leader (Philip Seymour Hoffman). Young, impatient, and probably navigating a chemical trough between Fabrics, I found the film's languid pacing and 137-minute running time to be gruelling work. I said as much a few days later when discussing it with Tom, one of my best friends from university and usually the one with the most interesting opinion to seek out, and probably steal, when it came to film. When it came to loads of things, in fact. But in this case, film.

Tom asked me if I'd watched much Paul Thomas Anderson before, and I had to admit that this was my first. I don't feel like mine was a childhood particularly lacking in film, but it must have been, as I've spent a lot of my adulthood telling people I haven't seen this or that, often something very famous and well-loved, to the point where my ignorance angers them. But Tom was always delighted by the opportunity to be your guide. He and I were living a few tube stops apart in south London, and his job working night shifts at a newspaper meant he, unlike most of my friends, existed in a pleasingly nocturnal parallel to my arduous professional schedule of doing anywhere between four and zero gigs a week. It was therefore not the most outrageously unrealistic thing for him to propose that we sink a couple of afternoons into educating me on the work of Paul Thomas Anderson. I was the student, and he was the Master.

Tom's crash-course off the back of this resolution consisted of *Boogie Nights* and *Magnolia*: the two nineties behemoths that announced to the world the talent and ambition of their director. And playing a minor but emotive role in both – a sweaty, love-struck boom operator in *Boogie Nights*, and a gentle, beleaguered nurse in *Magnolia* – was Hoffman, cementing himself not just as one of Anderson's key collaborators but as a character actor who would come to be acclaimed by most film fans as one of the all-time greats.

But no matter most film fans: the important thing was how much my friend Tom loved him. What I knew well by this point was that to be in the sidecar of Tom's enthusiasm for anything was one of life's great rides. A historian with a colossal sense of narrative and occasion, a sub-editor with a proud eye and love for detail, the verve of Tom's anecdotes and thank-you letters* gave a thrillingly epic sense of scale to the friends lucky enough to be in his orbit, weaving in and out of storylines like a prestige drama, revelling in the big moments and the bubbling subplots, flattering our callow lives with his roving narrative. His sparkling storytelling could take you as easily to a Civil War battle in 1645 as to a college ball in 2009, and he never forgot anything. He was an archivist with a foot in the present and an eye on the future, a nostalgic always in search of new memories, a raconteur and bon viveur in pursuit of all that was most silly and serious about life. This chapter is about him, but it would be a hell of a lot better if he'd written it, and a hell of a lot easier if I didn't have to write 'was' again and again and again.

Tom's infuriatingly impressive time management allowed him not just to excel at both work and play, a party animal

---

* This is a field I have often claimed as my own, including on television, but Tom was the true Master of this domain as well, in both punctuality and panache.

with a double first, but also to eat up more culture on the side than any of the rest of us. He and I shared many bonds, including Bond, most of them laughably on-brand for today's 6 Music Dad generation but a bizarrely heavy dose of almost aspirational introspection for a pair of feckless graduates. *Mad Men*, *The Wire*, The National, Bruce Springsteen: stuff to make middle-aged men contemplate their middle age, and to make pretentious twenty-two-year-old men *anticipate* their middle age. The grisly business of real life: it's messy and relentless but there's so much beauty and joy in there too. Enter Philip Seymour Hoffman.

Or, indeed, exit Philip Seymour Hoffman, a tragic loss at forty six, on February 2nd, 2014, a year after his Oscar nomination for *The Master*, and midway through filming what would be his final role in *The Hunger Games: Mockingjay – Part 2*. 'We should meet up to watch a couple more Hoffmans,' I proposed to Tom. This was a laughably bite-size challenge to my friend with his magnificent appetite for life and its quests, and his reply would come to define years of my life. 'We should watch *all* of them!'

This impish whim soon had a name: the Project. We would mourn and celebrate Phil – as we soon felt invested enough to call him – in the most total fashion, by working our way through his entire filmography in chronological order. Right, then. I paid my first visit to the Wikipedia page I have visited more than any other, back in the days when I still trusted it: 'Philip Seymour Hoffman on screen and stage'. Fifty-five films. This would be no small undertaking. I was nervous that it might become homework, but homework held no fear for Tom, who understood the Project to be so much more than that. This was a glorious adventure, at the magical intersection of fandom and friendship. As we sat down a fortnight later, February 19th 2014, to Phil's first screen appearance, in a *Law & Order* episode from 1991, him twenty-three years old on the show and us twenty-three years old on the sofa, I didn't fully appreciate that what we had just begun would come to constitute not just a patchwork quilt of individual memories but one of my major life achievements. An actor's entire canon! A cultural milestone, but more importantly, a hugely intimate shared experience with a best mate, the Project welcoming many viewers along the way but for the most part consisting of just the two of us. And I couldn't have anticipated just how grateful I would come to be for it, or why.

Which is not to say that it wasn't hard going at points. There was plenty of gold in the young Hoffman hills: his slimy college student (taken down by a blind, roaring Al Pacino) in *Scent of a Woman*, four Paul Thomas Anderson films in six years,* and his iconic cameos as the deliciously delicate assistant Brandt in *The Big Lebowski*, and the foppish, WASPish bully Freddie Miles in *The Talented Mr. Ripley*. Lines like 'This is our concern, Dude', and 'Hey Tommy . . . how's the peeping?' were instant classics, quoted incessantly. But we needed this cheer to offset some truly turgid fare: the inevitable minor roles in all manner of nineties drags and duds which weren't always easy to track down. *My Boyfriend's Back*, *Money for Nothing*, *Triple Bogey on a Par Five Hole:* this stuff was too niche for Netflix, NFI by the BFI. Instead, we were spending often sizeable amounts of money on Region One DVDs off Amazon Marketplace, or VHS tapes that could only be watched at Tom's parents'

---

* *Boogie Nights* and *Magnolia*, plus PTA's debut *Hard Eight*, and the Adam Sandler revelation, *Punch-Drunk Love*.

house, theirs the only VHS player left in town. What was the last thing *you* watched on VHS? Mine was *Joey Breaker*, a film about a movie agent who (and I am quoting its own blurb here) 'meets a remarkable Jamaican and has an epiphany', on November 18th, 2014.

Moreover, though we kept to the chronological remit as loyally as possible, the Project brought other dilemmas too. We watched every movie in its entirety, of course, even if Phil was in it for only two minutes, but what do you do for TV? We wondered if there were any other completists in the world on the same path as us, and if so, a nickel for their thoughts on *Liberty! The American Revolution*, a six-part, six-hour mix of documentary and historical re-enactment which Tom insisted we watch in full, across three sittings, on his parents' ancient PC, even though Hoffman was only in it for a few scenes. I didn't love *Liberty! The American Revolution*, but I trusted the process.

Thankfully, most films were getting easier to track down and, crucially, to enjoy. And we were making such good progress. In one of Phil's most-quoted lines, as real-life rock journalist Lester Bangs in 2000's fun-if-dated *Almost Famous*, he says, 'The only true currency in this bankrupt world is what we share with someone else when we're uncool.' Hoffman's gallery of loners and losers would take in much bleaker figures than Bangs, but those words struck a chord with us, two friends entwined by this not exactly uncool, but certainly unwieldy Project.

Various friends had dipped their toes along the way: Ed persuading me to play FIFA with him on a separate screen during a YouTube viewing of *Leap of Faith*,* Nina and Chris

---

* Steve Martin plays a faith healer in a Kansas drought, 1992.

cooking us oxtail macaroni during the awful *Patch Adams*.* Housemates would happily join us for at least a chunk of *Mission: Impossible III*, Phil's iciest villain in his biggest block-buster, but they would roll their eyes as we told them that we were going to be taking over the living room that afternoon for *The Invention of Lying*,† despite the fact that we'd both seen it before and hated it. This was one of our many rules: we watched everything, and even if we'd already watched it pre-Project, we watched it again. But even those without the time or inclination to watch the films still expressed interest, amusement and even admiration for the Project as it went on. Not everyone was able to ride in Tom's sidecar. But what a joy even to be in the motorcade.

My contributions from the sidecar remained pretty minor. I hosted the odd screening ('Another new location for the Project!' Tom excitedly declared, alongside other congratula-tions, when I moved in with my girlfriend in 2015) and chipped in for oven pizzas and iTunes rentals, but brought criminally little enterprise to the pursuit of our white whale: *Szuler*, the Polish-American film that Wikipedia listed Phil as appearing in before any other back in 1991. Tom was *obsessed* with finding *Szuler*. He emailed the producer, he slid into the DMs of various co-stars,‡ he emailed the Polish Cultural Institute. It was only after he managed to contact (on his second attempt) Pawel Luczynski, manager at Filmoteka Narodowa Warsaw, that the eagle finally landed. It was now late 2017, and we

---

* Robin Williams plays a laughter healer in a Virginia hospital, 1998.

† Ricky Gervais invents lying, 2009.

‡ 'Troy Ruptash says he can't help us,' Tom WhatsApped me giddily one day, 'but he says that Phil was a great guy!!'

were watching films like *The Ides of March*,* released two decades after the mythical *Szuler*. Finally, the myth was in our grasp, and we were sitting down at Tom's new flat ('*another location!!!*') in Brixton to watch the web link Pawel had sent us. What language would this film even be in? The answer: English, with Polish subtitles, and yet, in probably the great punchline of the Project, also dubbed over in Polish. We had no fucking idea what was going on in *Szuler*. We caught the odd snatch of background English, sandwiched between the Polish text on the screen and the Polish words in our ears, and deciphered that Phil was playing some kind of butler, but the inability to follow anything more than that was enough to make a man pine for even the Hoffmanless episodes of *Liberty: The American Revolution*. It was a truly magnificent waste of time. Now we really were on the home stretch.

Alas, though I was certainly emotionally invested by this point, the ongoing lack of organisation in my (now marginally busier) life meant I'd sometimes arrive at Tom's home so late that a screening had to be squeezed into a ludicrously clinical, often genuinely stressful time slot. Tom was generously tolerant of this behaviour, at least to my face, but it was still a shame, because when I *had* left enough time after that day's film to chew on it with him, I was always so glad of it, basking in the glow of my friend's enthusiasm or frustration for whatever we had just watched. Tom blown away by Phil's Oscar-winning performance in *Capote* ('We are truly entering the great man's golden age!'), Tom appalled by pretty much everything other than Phil in *Along Came Polly* ('One of the least believable relationships ever to grace the rom-com

---

* Ryan Gosling is really fit, 2011.

screen!'): both were equally invigorating. This was part of the fun of the journey, of course, tracing a quarter-century of a great actor's career, at first taking whatever role he could get, now alternating between passion projects and paydays, always respecting and improving even the crassest of the latter. Raindance! Make it rain!

Crassness-wise, amidst the cinematic progress elsewhere, the gender politics of *Almost Famous* (awkward) and *The Boat That Rocked* (appalling) made increasingly uncomfortable viewing. The schlubby pals or loser leads usually taken on by Phil were rarely embroiled in sex scenes* or sexist scenes, but his Oscar-nominated supporting role as bushy-tached CIA hothead Gust Avrakotos in *Charlie Wilson's War* was lost amidst the living room debate about the lasciviousness of Aaron Sorkin's script and Mike Nichols' direction,† the whole thing lamented by Tom as an 'egregiously problematic film'. Tom was no self-appointed morality czar, but time spent hearing his balanced and passionate takes on things was never wasted. He spoke generously of his own personal or professional challenges, was a fantastic sounding board for any such problems brought to him (I brought loads), and he always improved my understanding

---

* Though Tom did memorably note during 2012's *A Late Quartet*, 'It's always cowgirl with him!'

† We had been undeniably grateful for 'Hoffman hotties' like Diane Lane or Daisy Hall bringing some glamour to the rubbish we watched in the early days of the Project, but by the noughties we felt these writers and directors should have done better. Which is not to say I didn't spend much of the noughties in something of a proto-incel fugue state myself, with *Nuts* magazines under my bed at Eton and various other audiovisual fare cunningly concealed in a folder on my Acer laptop entitled 'Chemistry GCSE'. I did not do Chemistry GCSE.

of various big moments in British public and political life, which he watched unfold from the offices of an increasingly impressive CV of papers.

To hear Tom talk about his job – a sub-editor with no apparent aspirations to a byline photo, just a lover of news and history, thrilled to be in the engine room – was to be swept up, as ever, in his energy: to fall in love with newspapers, revel in their longevity and complexity, and to lament their slow commercial and – some more than others – spiritual decline. I felt honoured to be shown on more than one occasion Tom's scrapbook of every big front page he had worked on, approached with all the ceremony of a veteran getting his medals out of the attic, and it became the prism through which any major news event would be filtered: 'Is this making it to the scrapbook?' The royal family were frequent flyers, of course: Tom with as balanced a take as ever on their role in modern Britain, but a tingle down his spine and yours as he recounted the unique newsroom fervour around the various monarchy milestones. The biggest was yet to come, of course. In the least macabre or Republican sense, Tom spent a lot of time thinking about what would happen when the Queen died. In the months after the Platinum Jubilee, as her public appearances became sparer, there was the palpable sense of the time approaching, the whistle of history on the wind. Working on those tribute editions would be Tom's proudest professional hour.

We were already retracing the steps of one rich life, of course, and our Hoffman viewings offered frequent pause for rueful contemplation (on the days I wasn't running late for a gig) as we got closer and closer to its – and Phil's – end. Our hero felt fully evolved by now, in physique and repute, the command his characters had in the room and his name carried on the page. And we were all the more invested for having been by his side throughout. Nothing summed that up more than our rewatch (rules are rules) of *The Master*, in January 2018, five years after I'd casually lamented to Tom my boredom at the Screen on the Green. Tom had enjoyed it more back then than I had, but we were both adding a couple of stars to our reviews second time around as we watched the great man duking it out with Joaquin in one of the great cinematic two-handers. Phil's god-collared clash with Meryl Streep in 2008's *Doubt** had probably been the royallest rumble we'd watched him in so far, but this was human drama on a more epic, surreal scale, less about the specifics of plot and incident than two lost souls trying to make sense of the world, corralled and buffeted by forces beyond their control, against bounteous backdrops of ships and shopping centres, dinner parties and desert lands. It may not unseat (the Hoffmanless and therefore irrelevant to these purposes) *There Will Be Blood,* or even *Boogie Nights*, atop most people's Paul Thomas Anderson rankings, but the actor and director's interwoven careers – Phil and Paul, PSH and PTA – meant we were doubly psyched to see the two Ps at the peak of their powers.

What we and most people didn't know in 2012 was that Hoffman's dormant demons were on his shoulder once more, the addictions that had followed him as a younger man now back in his life and set to snatch it away little over a year later. It's not just a desperately sad story but a mildly incongruous one, a twenty-seven-year-old rock star's death for a middle-aged Hollywood doyen, a tragedy into which we could claim

---

* Shout-out to Amy Adams and Viola Davis in the support slots too! Four Oscar noms for acting, Jeremy, four? That's insane.

little insight as a mere couple of completists on the couch. What we had was the films, a life story on screen with plenty of ironies and overlaps to anyone with a gift for articulating this stuff. And Tom had that gift. On February 2nd, 2016, we watched Phil in one of his first leading roles, as a depressed, petrol-huffing widower in 2002's *Love Liza*. We'd not exactly been lacking in bleak films up until this point, and addictions of various kinds reared their heads throughout Phil's work,* but watching this film about grief and substance abuse, written by his brother Gordy, on the second anniversary of his death, was perhaps the toughest viewing of the lot. In the last scene, Wilson finally brings himself to read the letter from his late wife that has been hanging over him until now. 'Carry me in your heart,' she writes to him. 'I talk to you from there.' This redemptive conclusion gave a glimmer of hope at the end of a challenging ninety minutes. But Tom couldn't take much relief from this with the real-life events of 2014 still hanging over us. As he said wistfully to me that day, tongue only half in cheek, 'Sometimes life isn't like the movies.'

The final words spoken by a Philip Seymour Hoffman character in a film are themselves read by someone else in a letter, his death during the filming of *The Hunger Games: Mockingjay Part 2* necessitating some delicate rearrangement in post-production. The *Mockingjay* films aren't a patch on their two predecessors, despite the addition of Hoffman as Plutarch Heavensbee, but it was hard to watch him in it, knowing that Hoffman, not Heavensbee, would be snatched from us before

---

* His performance as a banker-turned-gambler in *Owning Mahowny* the following year saw him praised by Roger Ebert, in a phrase Tom loved, as a 'poet of implosion'.

the credits were even rolling. The Project was reaching its end. There was just one piece left in the puzzle. Our finale was to be a film from 2006 that Tom had long earmarked as the most potent of the lot (I hadn't seen it, obviously): Charlie Kaufman's sprawling, divisive play-within-a-play *Synecdoche, New York*. Tom was prepared to put chronology to one side for this one, too. We would do all the others, and then finish with *Synecdoche*, a film no easier than *Mockingjay*, but more fitting to Phil's legacy: a cultishly acclaimed, darkly comic meditation on life and theatre, rather than two stretched halves of a ponderous franchise finale.

Our pace of consumption had slowed, though, and it was about to hit two major roadblocks: the birth of my daughter in 2019, then the lockdowns in 2020. We could have watched *Synecdoche* on a Zoom call, I suppose: it would have been a 'new location' with a historic specificity Tom would have relished. But that's no way to wrap up. We talked about hiring a cinema for *Synecdoche* and inviting everyone who had joined us along the way, laughing at the contrast between the scale of the celebration and the melancholy of the film itself. But we never got round to it. I was certainly conscious of being genuinely reluctant to close the last door on this epic chapter of my life. And there were more lockdowns, and more milestones, namely Tom's wedding to Jess in August 2021.

Jess had been at university with me and Tom and they'd first got together at my parents' house in January 2013, on the day Paolo Di Canio helped clear the snow off the County Ground pitch so Swindon's game against Shrewsbury could go ahead. Their 2021 wedding had had to stare down bigger obstacles than could be resolved by one mad Italian with a shovel: it had been booked in since 2019, before any of us had heard of Covid, but the two-year engagement had turned into the most marathon game of corona chicken, multiple lockdowns of watching everyone else's celebrations getting canned while Tom and Jess held on, postponement deals declined, deposit refunds waived, regulation speculations changing by the week. They held on, and they won. Their wedding, spread over their two colleges back in Oxford, would have been a special enough weekend even without the glory of its very survival, a wild enough time even without it being the first full-scale party most revellers had attended in eighteen months. It was a joyous, sun-kissed triumph, full of grace and poetry, where Tom delivered a stunning and moving groom speech he'd polished for months and then unleashed specially devised dance moves into the anarchy of Covered Market nightclub 'Escape'. After legendary performances at his friends' nuptials over the years, he was now realising his ultimate ambition: to be an 'impact guest' at his own wedding. Jess and Tom moved into their first home together shortly afterwards: another new chapter, another new location. But still no *Synecdoche*.

In August 2022, Tom came to visit me in Edinburgh, as he did nearly every year, forever one of the great supporters of my efforts, but this time with a brilliantly on-brand bonus brief: researching the knights of the 17th century. This topic was broadly unexamined in most comedy shows that Fringe, but a key part of the postgraduate degree that Tom had started alongside his day job on Fleet Street. He and I crawled out of the same artists' bars at 3am, but only one of us was back at the Caroline grindstone a few hours later, deep in the archives of the National Library of Scotland, digging through the correspondence of Charles I, shedding new light on centuries-old mysteries. And then, suddenly, two weeks later, in September

2022: more history. A new King Charles. The scrapbook about to welcome some more front pages. 'Cometh the hour, cometh the man!' I texted my friend, the 'man' in question not so much Charles but Tom himself, the man now in the biggest week of his journalistic career, the man who thought so deeply about life and legacy, the man who had guided me through a five-year, fifty-five-film tribute to one actor, the man now playing his part in the national response to the most momentous public passing any of us would ever know. But I never got to hear about it, because that weekend Tom, too, was taken from us. He was killed in a road traffic accident: it could not have been more sudden, or more random, or more difficult to believe. There was no reply to 'cometh the man'. It was the last text I ever sent to him.

I don't know with any certainty what Tom would have made of me writing all this. In the weeks after his death, in the dreamlike horror of the official memorials and over the many miserable cups of tea in between, all sorts of laments poured forth, one of the most frequent being how we had lost the wisest person we could have talked to about this, had it happened to anyone else. As well as his insight, we had lost our collective memory bank, our best friend with his phenomenal recall and his dedication to preserving his and our stories, knowing that everything happening to us right now was our own future legend. Alongside other diaries, he had kept a handwritten journal of our Hoffman efforts, writing up a short summary of each (the ultimate lesson to erratic diary-keepers: they only have to be short!), when and where and with whom we watched, and what we thought. The journal occasionally zoomed out to that week's news, the various elections, referendums and scandals that might cast some shadow on our subject ('*Patch*

Adams seems all the more unsettling post-Savile,' he wrote in 2015). It was a minor – if never rectified – shame to me at the time that this journal was such a unilateral affair: 'I must do a review before we're done!' I said on more than one occasion, but never did.

Now, however, I did have a role. I typed up the journal to send to friends in 2023, and have re-read it several times since, hugely grateful for its existence but devastated by what it has come to represent. Tom leaps off the page in every sentence, his thrill at the hits ('We had a live one on our hands!') only surpassed by his fury at the misses ('An odious, flat, rotten-souled whinge of a film, watched with howls of anguish and rage').* And of course, his almost self-parodying dedication to its subject, a universally celebrated actor but one whose reputation was burnished at every turn here, even in the most insalubrious of settings. 'Phil, of course, turned in yet another selfless performance,' Tom wrote of Todd Solondz's *Happiness*, 'and seeing him shirtless, cleaning up his own jizz, was a remarkable demonstration of his allegiance to his craft.' Tom's phrasings of things are pilfered all over this chapter: I've laughed so much at his journal, and I've cried so much at it too. I miss my friend, and I miss the innocence of those quiet afternoons, and reading meditations on loss from someone you then lost is the most ludicrous of cosmic jokes. Sometimes life isn't like the movies.

Tom wasn't in fifty-five films, one *Law & Order* episode and a six-part documentary about the American Revolution, but he hasn't exactly left us short of material either: his extensive writings of fiction and non-fiction on various subjects, his vast

---

* This film's identity available upon request!

library of shared memories now passing into our collective custody, and the web of traditions, plans and ideas that we've used to forge whatever paths we can out of the dark. He'd already sorted my ticket for Bruce Springsteen in 2023 (just as he did in 2009 and 2013), and so, a year after the booking, in a whole horrible different universe, Jess and his parents and I held each other tight, as Bruce finished his own set with a whispered 'I'll See You in My Dreams'. Tom's post-wedding stag do in October 2022 was not cancelled, but upheld as the most raw and raucous of memorials. A sprawling community of his family, friends and fans cycled the length of the country in his name in 2024. And once a year since, on February 2nd, the day the world lost another great man, lovers of Phil and Tom alike have come together to honour the Project. More on all of the above in due course.

As I write this, it has been just over two years without Tom, and I am loath to wrap this period up in any neat bow, as if the lessons of such an experience can fill a hole that will remain, forever, just that: a hole. Life forces us all to confront its cruelty at some point: to snap ourselves out of complacency and take time wherever possible to be grateful, to cherish the good times, to tell our loved ones how important they are. Tom was living these lessons all the time: keeping his diaries, upholding his friendships, reminiscing backwards, planning forwards. Whether he was telling a story from four years ago or four hundred, he never let go of the thread that connected it to the now. He took so many photos: not just at parties and weddings but over short coffees and long walks, never disappearing into his phone to crop and filter but just getting the record in, surprising you with it at some later date, delighting you with your own everyday history. We didn't know how quickly and painfully we'd come to treasure these photos. We all take a lot more now. Tom truly knew that shared experience is life's most precious currency, and what enduring riches he gave us.

We carry him in our hearts. He talks to us from there.

CHAPTER 3

Fringe Concerns

In 2009, the freshers' year that I first got to know Tom then rolled thrillingly into the summer that I first performed at the Edinburgh Fringe. I made so many memories that August and so many more in the Augusts that followed, as comedy crept year on year from caper to career.

I recently and very belatedly hoovered up first the book and then the TV adaptation of *One Day*, both in just a few sittings, the climax just as shocking on page and screen. David Nicholls' story had been a bizarre blind spot for a decade and a half, despite being seemingly precision engineered for my own noxious nostalgia, and with so many of its reveries revolving around the Scottish capital. I have my own tantalising timehop of photos from Arthur's Seat, the extinct volcano in Holyrood Park which Dex and Em climb, in the bleary innocence of the book's first chapter, on St Swithin's Day 1988. Twenty-four years and one month later, August 2012, at the end of a bromantic night of our own on the Cowgate, Tom and I climbed it too, taking our tops off in the mist for reasons I can't now remember, but probably aren't *nothing* to do with single-sex education. It was, like so many adventures with Tom, the thing he always aimed these adventures to be: a multi-segmented quest we would remember forever. Dex and Em's graduation summer was now our own. Our whole lives were ahead of us. Whatever happens tomorrow, we had today.

I'm going to tumble back into that timehop now, in the spirit of Tom the historian, in the style of David Nicholls the annualist, and in the hope that another potted past will help us better process the present. But then I would say that. I'll always find an excuse for another potted past. *Back to the Future* is my favourite film, and the controls for my Delorean are always set for some distorted dreamscape of my own youth. I hope these dreamscapes give some idea of how much the Fringe means to me. I hope they capture not just my own evolution but the Fringe's, if only through its prizes and its prices. I hope we've got enough plutonium!

2009

Comedy Award winner: Tim Key
Comedy Award sponsor:[*] Foster's
Cost of a pint of Tennent's:[†] £3.30

Ivo Graham: performing as the youngest fifth of delightful if unavoidably undiverse mixed-bill show *The Lunchtime Club* (13:15, Tron, forty punters a day). My first ever ticket to Edinburgh, and an opportunity that was so much bigger than its fifteen minutes' daily stage time, though that was massive too. I used this stage time to mumble into the floor about student drinking games, a routine that won me 'So You Think You're Funny!' at the end of the month, the biggest moment of my life up till that point. The whole thing was organised by producers Jon Briley and Lisa Keddie, to whom I will forever be grateful for asking me, alongside Paul and Rachel, the cousins whose spare bed I was splayed on for far longer than any of us expected.

---

[*] Formerly Perrier, of course, and still, despite not sponsoring it since 2005, the word by which the Award still seems to be most referred, e.g. by Foster's winner Tim Key himself.

[†] The ChatGPT-assisted Tennent's inflation index is an only semi-satisfactory substitute for the main thing pricing more and more people out of the Fringe: the ballooning cost of accommodation. Every year brings more and more horror stories, and something simply must be done to put a leash on the landlords, but with such a vast range of horror stories it is nigh on impossible to knock it into any sort of average cost. Hence the pints.

2010

Comedy Award winner: Russell Kane

Comedy Award sponsor: Foster's

Cost of a pint of Tennent's: £3.50

Ivo Graham: performing for thirty minutes a day (drinking games and driving tests) as half of *Lunchtime Club* spin-off *Ivo Graham and Alfie Brown* (21:30, GRV, twenty punters a day). Then a dash across town to perform for twenty minutes a day (drinking games and driving tests, but faster) alongside Davey See, Naz Osmanoglu and Josh Widdicombe in *The Comedy Zone* (22:45, Pleasance Cabaret Bar, a hundred and fifty punters a day). The earlier show exposed me and Alfie in all sorts of ways we couldn't have anticipated: the latter show led to friendships that have set the course of my career ever since.

2011

Comedy Award winner: Adam Riches

Comedy Award sponsor: Foster's

Cost of a pint of Tennent's: £3.80

Ivo Graham: kicking heels on university year abroad in St Petersburg, not really moving things along much on the learning Russian or losing virginity front, instead preferring to spend my days reading Fringe reviews from internet cafés on Nevsky Prospekt. 'The longer we look at a funny story,' Nikolai Gogol wrote in 1842, 'the sadder it becomes.'

2012

Comedy Award winner: Doctor Brown
Comedy Award sponsor: Foster's
Cost of a pint of Tennent's: £4
Ivo Graham: performing under directors Sophie Duker and Dylan Townley as part of *The Oxford Imps* (15:15, Gilded Ballon, fifty punters a day), after starting each day splitting an underattended hour with growling voice of a generation, Liam Williams, in *Ivo Graham and Liam Williams* (12:30, Captain Taylor's Coffee House, ten punters a day). My material at the latter was mostly culled from a full show, *A Degree of Uncertainty*, that I'd performed at the end of my last term at Oxford, a show largely concerning my increasingly concerning non-loss of virginity. This Fringe was a hugely fun month despite the ongoing V plates, but worth missing the whole London Olympics for? Perhaps not.

2013

Comedy Award winner: Bridget Christie
Comedy Award sponsor: Foster's
Cost of a pint of Tennent's: £4.20
Ivo Graham: performing debut Edinburgh hour *Binoculars* (18:00, Pleasance Cellar, forty punters a day). A promising show with a mysterious title,* largely consisting of more adventures in virginity (now finally lost), including a fourth and final Fringe

---

* The title, a nod to something my brother had said at my expense the previous Christmas, was explained in the closing routine, but it was probably still too nondescript a name for a debut show. I'll brush past my relative pride/shame in my show titles as this history goes on, but many of them, including this one, would undeniably have made more sense if they were just called 'Eton Mess' like Flo suggested.

for my 'Never Have I Ever' routine. The show was waylaid in its final ten minutes by a quite bafflingly long story about buying discounted Ambrosia Rice Pudding with my grandmother while lodging with her in 2013. This year of trying to teach my beloved Babooshka (1928–2020) to use her television, in exchange for no rent and constant Charlie Bigham lasagnes, was a hugely special thing for our relationship. Nonetheless, the Ambrosia anecdote is the thing I petulantly decided to blame for my 'Best Newcomer' non-nomination.

2014

Comedy Award winner: John Kearns
Comedy Award sponsor: Foster's
Cost of a pint of Tennent's: £4.40
Ivo Graham: performing sophomore Edinburgh hour *Bow Ties & Johnnies* (20:15, Pleasance That, fifty punters a day). A great show with a great title, mainly boasting that I was now not just a non-virgin but someone's actual boyfriend. The show featured a routine about thank-you letters that I would later do on *Live at the Apollo,* and yes, the audience got a thank-you letter on the way out. I also banged on, not for the first or last time, about being posh, this year via the dynamite prop of a 1999 school magazine whose cover showed an eight-year-old me reading a *Match* magazine on a bench on my own, while more popular boys played croquet across the lawn. I blew this cover up to the largest size Ryman's would allow, and compare-contrasted it with the more ludicrously heroic cover star of 2008. This ludicrous hero was, of course, a family friend, and I referred to him as an 'Aryan nightmare' every day without seeking his or his parents' permission. Sorry, Mr Coleridge!

2015

Comedy Award winner: Sam Simmons

Comedy Award sponsor: Foster's

Cost of a pint of Tennent's: £4.50

Ivo Graham: performing third Edinburgh hour *No Filter* (18:00, Pleasance Beside, seventy punters a day). A weak show with a weak title, a cack-handed young fogey muddle through my increasingly serious relationship and my struggles with modern tech. The show featured one very silly routine about once having a Nokia 3210 without a working 7 button, and the various *amusing* modifications I would have to make to texts to write them without the letters PQRS. The audience got a letter on the way out of this show, too, thanking them for coming without using any of said letters, but that was just one of various ways that I was chasing the highs of last year and not really coming close.

2016

Comedy Award winner: Richard Gadd

Comedy Award sponsor: lastminute.com*

Cost of a pint of Tennent's: £4.60

Ivo Graham: taking a sensible year off, treading literal water at a Croatian wellness festival after the comedic water-treading the previous year.

---

* I was nowhere near nomination in any of the three years lastminute.com was the sponsor of the Edinburgh Comedy Award, but needless to say, it would be a very on-brand sponsor for most of my life and work.

2017

Comedy Award winner: Hannah Gadsby & John Robins
Comedy Award sponsor: lastminute.com
Cost of a pint of Tennent's: £4.70
Ivo Graham: performing fourth Edinburgh hour *Educated Guess* (20:15, Pleasance Beneath, a hundred punters a day). A great show with a great title, its riffs about privilege and politics hitting a fraction harder after the various electoral cataclysms that had occurred during my fallow year. The show used the premise of 'feeling guilty about not knowing enough about politics' as a very mealy-mouthed segue to its central 'stunt', that I'd learned all 650 MPs of the UK, a stunt that was quite rightly dismissed by some critics as 'not exactly comedy', but did serve me very well on *Pointless Celebrities* a few years later.* This show featured its own TV quiz throwback, a brutal

---

* As well as riding the constituencies of Pontefract and Pontepridd to the *Pointless* prize in 2022, the routine also saw me booked for Channel 4's election-night show in 2019, where I was told I would be reprising my *hilarious* stunt of 2017 and trying to learn the new MPs as they came in, in time for a quiz at 5am. Unfortunately, the 11pm exit polls proved so atmosphere-inhalingly depressing in both the studio and green room that most of the comedy bits, including my own, were abandoned, replaced by extended round-table analysis such as Stanley Johnson riffing about pilots in burqas and Amber Rudd threatening to deport Nish. What possible light relief could an Old Etonian comedian bring to this most gracious of victory parades? Though in reality a virtue-signalling leftist who'd spent the day campaigning for Labour in Bedford with Mark Steel, I am aware how outwardly, and perhaps still inwardly, I am just another champagne-centrist toff who won't be affected by any of this, so I was quite colossally relieved not to have to bring my 'let's see if I've managed to learn all the new Red Wall Tories!' vibe-murdering to the table in the wee smalls. That being said, DOA as my bit clearly was from the moment Huw Edwards revealed the scores, it wasn't *fully and finally* confirmed to have been cancelled until 3am, so I was still there in the green room for hours, in many ways the loneliest character of the whole enterprise, not even attempting any gallows humour with the rest of the sacked humourists, because I was sitting on my own learning the new MPs *just in case*. It was the night I learned the name Jonathan Gullis. It was a truly miserable night.

dissection of my 2009 humiliation on *The Weakest Link*, with video at the end to boot. The show packed this in alongside its own (entirely MP-based) quiz, and strong routines about family holidays, school reunions, and watching Jeremy Corbyn at Glastonbury. I had recently done *Live at the Apollo* and *Mock the Week* for the first time, and I felt ever so tentatively like I was on a roll. The MP quiz went much better some days than others, but the show always went well. I loved this Fringe.

2018

Comedy Award winner: Rose Matafeo
Comedy Award sponsor: lastminute.com
Cost of a pint of Tennent's: £4.80
Ivo Graham: performing fifth Edinburgh hour *Motion Sickness* (18:40, Pleasance Cabaret Bar, a hundred and fifty punters a day). An OK show with a Hot Chip title,* bringing my audiences up to speed on some rapidly escalating life commitments with a comedic hesitancy that betrayed the non-comedic hesitancy bubbling beneath. Solid if unspectacular routines about Chiltern Railways, Go Ape and buying a second-hand fridge, the latter featuring a topper about a Taskrabbit called Fernando ('can you hear the hum . . .') that was generously slid my way by Renaissance cheesemonger Charlie Baker. Charlie and our agent Flo were two of the first people with whom I shared the biggest news of my life halfway through that Fringe, the news that my partner was two months pregnant, that my show

---

* 'My third favourite Hot Chip song, and a cracker by Phoebe Bridgers', boasted the blurb. A needless level of detail for the Fringe brochure, but a solid early plant of my Bridgers flag in the sand, before she went massive in lockdown. Flat, fiancée, baby and Bridgers: I was ahead of the curve of *everything* in 2018! Somebody roll the windows down!

about whether or not I was ready to be a father was about to become very out of date. I was still touring this show, about whether or not I was ready to be a father, as a new father seven months later, and I was still touring it as a single father a few months after that. Who wouldn't get motion sickness when life is coming at them this fast?

2019

Comedy Award winner: Jordan Brookes
Comedy Award sponsor: the Dave channel*
Cost of a pint of Tennent's: £5
Ivo Graham: performing sixth Edinburgh hour *The Game of Life* (19:00, Pleasance Forth, two hundred and fifty punters a day). A great show with a great title,† in the midst of an offstage freefall which was by now well known to most of my

---

* I was very tempted to just put 'Dave', but despite the channel's domination of the UK panel show (repeat) scene this century, there really will be some people who read it as just a man called Dave.

† In February 2019, the month my daughter was born, but also the annual deadline for pinning the blurb (title) on the donkey (unwritten show), it felt fairly certain, however much my life stabilised or imploded between then and the Fringe, and however much I wanted to talk about it, that a title like *The Game of Life* would be a broad enough umbrella to cover literally any of the recent developments, not least the heavenly new actual *Life* we had welcomed that month at Kingston Hospital. If I had really got my shit together, we could have mocked up a poster mimicking 'The Game of Life' board game box, lots of different Ivos playing the game against each other, an almost queasily neat metaphor for my inability to settle on what kind of future I wanted. I don't and didn't have my shit together, though, so for the third year in a row I went for a generic shot of me staring into the middle distance, courtesy of sharp-shooting, Darude-blasting ex-flatmate Matt Stronge.

friends and family, but not my audiences. Insights about new parenthood boiled down to essentially not having enough time to watch TV opening credits, make a pot of coffee or (hello old friend!) have a wank. Oh, that this was the case: I had more than enough time for all of these activities in summer 2019. But even if the Fringe was only getting half the story, it was a very well-drilled half, with a genuine quotable one-liner about Eton advent calendars – 'the doors are opened for me by my father's contacts' – and a closing routine about interdental brushes which was probably the strongest stand-up I'd ever performed. I was grateful to so many people that month: to flatmate Alfie Brown, to pub quiz supremo Ed Strong, to honking Australian people-trafficker Rebecca Austin, and to Lily, Richard and Flo at Off The Kerb, keeping me and my Fringe on the rails in circumstances they can barely have understood themselves. On the last Wednesday of the Fringe, I was in a café on Nicolson Street.* watching my agent Flo get the 'your act's been nominated' phone call that I'd always dreamed of having a front row seat for. Jordan Brookes won the Dave and the ten grand.† and it wasn't hard to be pleased for him: as far as I was concerned, the nomination alone marked mission accomplished, and I could spend a glorious final weekend eating La Reine pizza, watching Ben Stokes tear up Headingley, and getting so drunk with my brother at Cabaret Voltaire that I accidentally locked

---

* Spoon, the first-floor brunchers' paradise which sadly made it through one empty lockdown but not the second.

† Jordan also then got to do some simply fantastic tweets about being the undefeated champion when Covid denied him any competitors in 2020 or 2021. A historic reign!

him out of our flat. And then it was Monday morning and it was time to go. A lot of heavy shit was waiting for me on the other side of the Fringe, but I could travel back to it with my self-confidence boosted rather than dented further. More than ever before or since, I'd needed Edinburgh to go well, to be a safe haven of pride and defiance as the rest of my life rumbled ominously ahead of it. I'm very lucky that it did. And I couldn't wait to see my little girl.

2020

Comedy Award winner: n/a

Comedy Award sponsor: n/a

Cost of a pint of Tennent's: £5 but stay away from the pub

Ivo Graham: navigating the last of the sun-kissed dystopia of lockdown one, which my ex and I had elected to spend co-parenting together in my childhood home, these five confusingly happy months marking the longest unbroken period I'd spent in that home since being cheerily chucked out to boarding school in September 1998. My own parents' unexpected quarantine on the other side of the world meant that we got full run of the house (arrest): all of the AGA, none of the aggro. We cooked some damn good meals in that AGA in lockdown one. And then we put our daughter to bed and watched *Normal People* together and went off to sleep in separate bedrooms. It was a fucking weird time.

2021

Comedy Award winner: n/a

Comedy Award sponsor: n/a

Cost of a pint of Tennent's: £5.20 but you'll need an app

Ivo Graham: making a very cost-ineffective one-day trip to Edinburgh to perform a single socially-distanced work-in-progress called *Hyper Reality* (Pleasance Rear Courtyard, 20:45, fifty punters in masks), at a very scaled-down Fringe, after a year gigging mainly in car parks and on Zoom. As well as slow-cooking with my ex, and coddling our offspring from waddling to toddling, the lockdowns were also spent doing something I hadn't really done, despite many parental pleas, since the late 1990s: tidying my room. I went to boarding school *and* hoarding school, you see: a joint honours that teaches you to treat your emotions like the rest of your possessions, and shove them out of sight under the bed. In 2020, I looked under that bed, literally and spiritually, for the first time in about twenty years, and the clutter I unearthed formed the basis of that year's work-in-progress and many shows beyond. What did you think was going to happen? I was going to throw the shit away and make peace with my past? No, I was going to file it, embellish it, and then wallow in it further, for money!

2022

Comedy Award winner: Sam Campbell

Comedy Award sponsor: the Dave channel

Cost of a pint of Tennent's: £5.50

Ivo Graham: performing seventh Edinburgh hour *My Future, My Clutter* (19:30, Pleasance One, three hundred punters a day). A strong show with a clunky-as-fuck title, a nod to a very niche album by The Fall that I haven't even ever listened to,* but also a nod to the fact that I had spent most of the last three years pondering my future and my clutter. I spent this show, which is available to watch on YouTube under the title *Live From The Bloomsbury Theatre*, reading through old school textbooks and tentatively revealing the collapse of my relationship, both threads sowing the seeds for later, even less comedic, adventures in my show, *Carousel*. My cry-jinks in the minefield of modern parenting were of course but a footnote to the rather more global crisis that had kept most punters away from Edinburgh since 2019. In the run-up to the Fringe, while the vaccinated vanguard got ready to squeeze and sweat into some of the least socially distanced rooms in the universe, comedians and commentators had been wondering what on *earth* we were all going to do about this unprecedented and definitionally universal

---

* I'm a very casual Fall fan, really just *This Nation's Saving Grace*, and I dare say the late irate Mark E.Smith would be furious about an Eton boy doffing his top hat to him at the Edinburgh Fringe. The title of this show should have been *Nuclear Fallout* but I didn't have the stones to go through with it. Its replacement, *My Future, My Clutter,* was momentarily funny in February and a pain in the arse all August. If this footnote is being read by anyone who might one day take a show to the Fringe, or any other stratospherically expensive arts festival, really do think about how many times you're going to have to say your show title out loud, and how many times other people are going to have to say it. Is saying it a pleasant or at least not unpleasant experience? Really think about whether it's a pleasant or at least not unpleasant experience. Unless you're explicitly going for unpleasant, as in the case of Mat Ewins' glorious 2018 usher-bamboozler *My Mistake! The Doors Are Not Open; The Show Has Been Cancelled. Do Not Have Your Tickets Ready!*

shared experience. Would we be trying to put the trauma behind us, or would we be unable to resist nibbling the low-hanging bat of jokes about Barnard Castle, Joe Wicks, etc.? Well, in my case it was yes to Barnard Castle, no to Joe Wicks, and yes to quite a long story about having a psychedelic breakdown about my ex's new boyfriend on a hot day at Peppa Pig World. I was the only piper playing *that* particular tune at Edinburgh 2022, and I felt weirdly proud of it, and I had a lovely month, eating lots of haggis and lots of mushrooms and persuading lots of comics to all buy the same blue jacket from the Scotland Shop on South Bridge. I'm wearing that jacket in a photo Tom took of us when he came to visit in the final week. It's the last photo he ever took of us.

And now it was time to think about Edinburgh all over again.

A rare piece of autobiography on commission;
a glimpse at the life behind the art. Biographers speculate that
the artist shared this spring 2025 brunch with her auntie Ginna,
auntie Georgia, thespian cousin Giles Havergal, and
a reliably face-pulling dad.

CHAPTER 4

Traitors and Trumps

After the whirlwind of the *Taskmaster* filming week had yanked me from the horror of that September, autumn and winter 2022 laid on further distractions, festive seasonings for the set menu of co-parenting, touring, and grieving my friend. The co-parenting part was getting ever more contentious, too: 2023 was shaping up to be a confrontational year on that front, and so I was happy to be distracted from that wherever possible too. We had a new King and a new Prime Minister, doing their best to follow the seventy-year and forty-five-day reigns of the Elizabeths that had preceded them. We had the bloodstained carnival of the Qatar

World Cup, England's quarter-final defeat to France the earliest exit of Gareth's four tournaments, but still providing his unrelated biographers, Ivo and James Graham,* with enough material for their respective Southgate shows later down the line. We had the first series of *The Traitors*, a national obsession over its three weeks on BBC1, and this too was something I would end up doing more stand-up about than anyone might have expected or wanted me to. I started a music podcast with my friend Alex Kealy, its dedication to celebrating and chronicling friendship and fandom very much its own tribute to Tom. Amongst other outings, we went to watch Franz Ferdinand at the Alexandra Palace, the band and its adjacent podcasts such a fixture of that autumn that I now can't listen to them without thinking of that time and feeling sad. Meanwhile, just before Christmas, my friends Craine† and Clare got married at the Union Club in Soho, and at the party afterwards, the furious competition between the wedding guests to whom they'd allotted half-hour DJ sets planted a seed that would grow into one of the most admin-heavy clubnights of all time.

With every comedian's Christmas comes the choice of whether to go back to the Fringe the following August, and this was a bit of a no-brainer ahead of 2023, when I would become one of the latest five beneficiaries of modern commercial phenomenon

---

* Ivo Graham's stand-up show *Grand Designs* and James Graham's rather more acclaimed play *Dear England*, both of which will be covered further later on.

† Craine is the lovely comedian and writer Tom Craine, whose first name will pop up later in this very chapter, but which is not an ideal first name to be dropping so soon in the context of the chapters just gone. There are a lot of Toms in this book and they are all people in their own right but it is still not *ideal* that they are all called Tom.

'the *Taskmaster* effect': a brief but potentially lucrative period where anything you could get to market by the time of (or within recent memory of) the show's broadcast would sell quicker than anything you'd ever sold before, and might ever sell again. My new stand-up show, and first in this new shop window, had its flimsy foundations laid out within the first few hours of 2023.

I had travelled to east London to see in the New Year, not for the first time, at casa Widdicombe, and on this occasion, with the first series of *The Traitors* a ratings smash that December, I had decided to dominate proceedings by forcing a bespoke game of it onto a decidedly mixed-ability party at Josh and Rose's house. A wholesome gaggle of young families had come round to the house earlier in the day to unleash their kids on the nation's favourite parenting podcasters,* before the

---

* Biting the hand that feeds is always a tasty treat, but it's worth underlining in a gushy footnote that not only have I loved and learned from a great many episodes of *Parenting Hell* as a listener, but that I appreciated appearing on an early episode in September 2020 as a delicately purgative outlet for some of my own domestic challenges at that time. Josh has lent his ear to more private overshares on many occasions, and I can almost always count on his kindness and discretion, even if he did once tell a story about me smoking a bifter on *Mel Giedroyc's Unforgivable*. I know Rob Beckett less well, but he, too, once gave me an extremely supportive dressing room pep talk about some of my co-parenting woes before I appeared on his own not dissimilarly titled panel show, *Undeniable*. 'At the end of the day it's just more people that love her, right?' he said, patting me encouragingly on the back before we went down to the studio and I dried my eyes in time to do a needlessly long monologue about *The Apprentice* Series 1–6. The most furtive and top-shelf counsel I got that summer, though, was from Judi Love, between scenes at *Backstage with Katherine Ryan,* in a chat we had to have in the bathroom, mics off like Tim in *The Office,* because our actual backstage was being filmed for the show. Wheels within wheels! Thanks again for that bathroom hug, Judi!

hellraisers went to bed upstairs and I took the wheel to steer the stiff necks into something genuinely stressful.

Josh's enthusiasm for the TV show of *The Traitors*, and my confidence that a sizeable enough majority of his guests would also be 'on team', meant that, for the first time in years, I felt I had the votes to get a proper parlour game over the line at a house party. Nearly a decade before, I'd been part of a friend-group that had been so obsessed with this same game – then under the name *Mafia* (they've rebadged it, you fool!) – that we'd gone away to Wales for the weekend and played about eight rounds of it in a row, sacking off meals and sleep in our collective zest to spend as little time as possible doing anything other than killing and banishing. It's a great format, and thanks to the TV show, with breakout star Wilf playing it almost as deliciously as Claudia Winkleman was hosting it, the format was now a national concern. Treachery is an addiction, and Britain was addicted. Time to push this gear into a vulnerable and unsuspecting family home.

I can lay no claim to Claudia's glamour or gravitas as a presenter, host and fashion icon. However, I had 'committed to the bit' as best as a man with no real instinct for costume or design can: by ordering a wig and a cape to Josh's house on December 29th via Amazon Prime. Ed Gamble's wife Charlie, joined by law to some of the most unapologetic body art in UK comedy, took my own gothic rizz up a couple of notches with a thick layer of eyeliner, furtively applied upstairs before I returned to the party, brought any non-*Traitors* related conversation to an abrupt end and started laying down the rules. As anyone who's ever tried to get any kind of game over the line at a party knows, especially if the party hasn't been specifically organised for this purpose and there are non-believers in your midst, you have to lay down these rules as quickly as you can in whatever brief window of authority you have managed to carve out for yourself. Not too many rules laid down early, but not too few. Enough that the basic principles of the game are made clear, and that people aren't getting tripped up on these basics later, and complaining (which they will) that you didn't mention them. But not so many rules that people are exhausted by the mechanics before you have even got started. It is the most delicate of roles: a pleading blend of supply teacher, charity fundraiser and, of course, open-mic comedian. Alex Kealy's attempt to explain the board game *King of Tokyo* a few months previously, in a hot hut in Cornwall that he had booked for his own birthday, was a bold but valid late-night pivot that might have got over the line if it wasn't for a cackling, non-contributing goon squad undermining him at every turn. I was part of that goon squad. We did not play *King of Tokyo* that night and a large part of me guiltily suspects I never will.

The downside of trying to organise a game at a party full of comedians is that these pricks are especially convinced of the brilliance of their own interruptions, and often with some statistical evidence behind them. Widdicombe has done *Mock the Week* twenty-three times. Gamble has done it thirty-six times. I have done it three times.* I couldn't get a word in edgeways then, so what hope did I have of getting it in now? The flipside, though, especially now that these flat-track bullies have gone on to helm formats of their own, is that they're no

---

* This league table of week-mockers – all the neater now that the stats, barring a digital reboot, are frozen in time – is another of my favourite Wikipedia pages.

strangers to the delicate mechanics of a fledgling panel show, and many of their producers were on the sofa that night. One of those producers was tiny-footed Woolyback Stu Mather, who prior to Widdicombe's *Hypothetical* had overseen *Never Mind the Buzzcocks* in its Simon Amstell period 2007–8, the very episodes I had watched over and over again on YouTube to guide me through nearly all of my hangovers and heartbreaks at uni.* Stu was sat between his partner in life Em Pickthall, and partner in *Buzzcocks* Kate Edmunds, two producing queens who have baptised and euthanised enough formats over the years to sympathise with the brazen burden of responsibility I had just voluntarily taken on. I had a strong core of support for the venture. Only a couple of the guests, Josh and Rose's friends from their daughter's school, were muttering entirely legitimate things about how they'd thought this was a normal party and whether this bit was going to go on very long. My responses: one, no it isn't, and two, the game will last until you are murdered or banished. To their relief and mine, these particular naysayers were murdered and banished extremely early on in proceedings. The game did then measurably speed up in pace and intensity without them, but I do regret that they later overheard me celebrating their departures. I oughtn't have so gleefully exclaimed that the game had been 'purified'. This language was not befitting of a notionally neutral gamesmaster and I apologise.

---

* There are only four series of Amstell *Buzzcocks*, three if you discount the (mostly) weaker guest-team-captain series, but this is more than enough for a 'specialist subject', and Stu has had to put up with quite a lot of 3am kitchen quizzes over the years. Give me a guest, Stu! Anyone but Dappy from N-Dubz!

We only played one game of *Traitors* that night, and its top-secret and randomly assigned villains were Ed Gamble, Em Pickthall, and Tom Craine. Craine, a prince of pratfalls who once brought a windbreak instead of a tent to Glastonbury by accident, was outed as a Traitor fairly early on in proceedings. Ed and Em, however, butchered and backstabbed their way to victory over the course of a delicious three-hour psychological assault. Murdered and banished guests, even those who had compromised the purity of the game in its early stages, remained rooted to the spectacle of the finale, sworn aggressively to silence by me, the guylinered budget Winkleman now drunk on power and also on Baileys. Murders were carried out in secret while the players sat in a circle with their eyes closed. Banishments were conducted on miniature chalkboards I had brought from home. The Hootenanny didn't get a look-in. At one point, someone's child knocked at the door, seeking parental reassurance after a nightmare, only to find a scene far more sinister than whatever they could have been dreaming of upstairs.* At another point, Ed realised his and Charlie's pre-booked taxi was about to arrive, and was urged by a banished Widdicombe to cancel it for the sake of the game. This was an exquisite thing for those in the know to watch unfold. Ed's cheeky charm has graced enough ad-reads to pay off a lifetime of cancelled taxis, but could he be persuaded to cancel this one, without agreeing to cancel it *so* quickly that his wife would be alerted to his treacherous designs at the next round table? Cazoo yeah he could. Ed cancelled the cab, survived

---

* And saw their parent Banished, live! No child should have to watch their parents' banishment live!

the round table, murdered his wife and won the game. Happy fucking New Year.

Two days later, I was telling most of this story at a new material gig, still buzzing from the success of the night and bringing such giddy glee to the retelling that even audience members who hadn't seen *The Traitors* were laughing or at the very least nodding politely. For one of the slowest starters in the game, staring down the biggest or at least most televised year of my life, this had kicked off 2023 very promisingly. January 2nd and I'd already had a banging night and written a banging bit. This lunatic in a wig's absolutely *flown* out of the traps!

Alas, old habits – not writing Edinburgh shows in time – die a bit harder than that, especially when loads of other shit's hitting the fan on the sidelines. In January, I had one new bit for my Edinburgh show. By July, I would have ... two new bits for my Edinburgh show. The sum total of those two bits: about fifteen minutes of stand-up! Hello disastrous preview season, my old friend!

Another well-intentioned Q1 decision that only served to solidify the hubris heading into Qs 2 and even 3: in February I did a work-in-progress hour at Always Be Comedy, the most delightfully but also dangerously positive audience in London, a borderline cult operation above The Tommyfield pub in Kennington, a church of giant LOLogy whose Haribo-hurling leader, James Gill, declares every guest 'the Maestro', and a man called Richard booms and claps so hard on the front row that windows rattle in neighbouring boroughs. Write drunk, edit sober, Ernest Hemingway apparently said, but if he did say that, which he apparently didn't, he might have added 'write at

Always Be Comedy, edit at literally any club other than Always Be Comedy'. ABC is the great deluder, the falsifier of dawns. Haribo is powerful stuff.

A few weeks after the blockbuster Traitoring on New Year's Eve, I had been invited to beat the January blues with a trip to the Alps, an all-expenses loliday courtesy of another disgustingly posh comic, Tower of London-dwelling* lothario Tom Houghton. The trip comprised two predictably nervy expat gigs in exchange for three predictably confident days on the slopes, a fantastically on-brand work perk where I even got a +1 for my starboy Harry 'Sweet Baby Griff' Griffin, Joe Lycett's tour manager and the sauciest thing ever to come out of Worcester. The high points of our journey out included dramatic readings of Prince Harry's *Spare* in English and French, playing boules in the departure gate with a potato I'd brought from home, and Sweet Baby Griff timing his phone to play Tyler The Creator's 'ladies and gentlemen we just landed in Geneva' the exact moment we landed in Geneva. The jape with the most long-term consequences for my 2023, however, was picking up a set of Harry Potter Top Trumps from WH Smith. This was an impulse purchase to cheer me up after I'd watched my potato get driven over by a passing baggage buggy, a small curl of a smile on its driver's face as he crushed our boules game into starchy smithereens.

The Harry Potter Top Trumps were a fairly random choice, I must stress, merely the game closest to the till in WH Smith: I wasn't satisfying some urgent need for Hogwarts on holiday.

---

* Tom literally lived at the time in the Tower of London. Poshness isn't a competition, but if it is, that wins.

94 YARDSTICKS FOR FAILURE

I had obviously devoured the books and films as a teenager, and in 2007, through yet more multi-layered twists of privilege, had got to not just meet but formally interview JK Rowling at Eton,* on the same night as an umbrella-clutching Steve McClaren saw his world-class but wet England side crash out of Euros qualification to Croatia. My attentions had been distracted that night, and my Pottermania had broadly subsided over the next decade and a half, not least due to its creator's increasingly furious ventures into debates that certainly hadn't been explored at School Hall, back in 2007.

Despite Top Trumps being boring and Harry Potter being tainted, the cards popped up a few times in the Alps, and a fortnight later at the Tommyfield, I'd not only got ten minutes out of Ginny Weasley's wand length, but I'd got forty minutes out of improvising a new set of Top Trump categories with which we ranked the bags of people on the front row. Size! Pockets! Water resistance! It doesn't sound much now, but it was absolute dynamite then. That's the Tommyfield for you! 'You've got to be careful,' I berated Richard Gill and his thigh-slapping support crew, 'if this is too fun I'll base my entire Edinburgh show around Top Trumps.'

---

* I was one of three secretaries of the school 'Literary Society', a position earned loosely on merit (no one else applied), but it was our predecessors who had actually secured JK's visit. On top of all the other inheritances that fall Etonians' way, this was a hell of a golden snitch to have waiting for us in office, and one we broadly failed to do justice to, by rushing through a heavily football-interrupted interview before cutting it short so that a much smaller crowd of VVIPs could join JK for a book signing. Many of those books were on eBay by the end of the week. Eton is a school which I was very lucky to attend, but it is, as if anyone needs reminding, a school powered by human greed.

It takes a top-tier foot-shooter to declare to a live audience the mistake they might make and then go on to make exactly that mistake. Six months later, I'd based my entire Edinburgh show around Top Trumps.

30·9·24

Men came to the house fore dind. all ovar the weld.

A rollercoaster of tension and release in a single tableau.
Witness the smaller diner's unbridled joy as the request for
soop is granted. Their global pilgrimage was not in vain.

CHAPTER 5

Cereal Killer

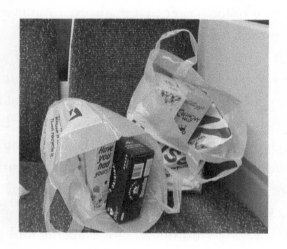

I spent a lot of summer 2023 questioning how, of all the things I could have been talking about onstage to the largest audiences of my career, I, a thirty-two-year-old man who'd barely engaged with Harry Potter since university, was now doing a stand-up show in which one of the biggest/only punchlines was 'Ginny Weasley's wand length'. My stand-up shows had, up until this point, typically been about the main things going on in my life. Was this the main thing going on in my life? No, of course not. But that was kind of the point.

A lot had happened in the run-up to my 2022 Fringe show –

moving out from my ex's, moving back in with my ex, the universal suspension of life as we knew it – but a lot had happened in its aftermath too. A break-up (broadly glossed over in this book), a bereavement (specifically addressed in this book), many hugely dispiriting and draining legal costs (some of them paid for by this book), and of course coming last on *Taskmaster* (the reason this book got commissioned). By spring 2023, my professional life was peaking and my personal life troughing* in a rollercoaster that made even summer 2019 feel like a ride on the teacups.

Through some foolhardy fusion of ambition and evasion, I'd decided not just to do one new show this summer but three, to spread myself across myriad ambitions old and new and leave as little time as possible to think about Everything Else. I declared to Holly and Lily, the Caledonian Mafia charged with bruing up my agency's Fringe operations, that I wanted to do not only a new stand-up show but also steer my leaking ship into the entirely uncharted waters of a theatre show *and* a weekly club night. Other agents and producers might have nipped at least one of these ideas in the bud within the first phone call, but that's not how Holly and Lily operate, nor the various other Off The Kerb bosswomen who'd be tasked with managing my multi-platform madness over the coming months. I'm so grateful to them. The theatre show and the clubnight were booked in. Their exact content – work-in-progress waffle and guest-heavy piss-up

---

* Huge caveat here of course: my daughter continued to be a source of relentless joy, my friends and family were absolutely there for me at every turn, and the last chapter literally just ended with a story about me going on a ski holiday. So this is, once more, quite a specific definition of 'trough'.

respectively – could be hammered out later down the line. But what was the stand-up show – lest we forget, very much the main show – going to be?

No one wants to see expressions like 'tonal spectrum' entering the fray at this stage, but there's no way round it, I'm afraid: I needed to work out where this year's show would sit on the tonal spectrum. To boil a whole dissertation into a merciful nine words: sometimes comedy is silly and sometimes comedy is serious. In one lane, Tim Vine, in the other, Hannah Gadbsy, both equally valid, all part of the increasingly taxed and tolled superhighway of delusion that we call the Fringe. As a comedian and indeed as a motorist, I have spent the vast majority of my life clinging cynically and selfishly to the middle lane. However, during the spring 2023 tour of my previous show, with its long routine about a jealousy-fuelled breakdown at Peppa Pig World, it did feel like I'd started to drift a bit too close to the hard shoulder of overshare.

The new *Taskmaster* fans were starting to turn up now, many taking their first and maybe only bite of this particular posh pie. I'm not the most complex of live propositions, sure, and they weren't the most demanding of propositioners: if anything, it was the opposite problem, where I quickly realised that the route-one camaraderie I could stoke merely by mentioning Frankie Boyle or the caravan was a much merrier jig than suddenly announcing to all these new recruits that I was struggling with the emotional reality of co-parenting. The ten-week sitcom formula of *Taskmaster* allows it to cut through the scripted efficiency of other panel shows, but there's still a difference between seeing the real person behind the facade (can't keep a jelly together) and the even more real person behind that facade (can't keep a family together). As cathartic as it had felt to pour my anxieties into stand-up at the Fringe six months beforehand, it was feeling more and more like a story I didn't want or need to share, certainly not to a hundred and fifty people in Teignmouth who just wanted to heckle me with Jenny Eclair's joke about getting money back from Eton. Falling out of love with one's show on the road is an occupational hazard for the touring comedian, but it did make me think about how I might avoid the same pitfall this time around. Alas, I was heading towards a different and rather larger pitfall.

My logic was sound enough. Touring a gloom-adjacent stand-up show had just left me feeling gloomier, and I didn't want that to happen again, especially with plenty more real-life glooms to contend with. Even if I did still want to scratch that particular itch, I'd booked my storytelling theatre slot in the tiny Pleasance Green, for the handful of ultras and completists to whom I could pour out my soul after lunch. The stand-up show, in the considerably larger Pleasance Beyond, would just be *fun*. It would be overambitious, and immersive, and everything that brought the lols and own goals to my *Taskmaster* stint. I'd spent more and more of the previous show's tour dates rushing through the serious material and devoting maximum showtime to whatever high-energy quests – or tasks, if you must – I could devise on the fly from audience suggestions. There are lots of those coming up shortly. There aren't, however, many boasts coming up shortly, or in the book at all, so please forgive this one now: I believe that on my day, I'm one of the most dedicated improvisers, committers to the bit, and carpers of diems in the game. What about a whole show based around doing that?

There is one particular gig to which I attribute this decision more than any other, and it was on March 2nd, 2023. This gig was the apex, and I think will always remain the apex, of one of the most desperate and relentless pursuits of my career: the mid-gig shop-pop.*

You may have some questions about the phrase mid-gig shop-pop, and my responses would be:

Who? Me, the ADHD goon whose book you're reading.

What? Usually some food that an audience member has referenced earlier in the show.

When? During an interval, or (if MCing) when another act is on.

Where? The nearest shop that sells the thing.

Why? Because, to misquote the tagline of a notionally resealable crisp: once you've popped to the shop, you just can't stop popping to the shop.

I am not the first comedian to have ever mid-gig shop-popped, and I am sure I won't be the last. But I'd be surprised if any comedian, anywhere, ever, has clocked up more mid-gig miles than I have over the last few years. Here, for example, is a list of ten shop-pops from 2023 alone. Not all of them were comedic successes, but those ones, alas, are all the more memorable for their hubris, colossal wrecks decaying in the desert of my desperation. Look on my shops, ye mighty, and despair.

---

* Not to be confused with the rather sadder side to the coin: the things in my life I've 'just popped out of' to do a gig, most damningly my friends Lylo and Abigail's wedding in 2018. There, I skipped the pudding, the speeches, and most of the dancing to drive from Wimbledon to die on my arse in (of all places for an Eton boy to flounder) Windsor. There's a reason we never did tutor outings to the Fuzzy Bear.

1. March 3rd, Brighton Dome: a multipack of Freddos from the Co-op, one of which was then thrown into the audience sellotaped to a frisbee.

2. March 29th, Leeds City Varieties: a full meal from KFC, for an audience member who wasn't there to receive it because he'd gone home at the interval.

3. March 30th, Hexham Queen's Hall: a bag of 'Sugar Free Soft Foams' from Aldi, for a sweet-toothed audience member who'd not incorrectly asserted that I'd never been to Aldi.

4. April 18th, Bristol Tobacco Factory: a Gü cheesecake from Sainsbury's, to placate a woman who said I'd disrespected her on her birthday.

5. May 4th, Folkestone Quarterhouse: cheese, onions and bread from nearby cornershop Memel, to make a sandwich that apparently made one audience member vomit from the smell alone.

6. August 18th, *Edinburgh Comedy Allstars* at the Udderbelly: some bleach at quarter past midnight from Rahman's Supermarket on Nicolson Street, for a man on the front row who claimed he'd rather drink bleach than go for a pint with me.

7. October 12th, Leicester Square Theatre: a meal deal from Tesco and a white T-shirt from Primark, the latter then defaced with a Sharpie backstage.

8. October 17th, Newcastle Northern Stage: an interval trip to the local 'secret Co-op', with ten extremely confused audience members I'd invited to join me during the first half.

9. November 10th, Harrow Arts Centre: three bags of sweets and a trifle from the big Tesco, distributed to

audience members who'd provided helpful facts about
a local park.

10. November 24th, Clapham Grand: pumpkin fritters to
    share with the front row, sadly Deliveroo'd to the venue
    as producer Owen Donovan refused to let me shop-pop.

But there is one that stands above the rest, one shop-pop
to rule them all, and this took place at and around a theatre
in Hertfordshire on Thursday March 2nd, 2023. Or, as I will
always remember this night, the Potters Bar Cereal Quest.

Going to MC a gig in Potters Bar was not a top life priority for me on Thursday March 2nd, 2023. I mean that with
great respect to the people of Potters Bar, and Alex of Anglia
Comedy who offered me the gig, and the solid wedge to MC a
gig at a relatively short distance on a Thursday night. But I
was in the middle of a national tour of my latest show, and
a lot of my remaining evenings were getting swallowed up by
a new and exciting but also extremely admin-heavy live music
podcast, and I wasn't making enough time for my girlfriend,
and I wasn't getting enough time with my daughter, and those
times mostly couldn't be the same times, and even if I should
try harder to stand by all the choices I've made in my life, I
can't truly recommend the various scheduling challenges that
said life choices have created.

Or, in short: I shouldn't have been going to MC a gig in
Potters Bar on Thursday March 2nd, 2023.

I'd reflected on that a few times in the days leading up to
the gig, but I'll tell you when the thought really struck home:
in my car at about 6:30pm on Thursday 2nd March, 2023,
when I realised that I was going to be late to MC the gig in
Potters Bar.

Should I have even been in my car that night? This was something I'd already debated to a quite insane degree on the day of the gig. If you have a car, and I'm lucky enough to, even though it doesn't have Bluetooth and I can't wait to upgrade it, every gig is a choice between public transport and your own wheels. Often the gig's location will make the decision for you: maybe your gig is nowhere near a train station – shout-out to Bordon, Gosport and Haverfield – or there are just too many connections to put your trust in. I love trains, but on top of the laughably escalating cost of tickets,* they've reached new heights of non-dependability in the infrastructural masterclass that has been life in the UK 2010–present, and you've got to be able to depend a bit on your trains, especially when you can't depend on yourself. I'm not proud, but as usual not ashamed enough to have ever properly mended my ways, to say that I have more than once blamed a fictitious train delay for why I'm running late to a gig, before that train delay has then ensued, leaving me standing furiously in a vestibule, watching the minutes rack up on an excuse cheque that I've already cashed as a lie, the boy who cried leaves on the line.

My Bluetoothless Skoda Fabia brings its own dangers too: getting stuck in traffic on the way to the gig, or struggling through motorway closures and drooping eyelids on the way back. In 2023 our industry lost a very sweet and funny man, Gareth Richards, to late-night driving, and though I do try to stop-revive-and-survive where needed, it's still my family's biggest anxiety about my career. The solitary confinement of

* And I know bus is an option too, and played a very dominant role in my life 2012–2017, but I haven't been to Victoria Coach Station since the pandemic, and I can't say I'm pining for her sweet post-apocalyptic vibes.

the car used to scare me too: those hours upon hours with my own despicable thoughts, with no sweet relief of just a little bit of phone, counting down till the services. 'Not long now!', I would think to myself, foot to the floor, seventy miles an hour *tops*, awaiting the lush dopamine of a light doomscroll in Leigh Delamere. But as the doominess of the scroll has loomed larger and darker in recent years, I've come to reach beyond any doubt my revolutionary conclusion that, get ready for this, my phone is actually *bad* for my attention span and mental health, hence the absolutely normal and healthy purchase of my iDiskk Phone Jail, one of my most beloved possessions 2023–present, the jail without which this book would not have got written. These days I increasingly look forward to driving, just because that's one of the only times I'm not on my phone. I don't necessarily want to do an eight-hour round trip alone in my car, a man can have *too* much mental health you know, but an hour there and an hour back? What a treat.

Potters Bar is an hour there and an hour back. I would drive to Potters Bar. That was the decision.

The decision lasted exactly one minute.

I faffed for too long at home, of course, so when I headed down to the car and loaded my destination into the Waze app, I was presented with a 7:52 arrival time, which was not ideal for my 8 o'clock stage time. I texted Alex at Anglia Comedy this news and set off, but before I'd even turned out of my street, Alex at Anglia Comedy had called to relay the even less ideal news that the gig actually was to start at 7:30, so he was not unreasonably dismayed at my 7:52 news. I was the MC, this couldn't just be shuffled round, and that even if Alex was in theory happy to tell the good people of Potters Bar to just talk amongst themselves for twenty-two extra pre-gig minutes, he couldn't on this occasion because opening act Ed Byrne had to head straight off after his set. For all its complicating of my own situation, I was intrigued to hear Byrne was doubling and dashing. I love the hot scent of other people's chaos.

What I did next was a pivot of really Olympic-level insanity. As soon as Alex hung up, I pulled over and consulted the London to Potters Bar train times for the fourth or fifth time that day. The burning question: was there a whiff of a diff? And you know what, there was a whiff of a diff: if I could get to King's Cross in fifteen minutes, I'd make the 7:20 that'd get me to Potters Bar for 7:40. A whole *twelve minute gain!* There could be no doubt about it. What I was in now was that ugliest of beasts, a pre-gig Dash. I dropped my car back home, legged it to the tube, got to King's Cross in sixteen minutes, and missed the 7:20 by seconds. I would now be taking the *not just later but slower* 7:35 that would get me to Potters Bar for 8:15. From the jaws of defeat: heavier defeat.

I was apoplectic with myself on the 7:35. For getting myself into this whole damn mess, and more specifically, for having taken my car back home to park it when I could have just left it on the street *for free* and got to King's Cross more quickly. There are always big lessons and small lessons in life. I need to get better *about* being late, but I also need to get better *at* being late. By dint of its delirious and disastrous late switch in mode of transport, this was a unique entry in my life's vast catalogue of punctuality prangs. The yardstick for failure measures this one high. I passed the barely believable news on to Alex at Anglia Comedy, and he confirmed that Ed Byrne would have to go straight on, and I, the man who was booked to welcome him to the stage, ought to just about get there in time to welcome him off it forty minutes later. I could MC us into the break. This was not the end of the world, at least anywhere outside my head. Sure, I had just laid bare for the umpteenth time the unimproving calamitousness of my own decision-making, but the punters of Potters would not mind about, or even know about, the late switch from Graham Then Byrne to Byrne Then Graham.

They did know about it, of course, because I told them immediately upon my arrival: the consummate slickness of Ed's crescendo being at quite dramatic tonal odds with me then bursting onto the stage and straight into an apologetic rant about my dreadful choices. Then it was the interval, and I could go to the green room and apologise again to Alex from Anglia Comedy, and prepare for a surely more relaxing second half.

It does not feel like a colossal spoiler by this point to say that the second half was not more relaxing.

I can't remember exactly how I even got on to the topic of cereal after the interval, but it was broadly a combination of two things: (1) I tend to dedicate nearly all of my stagetime, at any gig I am MCing and many that I am not, to rabbiting on directionlessly about whatever trivial (and occasionally non-trivial) shit is on my mind, and (2) cereal is almost always on my mind. Suddenly I was in a very long conversation with a man in the audience called Richard who claimed, quite fantastically, that he had seven different cereals in his house, one for every day of the week. Who cares if it was true or not: whether Richard was a bona-fide breakfast bet-spreader or a cocky Kelloggs confidence trickster, we were about to get a fantastic list. Writers at Would I Lie to You? spend weeks cooped up in offices trying to pitch statements as perfectly on the Fiction Faultline as Richard's week of cereal. Which was, by the way, from Sunday to Saturday:*

Sunday: Chocolate Granola

Monday: Fruit Granola

Tuesday: Shreddies

Wednesday: Crunchy Nut Corn Flakes

Thursday: Bitesize Shredded Wheat

Friday: Weetabix

Saturday: Flahavan's Porridge

There are all sorts of options available to an MC when presented with such gold. One of them is, quite simply, to leave it there: when the user-generated content is that good, and Richard has anointed himself an instant legend in the room, why try and top it? But perhaps a good MC interrogates the choices, perhaps they ask what Richard's family think of this, or what cereal he eats when he's on holiday. Perhaps they make an *ingenious* topical reference to the Craig David song 'Seven Days', one of the most frequently crowbarred songs into *Mock the Week*'s 'if this is the answer, what is the question?' round alongside '99 Problems' and '500 Miles'.

I would be so well served in comedy, and in life, by slightly more frequent recourses to these swift, efficient, tried-and-tested approaches. Unfortunately, in my head I was already halfway to the shop. Richard finished listing his cereals, everybody laughed, I brought on headliner Stephen Bailey, and then I immediately went back to Alex from Anglia Comedy, to ask if there was anywhere nearby that I'd be able to buy these seven cereals during the twenty minutes Stephen was onstage.

---

* Calendar-wise, I'm a Monday to Sunday guy, but this is Richard's world, and we just live in it.

Given that I was late to his gig, forcing Ed Byrne to (pardon the phrase) bring himself on, and I was now proposing to leave the premises early, potentially forcing Stephen Bailey to (pardon again here) bring himself off, Alex from Anglia Comedy was extremely kind/mad to even let me out of the building, let alone advise me on local supermarkets. The good news: there was a small Sainsbury's just down the street. The bad news: I didn't trust that I'd be able to get anywhere near the Full Richard in a small Sainsbury's. My working week is a small Sainsbury's. I get my Special K and the occasional multipack for my daughter there, but you ain't getting Flahavan's porridge in a small Sains. Alex from Anglia Comedy winced. 'Well, if you wanted to get all of them you'd have to go to the big Tesco, and that's basically out of town.'

If my casual disregard for my professional obligations can in any way be compared to a bull, and for these purposes I think it can, rags don't come redder than 'basically out of town'. The big Tesco was twelve minutes' walk away. I've written extensively over the years about the almost sexual thrill I get from shredding these kinds of estimates. I can run a twelve-minute walk in four minutes, and Stephen was doing a twenty-minute set, so if I ran there and ran back, that would still give me the best part of ten minutes to pick up the cereal. And I wouldn't need more than five! Quite astonishingly, getting to the big Tesco just outside Potters Bar and returning with seven specific cereals in the next nineteen minutes only registered in my shop-popping WinViz as a medium difficulty enterprise. Game on. Alex escorted me to the stage door and bade me good luck as I disappeared into the black Hertfordshire night.

The big Tesco just outside Potters Bar is up a pretty winding and climbing main road, so that wasn't ideal for me on the thin stretch of pavement next to it, but my body was about 90 per cent adrenaline at this point, so I *charged* up that hill, confident that this incline would be my friend when I was sprinting down it again in five minutes' time with seven packets of cereal. And it really was five minutes: I *nailed* the turnaround at the big Tesco. It wasn't exactly a hive of activity at 9:45, and I was definitely its buzziest bee. Conditions were perfect for a supermarket sweep, and getting nuclear-bunker quantities of cereal really is the best kind of supermarket sweep I can imagine.

My efficiency in Tesco bought me time, if anything, to slow the pace on the way down the hill, as demanded by my loot, and on top of everything else to try and film a bit of the run for the social media #content I was already eyeing up when this was done. Running with seven bags/boxes of cereal, including a full kilo of Flahavan's porridge oats, was a physical challenge I'd unsurprisingly never engaged with before. And there was a bonus heart attack in store upon my return to the Wyllyotts, when the stage door I'd left ajar was now closed, raising the quite ludicrous possibility that I had made it back to the building in time only to be left out in the car park with £28 worth of cereal. Thankfully, some panicked knocks got Alex's attention on the other side, and he smiled in disbelief when he opened the door to see my loot. Somehow this gave me the gumption to start asking more things of him: could he film my return to the stage? Could he get the sound technician to cue up the theme to 'Happy Days'? Could the house lights be brought up so I could throw the porridge oats for Richard to catch? Alex said yes to the first two questions and looked quite concerned at the third. But never mind that: Stephen Bailey was wrapping up his set and putting the mic back in the stand. The most impatient members of the Potters Bar audience would be reaching for their coats, assuming they would soon be free to go. They assumed wrong.

In most standard MC roles, the job of 'wrapping up at the end' can last as little as thirty seconds: a thanks to the acts, a thanks to the venue, a promotion for the next night, and perhaps some final callback to one of the night's running jokes. Well, I had that final callback all right, but it wasn't going to be done and dusted in thirty seconds. I returned to the stage, raised another cheer for headliner Stephen Bailey, and followed it by requesting a cheer for the 'real hero of the night' (sorry, Stephen, sorry, Ed Byrne, sorry, Alex from Anglia Comedy): Richard, the man behind the week of cereals. 'It is a week I hope to recreate!' I announced, before disappearing into the wings and returning with the loot. I laid out the cereal on the stage. How did the people of Potters Bar react? Well, there's no two ways about it. This is the kind of boast I make only occasionally amidst a life of relentless embarrassment and apology, but the people of Potters Bar went absolutely fucking bananas.

They couldn't *believe* I'd gone to the big Tesco. I regaled them with my trip before cueing the 'Happy Days' theme, and danced down the line from granola to porridge in time to the lyrics.* Sunday, Monday, happy days, Tuesday, Wednesday, happy days. My inability to resolve the various problems in my professional and personal lives meant that too many days of late had not been happy ones, but for this blissful minute

---

* Richard's Sunday-first ordering really helped, as it happened.

onstage in Potters Bar, dancing my way around Richard's week of cereal, none of that mattered.

And as the pendulum swung back once more from impasse to impulse, I decided, much as I had at the end of my first *Taskmaster* episode, to risk it all with a rogue throw. I scanned the room for Richard once more, and I picked up the Flahavan's porridge, a bag described by its own blurb as a 'jumbo kilo'. It had already been established, at the start of that same *Taskmaster* episode, that I don't know what a kilogram is, let alone a jumbo one. But it's certainly a unit that shouldn't be thrown at an audience member in Potters Bar. I am a fast man but a weak man. I've never thrown a kettle over a pub. I used to dread fielding on the boundary in school cricket because I literally couldn't get the ball all the way back to the wicket in one go. So what hope did I have of lobbing a jumbo kilo of porridge to a stranger in row H without decapitating someone else in between? Alex at Anglia Comedy had not brought the house lights up. This couldn't stop me. Nothing could stop me. I pressed the Flahavan's to my chin like a shot putter before hurling the porridge into the darkness.

By the summer of 2023, my ventures into physically exertive comedy would have more of a stench of desperation about them. But that's because on Thursday, March 2nd, at the Wyllyotts Theatre in Potters Bar, a gig I'd done my utmost not to make it to at all, I had pulled off what I'm not afraid to call the heist of the century. I'd run for the cereals, made it back with the cereals, done a mad tribal dance around the cereals, and then decided, in a topper that could have quite literally topped someone, to throw the cereal towards the audience in the hope that a man called Richard would catch it. And Richard did catch it! Can you imagine the cheers? All the other griefs and grievances of my life drowned out in the wheaty whoops of the Wyllyotts. Who wouldn't start to believe their own hype on a night like this?

The artist's use of multiple exclamation marks gives maximum emphasis to this piece's message, but its protagonist's rolling eyes acknowledge the deeper truth, that this advice is often easier to dispense than heed.

CHAPTER 6

Beautiful Burnout

I'm aware that the sweaty quests of the last chapter may have been a genuinely stressful reading experience for those whose well-ordered lives do not involve this kind of comedy cardio. Whenever I write about running to shops or trains on social media, I receive messages from friends expressing occasional amusement but often other emotions too, emotions like concern, pity or outright rage. Katie Storey, an elite gagsmith whose appetite for risk in other areas of her life included a long riff about consent in her own bride speech, will message me after pretty much every one of my social media Dashes, begging me to change my ways. Tim Key, the lager-spattered lockdown laureate who has been subjected to much of this second-hand adrenaline after gigs and football games, generously or damningly christened the lifestyle in two words that fully capture the suffocating compaction of its constituent parts: 'No Air'. In recent years, I have received multiple comparisons of my behaviour to the 2019 Safdie brothers' film, *Uncut Gems*. My goods are of rather lower commercial value than the million-dollar opal Adam Sandler is trying to rescue from Kevin Garnett, but other aspects of the operation, from the co-parenting juggles to the obsession with The Weeknd, mimic the frenetic churn of my daily life with uncomfortable accuracy. I'm yet to pop to the shops during a gig to buy an audience member a jar of Bonne Maman or Hartley's Strawberry Seedless, but I hope one day to tell that story and I already know what that story is going to be called: Uncut Jams.

So if you've found all this writing about running to the shops stressful, I'd like to apologise. The good news? This next chapter is not about running to the shops. The bad news? This next chapter is about running marathons, and that's an insufferable lifestyle all of its own.

Being an incurably late man has provided me with daily running training for pretty much my whole life, but I was also dragged into it young by my similarly tall and tardy dad, himself a long-distance nearlyman with a semi-plausible story about an inter-school race in 1974 that he'd have won if his opponents hadn't mixed up the signposts. My family moved to Sydney from 2001 to 2003, and we lived in Vaucluse, and if you know Sydney, you'll know that makes me just as much of a posh twat on that side of the world as I am on this one. Our sunset circuits of Vaucluse's South Head, pausing to swim the length of Watsons Bay and then drip drying home for dinner, were some of the happiest constants of the brief non-boarding Sydney Grammar School chapter of my childhood. As we and sixty thousand others panted down Bondi Beach to complete the 14km 'City2Surf' in August 2002, a sun-kissed adolescence stretched invitingly ahead of me. But then we moved back to England and I was incarcerated once more.

At Eton, I channelled a lot of my homesick energies into the annual 'steeplechase', a five-mile circuit of Dorney Lake, where Team GB would take four rowing golds at London 2012. The latter was still just the twinkle in the eye of a philandering mayor, but this steeplechase was already my personal Olympics. The ceremony of the race was not universally respected – some of the cooler cats would bunk it off early to smoke under a railway viaduct – but for me and the rest of the future Strava dweebs it was the biggest day of the year. Some of us had nothing else. I came 14th out of 250 in 2007, and I'm afraid to say that was about as good as being a teenager got for me. It really could have occurred to me to do a marathon a bit sooner than nine years later, but anyway, never mind, in 2016 I did my first marathon, in London, and I loved it, and I did it in 3 hours 17 minutes without hitting the famous wall, so by this point there was definitely evidence that I was a not-bad amateur runner. And even then it took me another four years and a pandemic before I really started capitalising on it.

The basic science of running to feel better had long been available to me, but I only *properly* started turning miles into smiles in lockdown one, which I was lucky to spend with my family and a garden, but which was also obviously a period of Great Personal And Global Insecurity which went on much longer than that tousled twat told us it would. In between mornings reading *I Want My Hat Back* and afternoons hosting *The Lock Inn Pub Quiz* on YouTube, I would spend my government mandated hour of exercise running laps of the village, listening to Elis James and John Robins' *Isolation Tapes* or the third Haim album, even throwing in some sit-ups back in the garden if parenting/quizzing commitments allowed. I'm going to come out and say it: I was a *specimen* by the end of lockdown one. Running had gone from a nicety to a necessity, in a life increasingly dominated by adult-themed anxieties and self-inflicted stress.

The most adult-themed anxiety in the Graham family, and the least self-inflicted of our stresses, is my mother's multiple sclerosis, which has been chipping away at her mobility for twenty years now: a huge physical wrench for her, and an emotional one, too, for her and the many, many people who love her. The disease has, needless to say, completely changed her life, while still making slower progress through her nervous system than it does for many MS sufferers. The latter include Lana, the late mother of Maccabees guitarist and fellow MS Society ambassador Felix White, whose own book I have plenty of kind words for, especially if you are also interested in cricket. Alternatively, in the fictional realm, there is Susan Kennedy of *Neighbours*, who got MS on the show at about the same time as my mum got it in real life, and immediately went blind in a car park. As a never-miss-an-episode *Neighbours* fan

2001–8,[*] I rarely complained about the various poetic licences the show took, but this particular storyline wasn't ideally timed from my perspective. My mum had had more localised flare-ups earlier in her life, but it was only recently that she'd received the more long-term 'secondary progressive' diagnosis and started to contemplate how to discuss it with her children. 'They don't watch *Neighbours*, do they?' she recalls one friend asking. Well, yes, I did. Sometimes twice a day.[†]

Anyway, my mother's own trajectory was not the same as Susan's, but it has taken her, over the past two decades, from walking occasionally with a stick to sometimes being pushed in a wheelchair, to now being a full-time resident of the 'mid-wheel drive chair', described on its website as 'rugged, robust and responsive', and rather distractingly named the Quickie 500. My family, amongst other less disability-adjacent privileges, is

---

[*] For my first few months at Eton, where we watched *Neighbours* in the common room every day between lunch and Field Game, I was fresh back from two and a half years living in Sydney, meaning that while I had to endure the nickname 'Skip' and jibes about my faintest hints of an Aussie accent, I did arrive with a term's worth of *Neighbours* spoilers, the home nation's broadcast schedule being some way ahead of its coloniser's. I enjoyed wielding these weapons in my head more than I ever did in reality, but it was a soft power I took great comfort in while it lasted, until the pommies caught up and my tormentors (friends who teased me occasionally) could sledge me without fear of having their soaps ruined. I revelled in this situation on a comedy set filmed for Australian television at the 2018 Melbourne comedy festival, and you can view this set on YouTube if you're so inclined.

[†] Yes, I'm aware this is quite literally the title of Josh Widdicombe's book, but it is also, probably, the single (double) area in which my teenage life overlapped most with his own.

lucky to have been able to adapt itself around this situation with resources not available to all of the MS community: not just enjoying the benefits of a robust Quickie but also fitting the family home, my childhood home, with lifts and ramps, and getting regular support from carers whose lives were further burdened by our family last year when I gave their sons Swindon Town shirts for Christmas. My mum's resolve at the centre of all this change, to keep doing the things she can do for as long as she can, and accept the things she cannot with far more grace than most people would manage, is an inspiration to us all. My father, too, has adapted to this increasingly challenging chapter of their lives with gravitas and gusto, though he did also leave her at home on her birthday last year to go and watch a Steve Hackett concert on his own.

My siblings and I are not affected a fraction as much by the situation as Dad, or Mum herself obviously, and for the first decade of my mum's developing condition we were relatively detached from the situation, away at school or uni or larging it in London while the stairlift installations and Steve Hackett negotiations played out elsewhere. But for the last ten years we've been more involved, both with help at home and fundraising elsewhere. And the latter has stayed very much within my skill set. Brought into the MS Society fold by its chief comedy liaison, Brand New Heavies fan and semi-retired Pretty Boy, Lee Dainty, I started doing gigs for them in London after university, and did my first marathon in London in 2016, sponsored by some pretty chunky debut donations from deep-pocketed family friends, only some of whom had been in love with my mother in their twenties.

I hosted more MS Society fundraisers over the coming years, and they remain some of the proudest but also the most cómedically enjoyable nights of my career, such as the ten minutes I spent being sold a delicious lie about a Norwegian flag by a confidence trickster called George in 2021. But I wasn't back in my orange running vest until Brighton in 2022, a marathon I wouldn't have been able to participate in at all if an audience member called Annabel hadn't picked up my accreditation for me the day before. Even more shambolic was the 50k 'Machathon' I organised at the Machynlleth Comedy Festival a month later. This DIY ultra consisted of me, and a revolving cast of locals and legends, doing ten consecutive loops around the town, this town that means so much to the UK comedy industry, transformed once a year into a West Walian whimsical wonderland. The Machathon was not without its casualties – Alex Kealy had to retire early after treading, like Alan Partridge, on a spiiike – but it concluded, extremely movingly, with me being first officially announced as an MS Society ambassador and then presented with a tray of Ferrero Rocher outside the Mach Arena. The Society really were spoiling me. What next?

Answer: two new milestones, in the shape of one and a half marathons in April 2023. First the half, pushing Mum in a chair, and then the full 26.2 miles on my own a fortnight later, London again, this time not just running for endorphins and general philanthropic kudos but a real time target, the iconic and just-about-realistic Sub Three Hours. I'd read a very fortifying book by the comedian and reluctant sandwich sharer Paul Tonkinson, who had pulled off a hugely impressive Sub Three at the age of fifty with a fairly radical overhaul of his wine and cheese habits in the months leading up to it. So, from the start of 2023, the New Year I woke up to with post-*Traitors* guyliner smudged across my pillow, I banished my own vices of beer and crisps from my life. Beating my first and best

122 YARDSTICKS FOR FAILURE

marathon time – 3 hours 17 in 2016 – by over a quarter of an hour, seven years later, would be no mean feat. Time to pop shut the Pringles, pie off the Pipers,[*] and pour away the pale ale. I was now a miserable disciple of the Lucky Saint.

The half marathon that April was a collective triumph that brought my whole family together and which I hope will be repeated for many years to come. On Good Friday, all five Grahams, who dine together on high days and holidays but still aren't all in the same place nearly as much as we'd like to be, converged on east London. We were joined by my uncle, cousins, and my oldest friend, Julian, renamed Emergency Julian after the various shoulders and spare beds he and his masterchef wife Rose provided for me to snivel on after my break-up in 2019. Emergency Julian is a true marathon evangelist, the first person to introduce me to the phrase 'you never regret a run'. We certainly weren't going to regret this one.

The event that day was a mixed 5k/10k/half marathon, put on by a huge and pleasingly responsive company called RunThrough, who host these across London and the UK all year round. The fully tarmacked circuit of Victoria Park, where I trained for my first marathon back in 2016, would now be welcoming me and Mum in the superbly ergonomic, but thin-wheeled, Delichon Delta Buggy. This buggy, most famously and movingly used by Leeds Rhinos legends Rob Burrow and Kevin Sinfield, had been kindly lent to us by a mobility sports pioneer

---

[*] Pipers Longhorn Beef, and Pipers Wild Thyme & Rosemary, in their brown and purple bags respectively, absolutely dominate the crisp landscape at the Graham hearth. If you've come round for Sunday lunch and there aren't any Pipers crisps on the table in the half-hour leading up to it, something has gone badly wrong behind the scenes.

(and long-distance runner himself) called Martin Davy, and I'm so grateful to him. Mum could have driven round the course in her own chair, but it doesn't need pushing, and, despite its name, isn't actually much cop in a competitive environment. No one ever won a race in a Quickie 500.

This would be my first ever run pushing Mum in the chair, but it was also my dad and brother's first half marathons, and my sister's first 5k. Each of us broke a personal barrier that day, and we were all buzzing from our barrier-breaking afterwards. It was a big day for MS Society fundraising, but also a huge day for Team Graham. My mum was very forgiving of the speed at which I pushed her through some of the sharper turns, enabling us to do the half in a very respectable 1 hour 35, a time that she used, amongst other distractions, to do the Wordle. Meanwhile, my dad, who had insisted that he'd be fine as long as he stuck to his rigorously assembled playlist of songs at 150BPM, nearly all of which appeared to be by the band Editors, got quite tired in the final lap, and my sister went to do the last bit with him, which was a very moving sight itself, although he has since said that having to talk to her distracted him (and his heart rate) from the playlist. Running is a wonderfully social sport, and also, at times, a hilariously antisocial one. But Dad's smile had returned by the time we all posed, with Uncle James, and cousins Alexander and Katie, and Emergency Julian, in a photo that was not hard to nominate as the first slide of my '2023' Instagram round-up. If it's the sort of thing that might be vaguely relevant to you and your family, I cannot recommend doing a big run together highly enough.

Two weeks of carb-loading and then I was back in Greenwich for the big day. The even bigger day. The race with myself for Sub 3, a race in which I was feeling tentatively hopeful.

My best ever time remained 3h17 in 2016, but I had done a lot of running since then, and completing a half marathon in 1h35 while pushing a wheelchair certainly boded well for completing a whole marathon in 2h59 while not pushing one. This race was also for the MS Society, and also for my mum, but I couldn't pretend those priorities were any higher than third and second here. In the words of *Breaking Bad*'s Walter White, another family man corrupted by chemicals: 'I did it for me. I was good at it.' And, with my weekly *Taskmaster* humiliations – however jolly – now being broadcast to the nation, and various personal struggles sapping my confidence in private, I needed to be good at this. I wanted to be the one who knocked on the door of Sub 3.

My brother would be by my side for this one, too, although not literally by my side for nearly any of it because, and there's no dancing round this, I was late. We had arranged to meet in Greenwich but it wasn't as easy as hoped to find each other at the start line of literally the largest marathon in the world. I arrived ten minutes after Ludo, and set off ten minutes after him too. This wasn't a complete disaster – your time doesn't start till you do – but it was still a pretty schoolboy error. On top of this, I hadn't got myself a proper runner's watch, meaning that I was reliant on checking a phone that was already down to 70 per cent battery when I set off, and I hadn't even brought a portable charger. The thought of running out of battery midway through the race ensured that I was in a state of dread almost as soon as I got going. Then, as the rain started to fall harder, soaking my shoes and my phone screen, and making it harder to overtake the (sorry again about this, we're all heroes but) *slower runners* whom my lateness had doomed, nay demeaned, me to start alongside, the pessimism lurched from gloom to doom. This was the biggest race of my life, and I had thrown it away before I'd even begun.

I had told a lot of people about my hopes for this run, mainly when explaining the 'no crisps or booze' dietary commitments I'd attention-seekingly clung to since New Year. I'm not too fussed about booze, but I really do *love* crisps. More seriously, my increasingly isolationist obsession with Sub 3 had heavily contributed, alongside other factors, to my latest, and saddest, act of romantic self-destruction. I was boozeless and crispless and girlfriendless, I'd surrendered invites to two weddings, and was I now going to render that all for naught because I'd left home late, and, irony of ironies, not bought a watch? Even if I could read my phone screen, which within the first wet mile I no longer could, I still didn't know exactly how fast I needed to go. I was pretty sure, however, that I was currently falling a long way short of it. You fool! Few people can have been running those early miles of the marathon, the crowds whooping and cheering twice as hard as the rain was falling, in more of a black cloud of self-reproach than I was. Not running a Sub 3 marathon is not an unforgivable crime in itself. It was only ever a distant dream, and I'd taken care to emphasise that to everyone I'd told about it, as I pushed away their pints and Pipers in the preceding months. But nonetheless, to fall short in this way, after everything? The phrase 'yardstick for failure' was yet to enter my life, but make no mistake about it: this would be one of them.

And yet. And yet. As the miles ticked by, and the rain stopped, and my shoes dried, I slowly, thrillingly, began to claw the minutes back. The roar of the crowds through Deptford, past the Cutty Sark, and over Tower Bridge was every bit as exciting as I remembered it, as transcendent an experience as any marathon evangelist will tell you it is. I was music-free as I soaked up the city and conserved my phone battery for the first half, then the headphones came out as the crowds thinned towards the Docklands. I turned first to my favourite DJ set of all time, the Dekmantel disco odyssey of Palms Trax, and then to Underworld's 'Beautiful Burnout', the song I'd run to since watching it in a play of the same name at the 2010 Fringe, the song whose ominous pulse would soundtrack the race as I recounted it in my own theatre show later that year. As my legs started to leaden with a third of the race still to go, I thought back to Paul Tonkinson's book, and the mantras he'd clung to in these moments, the demons from his past that he'd summoned up to propel him over the Wall and on towards glory. I summoned up my own demons in this moment: my guilt about my break-ups, my anger at the ongoing obstacles between me and my daughter, my increasingly public persona as a man out of control. This, however, was in my control. I had to believe I could do it. There were so many people rooting for me, and the two main ones were just a few blocks away.

At mile 19, Canary Wharf, there they were: my mum and dad. They were in the exact same accessible spot that they were in 2016, with my then girlfriend, now co-parent, back in the simple times. I was so proud to be doing this for my parents, and knew that they would be proud of me whenever I finished, but I did also know how carefully Dad would have been following my split times on the marathon app. I got an emotional hug from Mum and a statistically useful hug from Dad, shoving me straight back out into the race with a wave of his phone to let me know that my brother wasn't far ahead, and nor was the Sub 3 group. If you can catch him, you can catch them.

A mile or so later at Limehouse, I caught him. My brother is five years younger and less grey-haired than I am, but he is still the person most similar to me in the world, and to the rest of the race we would have looked like two twins in an ecstatic orange blur as we charged, cheering, towards each other, in our matching MS Society vests. I was so excited to run together for a bit, to share this historic moment with him,* but he urged me to push on if I could, and I could, so I did. Now the calculations were getting simpler: never mind the minutes per kilometre, I just knew I started at 10:15, so I had to finish by 13:14. And I was increasingly certain that I could. I didn't feel great, but I didn't feel terrible. I felt a lot better than I did at this point in Brighton. That's the no crisps talking! I kept going and soon I was at Westminster at 13:12 and the Horse Guards Parade at 13:13 and then holy shit, holy shit, I was *crossing the finish line* at 13:14. I was getting interviewed by the Marathon's social channels about my nipple chafing before

---

* After years of him growling and groaning whenever I banged on about running, my brother has the bug too now, and I'm so pleased to share it with him, however competitive it may yet become. After pipping me and 198 other *Peep Show* fans to the Megatron in the Dobby Club's inaugural 'Accidentally Run to Windsor' marathon in October 2024, my brother then went from the world's newest marathon to the oldest, running to Athens like Pheidippides a few weeks later. The latter was a team effort alongside several other school and uni friends in memory of their own dearly departed friend Sam, a Russianist who took his year abroad much more seriously than I did and showed similar endurance at a very cold goalless draw between Swindon and Stevenage in December 2021. I was so delighted for my brother and his Athenian crew. But I was also *delighted* to see that his time, 3h11, while hugely impressive, was still some way short of my current PB. One day he will overtake me, and then I'll have to try and overtake him back, and that's where the real games will begin.

I'd even had a chance to check for certain that I'd done it. But then I got my phone back and my first text was from my uncle James, monitoring the app through his magnetic glasses, and the text confirmed that I had, I'd done it, I'd fucking done it! Two hours fifty-nine!

And then, suddenly, Ludo was there too, and then there waiting for us were his crew: his earthly delight* of a girlfriend Giulia, and the big society of his university rave squad, all of them under a barrier bearing both of our names. And one more of my own legends had come to surprise me, a friend I'd known for nearly twenty years, but who over the last few years in particular had come to be the friend I depended on most in the world, a friendship I will try and sum up later, but which, in short, is based on a shared love of music, comedy, and Krispy Kreme donuts. Alex Kealy and I have laughed in the face of cardiac arrest over many a Mixed Dozen over the years, and seeing him waiting for me with a box at the race's end was a very moving sight even before I saw that the box was full not with Kremes but with crisps, packets and packets of crisps, a bulging selection of all the flame-grilled, deep-ridged kings I'd denied myself since New Year. The tragic truth is, of course, that at this exact moment in time I'd much rather have had a donut, but I clagged my parched mouth delightedly with Monster Munch all the same. I love this man and his contempt for the clag!

---

* In case this has the slightest hint of any shade on my brother's girlfriend, someone I could not praise highly enough would it not be for how much it would embarrass her, let me break open the in-joke by confirming that Hieronymus Bosch's *The Garden of Earthly Delights* was the theme of her recent 30th, a top-tier party which ended in a rave at the Pickle Factory, me still dressed in my priest's cassock.

Alex accompanied us on to a pub garden in west London, where the whole family cheered as we arrived, and my dad was showing my splits to anyone who'd listen and saying how I just got faster and faster, and my mum was so proud too even if she didn't really understand the splits thing, and my little girl wasn't there but she will be next time and there will be a next time. The first crisps of 2023 were followed by the first booze of 2023: I drank three pints in ninety minutes, and they went straight through me, of course, so I was in quite a bad way when it came to that evening's commitment of presenting Club Employee of the Season at that evening's EFL Awards. Most people wouldn't have taken that gig (glamorous but unpaid) on the day of the marathon. I've got two words for you: no air.

The apostrophe inflation reaches the next generation, in a piece that flatters and delights its subject, whose body language onstage is often considerably more reserved than this.

CHAPTER 7

Organised Fun

Running the marathon in under three hours was and remains the defining sporting achievement of my life, all the sweeter for having snatched glory from the widening jaws of regret. But now it was over, and the joyless claustrophobia of my marathon-training life was replaced with a more familiar foe, the directionless panic of my non-marathon-training life. I was, literally and spiritually, back on the crisps.

My series of *Taskmaster* was now live, broadcast for ten

consecutive Thursdays through spring 2023. I spent most of these ten Thursdays on tour, enjoying the rousing but reproachful reception of people who'd come to see me because I was on their favourite TV show, but didn't appreciate me scheduling my visit so as to directly clash with that TV show. And fair play, that was disrespectful. The mid-gig shop-pops for Sugar Free Soft Foams in Hexham, or cheese and onion sandwich fillings in Folkestone, at least went some way to giving the people the second-hand stress of the 'Ivo Graham on *Taskmaster*' experience. And then I'd get into the co-parenting material, and make people wince even harder than they had at my smelly sandwich. If I wanted to make people weep at the Fringe, with or without live onions, I could do it in the work-in-progress theatre slot I'd booked in for the last ten days of the month. This would be titled *Graham in the Green* because it was in the Pleasance Green. The main show was titled *Organised Fun* because, well, that was what it was going to be. The phrase 'organised fun' had cropped up repeatedly – in praise and damnation – throughout my various Traitoring and Trumping so far that year, and it would almost certainly encapsulate whatever clumsy cabaret of games and shop runs I ended up presiding over in August.

In May, I donned a nearly ironed shirt to film *My Future, My Clutter* live at the Bloomsbury Theatre, and that was the previous tour done. Now surely the Edinburgh planning must start. But still the distractions kept coming. I recorded an episode of *Saturday Kitchen*, where I upset some viewers with my disrespect for the tiramisu. I recorded an episode of *Would I Lie to You?*, where Lee Mack correctly outed me as not knowing which way to hold a flute.* I recorded an episode of *The Weakest Link*, a history-repeating ordeal which will get its own chapter later on. I recorded a series of *Unite*, a Radio 4 sitcom where I play a chinless wonder called Gideon struggling

---

* *Would I Lie To You?* is as fresh and authentically improvised as such a prime time institution could hope to be, but they do give you a small hint as to what you might have to lie about in the 'This is my . . .' round, because if you balls that one up, there's two other people's stories at stake too. An hour before the show I was warned by producers Rachel and Peter to 'have a quick think about what playing the flute might be like', which isn't the biggest mountain of homework compared to some panel shows, but which I did then fail to do at any point in that hour, distracted by a delightful video call from my daughter which ate up most of the flute revision window. I realised my omission, panicking, in the corridor into the studio, phone back in my dressing room. I didn't even know which way you hold a flute. Left or right? I had a not hugely unlikely premonition of being asked that exact question by Lee Mack very imminently. There was nothing for it. I had to beg the help of the closest non-panellist to me in the corridor, Sinitta's PA. Unfortunately, Sinitta's PA didn't know which way you hold a flute either, or perhaps did know and was withholding the information, knowing that my ignorance would be for the benefit of not just the show but Sinitta herself. I asked Sinitta's PA to Google image 'how to play the flute' and, clearly perturbed by the panic in my voice, he obliged. Alas, the page was still loading when Rob Brydon called my name, and by the time the pictures had loaded I was already walking on set. An hour or so later, I claimed during the 'This Is My' round to have been part of a woodwind trio called 'Tooty Flooty', and sure enough, my opposing team captain Lee Mack asked me which way you hold the flute. I can't remember if I got it wrong or merely conveyed enough uncertainty to rule me out regardless, but either way: no one believed I was in Tooty Flooty. Sinitta chuckled away alongside Lee throughout my ordeal, and I spent most of the drinks after the show glaring across the room at the PA who had not been able or willing to save me.

to adapt to his new step-family.* The funniest thing I probably appeared on in that period, and a current that bore my boat further back into the past, was an episode of Radio 4's *My Teenage Diary*, where I narrated excerpts of my excruciating university journal to Rufus Hound and a live audience in Bethnal Green. These included excerpts such as 'I join Penelope at Georgina's, where I eschew the usual bruschetta in favour of a chicken spicy salad. Hurrah!' This diary was a goldmine of comedic embarrassment – real Ivo was so much posher than fake Gideon – and a tantalising time machine to that age of undergraduate innocence, spotty and smelly and probably in a bit of a tizz about Finals but still, fundamentally, able to bat all that away merely by bravely eschewing some bruschetta, the *usual* bruschetta, this balsamic-flecked millstone around the neck of my student brunches.

These and a million other distractions meant that I drifted through preview season without ever really deciding what *Organised Fun* was going to be, improvising Top Trump games and telling longer and longer versions of my *Traitors* story, but not ever gaining any sense that it was turning into a proper show. Many of its other constituent parts would not make their debuts until the Fringe itself. One of these, after an introductory montage of my *Taskmaster* facepalms collated by a man called Kevin in Philadelphia, involved a slide onscreen asking a self-selecting audience member to 'choose Ivo's outfit' at the

---

* My stepfather and -brother in *Unite* were played by Mark and Elliot Steel, who drove me to my first ever Glastonbury in 2014, turn up to play comedians' football together most weeks, and who I truly believe would be a most welcoming home to me should some tragedy befall my parents, my godparents, and all of the other family friends who I feel sure would step into the breach if required.

start of the show. Said volunteer was then instructed to select a shirt and trousers from multiple choices on a clothes rail and move them to another rail near the wings. I would then reach out, grab this rail and have to get changed offstage in a *hilariously* short countdown,* so short that I was usually doing up my shirt buttons or even my trousers as I took to the stage, almost always in the most garish combination of the clothing options that had been hung out, a pink shirt and some paisley pyjama bottoms, any claim to dignity forfeited within seconds. But wasn't that the *point*? To be undignified? 'Humiliation's your thing, isn't it?' my brother had replied, when I (correctly) confided in him pre-*Taskmaster* that I thought it was going to be quite humiliating. Well, yes, but there's a difference between harnessing the humiliation, and quite literally exposing yourself as you take to the stage, a festival funster flying low, flashing a fearful fanbase of neurodivergent children. In some ways, over twenty-five nights of quick changes, it's a miracle I didn't.

Another idea I was hoping to include in the show, and a proposal that I only now fully appreciate the madness of a year on, was the other completely untested bit of business, which is that two other self-selecting audience members would be forced to race to a nearby shop during the show to buy a Meal Deal of their choice. I had got so much mileage out of the mid-gig shop-pop this year: now other people were going to do those miles for me. Why a Meal Deal? Well, I am a

---

* Set to the song 'Sunsleeper' by Edinburgh's own Barry Can't Swim, who by the following year was one of the biggest DJs in the country. So I was at least ahead of the game on that front. A thin silver lining, especially when I now cannot enjoy that song without memories of furiously fumbling the buttons on a floral shirt.

miserably frequent flyer on the Meal Deal front, confident that few people in the world have had more Sainsbury's tomato and mozzarella wraps than me, so I was genuinely interested to see what other people's choices would be, a month-long Meal Deal data harvesting exercise. Perhaps the volunteers could then be given a speed eating competition on their return. I was increasingly certain that I wanted the show to be a series of interconnected games, partly a nod to *Taskmaster* itself, and partly because of a trip I'd taken that May to visit friends living in Ghana, a dizzying group holiday that was given a constant competitive edge by our rolling 'modern pentathlon' of ball games on the beach and word games in the car. I had been complimented, or at least affectionately teased, by my friends on that trip, for my inexhaustible appetite for anything with a competition format. But quite a few people would be exhausted by it at Edinburgh 2023.

The first of these was Will Hall, a younger stand-up and ball of PowerPoint assisted neurosis after my own heart, whom I'd spent several hours bonding with on the hottest and darkest day of the year, Adam Brace's funeral. This service was held at a sweltering crematorium in Manor Park so stuffed with mourners that I was shoved up against the back wall and at one point pulled some blinds down by accident during a reading. As the June sun beat through the now blinds-free glass behind me, a late-era *Live At The Apollo* line up took turns to read eulogies, and Adam's friend John clattered our stumps down with the unlikely emotional yorker of the cricket, getting out a portable radio to play thirty seconds of Test Match Special because, as he quite rightly observed, Adam would have been appalled by this clash with the first day of the series, and would have insisted on a score update at some point during proceedings.* Ashes to ashes, dust to dust. I don't want to go to any more young men's funerals.

Will would be helping with the Top Trumps section of my show, taking data from an audience questionnaire and turning that data into playing cards backstage. This routine was not something we rehearsed at any point pre-Edinburgh, and it would send us both quite mad over the next month. Every day in Edinburgh, I wandered into my queueing crowd pre-show, brandishing a series of laminated QR codes that linked to an online survey about how far each person surveyed had travelled to be there, how many Fringe shows they'd seen, etc. At the same time every day, Will would be legging it over from his own show and crashing into a chair backstage to start transferring this data onto Microsoft PowerPoint. Every day, he managed to just about copy, paste, print and cut the Top Trumps cards in time for the point about halfway through the show when the modern pentathlon demanded them. I was always so grateful to see him there, waiting side of stage with a freshly minted deck, but each time his sweaty brow betrayed the mania it had taken to mint it in time. Still, what small price two men's mental health, for the rich reward of turning an audience into a set of Top Trumps in under half an hour? Ah yes, what fathomless riches.

The other person joining the Trumping payroll in Edinburgh, and signing up in fact for a rather longer-term sufferance, sufferance I do not want to trivialise here, was plate-spinning technician-turned-producer and director and quite a lot of other things Luca Dunne, her very surname

---

* And we didn't get one! It was tea! We got Aggers and Cooky burbling about the Edgbaston catering, and it was all the more perfect for it.

an affirmation of a task being completed. I added Luca and Will to a WhatsApp group called 'Ocean's Three', indulging my laughable fantasy that this show was a heist and I was George Clooney,* executing a perfect hit job on the Bellagio of my own reputation. This was in addition to the 'Ivo Fringe 2023' WhatsApp group populated by Lily, Holly, Yeva and Kelsey from Off The Kerb, a crack team of festival problem-solvers without whom I would not have got anywhere near the Bellagio at all. Everyone involved was aware pre-Fringe of what a shambles I was, but no one was quite ready for this year's new flavours, shrouded in mystery until the eve of battle and then announced on a terrifyingly long email I'd typed up and sent to all parties on that great galvaniser of gagsters and goons: the train to Edinburgh. With a level of detail that can only be achieved by having three coffees before Darlington, the email laid out a minute-by-minute breakdown of how the modern pentathlon would proceed, specifically its most ambitious and untried feature, the Meal Deal Dash. I had decided that the Meal Deal Dashing audience members should be rigged with GoPro cameras as they left the venue, and that footage would then be collected and uploaded fast enough on their return that we could watch it back, like on *Taskmaster*, at the end of the show. A manic masterplan,

---

* Clooney as Danny Ocean is, for me, second only to Clooney as Ryan Bingham in the 2010 Oscar nominee *Up in the Air*, which my friend Youngsie and I love, despite its clear damnation of Bingham's spiritual loneliness, for just how quickly and efficiently the man travels through airports in it. I shared this love with the comedian Charlie Baker, and we now text each other about the film, often just the word 'Clooney!' when we're trapped in a queue at passport control or baggage reclaim, falling once more short of our hero's handsome glide through speedy boarding.

written up the day before the show opened, by a man with no experience of doing any of this before.

Roped in to provide quite vast quantities of eleventh-hour technical support was comedian Stuart Laws. Stu is one the all-time great committers to the bit, habitually dedicating entire Edinburgh shows to flipping beermats or saying the word 'never!' over and over again as Michael Caine, as well as showing a loyalty to the gilet that is unparalleled in comedy, if not in some regions of my extended family. Stu had directed my Bloomsbury filming and now was helping me road-test the Meal Deal Dash, because he, like me, loves a run, because he, like me, loves a jape, and because he, unlike me, owns GoPro cameras, GoPros he was theoretically happy for me to strap to two audience members a day to document their Dashes. What if they just didn't come back? Go to Ivo Graham's show, my rival Oceans would be instructing their crews this month: it's the easiest heist in town. You yawn through a twenty-minute story about *The Traitors*, you put up your hand when he mentions Meal Deals, and you get sent out into the street with a £249 camera. This threat would have to be risk-assessed, but only after Stu and I had road-tested the dash. We fixed up the GoPros and raced to the Tesco's on Nicolson Street for our sandwiches, snacks and drinks.

The good news was that we raced there even faster than I'd expected, there and back in under four minutes. The bad news was that, welcomed to Edinburgh by a predictably but inauspiciously wet July eve, it was a dangerous Dash, up and down slippery cobbled slopes, that nearly put me on my arse more than once, and this was me, a seasoned Edinburgh-dasher with this particular route coded into my internal sat nav for over a decade. What about the legions of Fringe first-timers armed with nothing more than – and I was a lunatic to think this would help the proposal in any way – a laminated map? If two people a day were being asked to do this, for a month, even if you tried to pick the most athletic-looking audience members you could, one of those fifty athletes was going to sprain an ankle. This would surely raise a few eyebrows with the Pleasance's risk assessment team. But we wouldn't get their verdict until the next day. In the meantime, we watched the GoPro footage back, and agreed that it was very funny, mainly because at the Tesco checkout my head-cam had captured me entering my PIN into the machine. This blundering breach of my own privacy might make a funny sequel to 2021's Doubletree by Hilton incident, but would also mean warning my prospective Dashers that they were about to potentially forfeit not just their physical safety but their financial security. Still, it would all be worth it when they arrived, panting, back at the venue, and were immediately forced to wolf down their Meal Deals as quickly as possible.

The tech rehearsal complete, I and the multiple other people embroiled in this insania headed out for a nervous but excited team dinner, in an actual restaurant, and I went to bed that night with my big dreams still intact. I then woke to the news that the Meal Deal Dash had indeed failed all of its risk assessments. Sorry, Ivo: you can't send audience members out of the venue and you can't give them GoPros and you can't get them to eat onstage. You can still do this Top Trumps thing, I guess. Good luck with your opening show in eight hours.

A risk assessment is a fairly binary yardstick when it comes to failure and success: I had, in the space of barely a day, devised a whole new plan for my show and then had it quite understandably vetoed by the authorities. It was a stressful and ominous start to a high-pressure month at the Fringe, and I wasn't going to get anywhere by pleading with the Pleasance to reconsider. The modern pentathlon was hurriedly rejigged so that it now consisted of the two daily audience volunteers (1) running offstage to get changed into Primark replicas of my Taskmaster outfit,* (2) taking a quiz of questions I'd got wrong on *The Weakest Link*, (3) trying to catch Mavrix moon balls bounced at them by team-mates on the front row, (4) playing Top Trumps against each other using members of the audience, and then (5) helping me collect donations for the Trussell Trust at the end of the show. The whole thing was bedlam, a blur of half-baked bodges someway propped up by the enthusiasm of the pentathletes and the team behind the scenes, but the most ludicrous marathon of mayhem for me, the madman in the middle, running around in my pyjama bottoms. *Organised Fun* was a ludicrously on-the-nose title for

---

* You laughed at *my* quick change, now I can laugh at yours! I did try and provide a decent pile of sizing options, and all large and soft enough that they could be pulled over the audience members' pre-existing outfits with ease, but it was still not ideal for them, or for Matt Forde, who was sharing a dressing room with me that year. Fordey is not just the best impressionist in the game but one of the most infectiously upbeat people I have ever met, even that month as he was battling with a sciatica that would reveal itself in the autumn to be the big C, a tumour at the base of his spine. Having only written a pretty hurried scribble in his hospital visitors' book that autumn (I was running late for a gig), let me say this now to Fordey: your attitude over the past year has been an inspiration to so many people, I am so pleased that you have recovered and that Forest are doing so well, and I am so sorry again for that time that two of my audience members ran into our dressing room and, because I hadn't warned you that this was part of my show, you thought you were getting robbed and shat your pants. Perhaps for the final time.

this show, which was rarely both and sometimes neither. And there was so much more chaos to come.

With this first rollercoaster spluttering into life on the Wednesday, it was next time to cut some more red tape on the Friday: the first ever *Comedians' DJ Battles* at the Assembly Underground. The idea of nightclub knockout tournaments, of having some needlessly competitive measurement for who's laid down the best tunes at a party, had been an obsession of mine for some time, ever since I watched comedy promoter and Rage Against The Machine disciple Will Briggs, one of the least angry people I've ever met, drop 'Killing in the Name' at Craine and Clare's wedding in December. As a room full of TV producers in their forties bellowed 'fuck you, I won't do what you tell me' in unison, shaking the members' club basement with their collective disrespect for the Man, Will leant in to the DJ up next and in a delicious moment of bravado in the booth which I'm so glad was caught on video, shouted, 'You're fucked, mate. You're fucked.'

Two months later, I had asked my Fringe producers to book in a weekly slot at the Assembly under the title *Comedians' DJ Battles*. This route-one Ronseal of a name may be changed for future ventures, although changing it would mean retiring the £400 neon sign I ordered on the train to Edinburgh in July. Beyond the spring admin of writing a silly blurb and posing for a photo hovering over some decks, decks that I did not and to date still do not know how to use, I had, once more, given very little thought to the night, beyond an obsession with its fundamental ethos: that people would be encouraged to be, at all times, 'absolutely having it'. I have loved this very basic credo ever since I read it in a YouTube comment about a man in leopard print convulsing to Four Tet at Glastonbury.

It is, to use another thing I like to shout in people's ears on dancefloors, 'what it's all about'.

As the seriousness of other aspects of my life has ratcheted up in my thirties, I have cherished the wild abandon of the dancefloor more than ever, and it was a real source of pride to create one at the Fringe, where there are lots of rooms in which you can sit up lamenting your reviews into the night, but not so many where you can shake them off. But would it actually work? If I built it, would people come? Walking into the Friday tech rehearsal and seeing the neon sign already mounted on the wall was the first time I truly believed. By the time we opened doors at 11pm, and ribbon-cutter Alexandra Haddow* dropped the Arctic Monkeys' 'Dancing Shoes', the first track ever to be played in a Comedians' DJ Battle,† the Underground was sold out, and there was one thing on our mind: absolutely having it.

I was living once more with my beloved Alfie Brown, co-star of my first two Fringes, cohabitor of my last five, a magnificent unbroken‡ run in the same reasonably-priced (by many standards but especially by the Fringe's) New Town flat that we hope to rent in August perpetuity from a man called M.W. Barber. M.W. Barber (and I do know his first name, but if a flat says

---

* The host of *Indie Amnesty*, a fantastic comedians' clubnight that long predates *Comedians' DJ Battles*, and with very much the same rowdy ethos, if not the tournament format.

† I tend to steer my ship towards the padded shoulders of the 80s more than the knackered Converse of the 00s these days, but I will never forget that first Arctic Monkeys' album, and very much intend to host a twenty-year anniversary clubnight in January 2026, where it gets played in full, with the pauses, as Alex Turner and Andy Nicholson intended. Pints during 'Vampires'!

‡ Apart from by Covid obviously.

M.W. Barber on the door it's just more fun to say M.W. Barber, isn't it?) is an artist with a lot of house plants, who summers in Barcelona, and I've never met the man but every year our bond deepens. I hate to be too much of a dribbling landlord-stan, but, on top of the peaceful ambience of the home itself, M.W. Barber delivers in three ways that surely mark him out from most of the vultures rapidly inflating the Fringe into extinction: he doesn't hike up the rent year on year, he doesn't demand a cleaning fee, and he occasionally texts if you get a good review.

In 2022, Alfie had been in line for quite a lot of texts from M.W. Barber, and his blistering show *Sensitive Man* saw him nominated for the main Comedy Award, whose official photo-shoot marks him out as surely the most hungover nominee in the show's history. On the triumphant day that earned him that hangover, as he waved taxis down with his gong on the Grassmarket, I declared our home (in which I'd celebrated the same news in 2019) as 'Two Nom Towers', a nickname that only deepened our resolve to return there in 2023. But Two Nom Towers has witnessed a great many chapters in the rolling soap operas of mine and Alfie's lives, and 2023's chapter was a rather less jubilant one.

The occasional horribilisness of my annus had been more than matched by Alfie's own, a semi-consensual blaze of social media trial-by-fire in the spring through which I (and many other pals and producers) had been far less of a support to him, than, say, his longtime director and best friend, Adam Brace, who had then not hugely helped proceedings by dying of a stroke that April. On our first day back in M.W. Barber's home a few months later, we'd swapped notes on our respective fears for the month: Alfie's that doing any Edinburgh, especially this Edinburgh, without Adam, would be impossibly lonely, and mine that the current co-parenting cold war in London would stop me seeing Edie for the month. Her mother had brought her to the flat in utero in 2018 and then out of it in 2022, the latter a triumph of surface-level happy familying in the Julia Donaldson tent that looked unlikely to be repeated this time around. No noise has been as consistent an aspiration and a thrill in my Edinburghs 2009–present than Alfie's great roar of a laugh, so the sad silence of our Scottish sorrows was all the louder for its lack on this particular afternoon. Fortunately, Alfie broke the tension quickly enough. 'Well, this isn't very Two Nom Towers, is it?'

The flat has now been cathartically rebranded as Two Ignom Towers, and the friendship is all the deeper for it.

Alfie, who has silly voices and showtunes coursing through his vile nepo bloodstream,* joined us at the first night of *DJ Battles* to gyrate wildly over '9 to 5', and this even temporary exorcism was one of many memorable sights and sounds of the Underground that month, alongside Alison Spittle's Shrek costume, and a nineties megamix courtesy of Jess Phillips MP. In this three-pronged fever dream of a Fringe, *Organised Fun* was only occasionally fun, but the clubnight was delivering in spades. As for the third, definitively non-fun, prong, the halfway point of the Fringe was fast approaching, and with it the low-key premiere of *Graham in the Green*, the hour-long storytelling show that of course I had once more given next to no thought to since booking it in back in February. Luckily, I had one tiny sliver of time to pull something together, and that was back on that most familiar of panic chambers, the London North Eastern Railway.

---

* The chameleonic Jan Ravens and the late great composer Steve 'Glenn Ponder' Brown.

It had been resolved over the course of an expensively mediated Zoom call, not my favourite two hours in M.W. Barber's home 2018–present I must say, that Edie would indeed not be coming to Edinburgh, and that I would go down to her instead: not on a day off, because I didn't have one, but on one of my days 'on', a ludicrous risk by anyone's standards but my own. This wasn't even my first ever mid-Fringe Dad-dash: I'd flown down and back in a day in Edinburgh 2019, a quite grotesque carbon footprint merely to push a pram round a pond for an hour, but a push that meant a hell of a lot then, as this meant a hell of a lot now. Although not enough for me to have actually worked out my travel arrangements yet.

A few days before the halfway point, I'd been joined in Edinburgh by two more best friends, pillars of my life more than meriting a quick paragraph or two of origin story: my university roomates, Matt and Poppy. Matt was initially my sole university roommate, and I'd fought off several other suitors for that privilege at the end of our first year: everyone in college loved or fancied him or both, and I was desperate to bask in his reflected glory in our set at the top of Staircase 7, two single bedrooms opening onto our bombsite of a shared living room. Staircase 7's central location made us a major pit stop on events like 'the alcoholic tour of the college', a toxic turbolash for which Matt and I bought twenty bottles of Everyday Vodka from the big Tesco in Cowley, dragging it back over Magdalen Bridge in wheelie suitcases.* I didn't want to bring too leering a second-year energy to these fresher events, but I was unde-

---

* Wheelie suitcases full of booze would be a feature of 'Partygate' in 2022, but it's worth reiterating that despite Matt being a sometime civil servant and me being a full-time posh twat, neither of us were involved in that one.

niably keen to shake off my virginity at some point, and felt
that these odds could only be improved in the orbit of Matt,
himself rebounding out of an impressively long-term, but now
unworkably long-distance, relationship with his high-school
girlfriend back in Harrogate. What wild oats might be sown
by these two swashbuckling sophomores, with their combined
history of one sexual partner and one 'So You Think You're
Funny?' award? Unfortunately, we both bungled this grubby
gameplan: Matt let me and himself down by getting another
girlfriend within weeks of the autumn term starting, while my
semi-ironic Thomas the Tank Engine duvet had still welcomed
no visitors as I packed it back into my parents' car the following
June. I had dreamed of being Captain Oates, but I would be
out in the cold for some time yet.

For all my fury at my friend's betrayal, as I tanked quietly on
the other side of the wall, it was a betrayal for which I would
eventually end up being very grateful. Matt's relationship with
Poppy, the first-year mathematician with a room at the bottom
of our staircase, proved to be not just some sham marriage
of neighbourly convenience, but a civil partnership of true
longevity, and one that would yield surprising geographical
ambition from two people who couldn't even be arsed to cross
the quad for a snog. Their decade and a half together has seen
them through a twenties split between London, Manchester and
China, to a grown-up life with a farmhouse and two children
in north Yorkshire, via a ten-month sojourn to Ghana in 2023,
an adventure most young parents wouldn't have the stones for
but which gave me and everyone who visited them a week we'd
never forget. My own adult life has seen me reside as the third
wheel to a lot of great couples, but they were my first, and
while I initially insisted that Poppy was the third wheel, and

the nickname Yoko persists to this day, she has become just as integral to my life as the as-yet un-assassinated boyfriend that she stole from me in 2009.

Poppy and Matt have come to support me at nearly every Fringe, and in 2023 they found me wobbling at the halfway mark, about to pile an already overflowing plate with a theatre piece that I was still yet to write a word of, its premiere two days away, with the small matter of a trip to London in between. I was, it would be fair to say, shitting it. But my sleep-deprived disarray held few remaining surprises for two best friends who had weathered fifteen years of my Pro Plussing dissertations and co-parenting disasters, and who had, like most other frequent flyers, learned to enjoy or ignore the turbulence. I was not travelling by plane this time, instead heading down on the last train to London, straight after the end of *Organised Fun*, and coming back the following afternoon, having seen my daughter, but also, hope against hope, having done my work. Matt took me to W. Armstrong & Son, my favourite vintage shop in Edinburgh, where he steered me away from the shirts towards the less familiar terrain of the hatstand. He took down a beret and placed it on my head with a formality that was at once ridiculously silly and deadly serious. 'This is your writing beret,' he said. 'You're going to get on that train and you're going to wear this beret and you're going to write your show.'

That evening, I wrapped up another frantic pentathlon at the Pleasance Beyond, made the 19:58 with seconds to spare, and I sat on that train and I put on my beret and I wrote my show. I got a few strange glances for the beret, much as I'm getting a few strange glances for it now in this Caffè Nero. It's still my writing beret, a superstition that I will honour whenever I can, forever grateful to Matt for spurring on the essay crisis that would become the best show I've ever done. The show was what I had long wanted it to be about – my memories, my regrets, my uninnocent elegant falls into the unmagnificent lives of adults* – but it was now also about this very journey south. My whole life had led me to this train and now I was pouring my whole life out on it.

I got in to King's Cross at quarter to one in the morning, with several thousand words written and a props list bubbling in my mind. The fridge waiting for me at home was pretty empty after a fortnight away, but the fridge door itself was an embarrassment of riches, a collage of magnets and mementos that I had long started to consider the main art project of my life. The expired sell-by dates that shamed the yoghurts and vegetables inside the fridge were badges of honour on the gig tickets and wedding invites outside of it, a mosaic of my life where Edie's drawings jostled for space with postcards and Polaroids, banknotes and beermats. This is how I would tell my story, through these things I'd never thrown away, these portals into the past that lived on my fridge and in my head and a hundred other messy piles in between.

For all the gush and rush of the commute, the main excitement was waiting for me in the morning. I leapt out of bed at 7am, did one final raid of the interior and exterior of the fridge (some crusty Onken and a 2012 Swindon stub), and went to pick up my daughter. Her shout of 'Daddy!' at the door is the happiest noise in my life after even two days away, so was

---

* Richard Roper has quite legitimately requested a footnote explaining that this is a lyric from one of my favourite songs by The National, swift-whispering merchants of mid-life melancholy who probably still just pip LCD Soundsystem as my favourite band of all time.

quite the wrecking ball after two weeks. We did our now very well-honed re-enactment of *The Tiger Who Came to Tea*, went for a swim at our favourite pool, then I dropped her back with her mum for lunch and headed back to King's Cross. It was the tiniest of cameos in a month away, and I don't ever intend to be in this position again, but nonetheless to have got to her at all, and to have had a roar and a splash in the August sunshine, was pure heaven. Now to get back on the train and write it up. I made the 1pm in decent time but this was only fulfilling my own half of the bargain, punctuality-wise: the train was due to arrive forty-five minutes before that evening's *Organised Fun*, so any delay at all would be a disaster. Whatever the erratic quality of the show, three hundred people had booked to see it, and nobody bar Luca knew just how close to the start I was planning to arrive. Luckily, we arrived at Waverley within the specified four and a half hours, four and a half hours I used to polish off my first draft of the new show. Missions accomplished. Back into the Pleasance with minutes to spare. No one lives like you do.

The theatre show began the next day and I was immediately thrilled by what it had become and what it might yet turn out to be. It was listed as work-in-progress, the show's freshly written and printed script in my hand throughout, and audiences were small, but they were supportive, supportive in all sorts of ways, coming up afterwards with compliments on the show or semi-therapeutic reassurances that it was 'all going to be all right'. Some of them had been crying. That's a cynical thing to take too much pride in, but after all the ball games in the big room next door, it felt good to have some emotional heft in the solipsistic sanctuary of the Pleasance Green. I short-cutted to this heft with a soundtrack, introspective instrumentals by

Bonobo and Underworld, songs I'd long dreamed of sullying with a navel-gazing monologue of my own, another dramatic dream facilitated by Luca's sleight of hand in the tech box. Was this theatre? It certainly wasn't comedy. My aunt and my brother, regular Fringe visitors and two of the people in the world closest to the show's content, came to watch it in its first week and were gratifyingly non-horrified by what they saw. *Graham in the Green* swiftly became the hour I looked forward to most each day.

Organised Fun continued to be the most stressful hour, not helped by a *Guardian* review a few days later which crystallised most of my private anxieties about the show into print for all the world to see. But the show must and did go on, some days better than others but resulting either way in a surge of adrenaline at its finish that fuelled some more epic Edinburgh nights, two of them in my own club. The final *Comedians' DJ Battles*, on the last night of the Fringe, went on until half past four, and ended with another insane train dash, to the Monday morning's first chopper out of Saigon,* back to my little girl.

While the rest of the dancefloor stumbled off to bed, or to attempt a woozy dawn ascent of Arthur's Seat, I was accelerating into action, pausing only to pose for a final photo with Ocean's Three and Off The Kerb, the heroes who had propped me up all month and been thanked with little more than matching pairs of *DJ Battles* T-shirts and fluorescent

---

* My friend Henry Perryment, fellow 2019 nominee and champion of the reckless all-nighter, was the first person to recommend me this train, many years before I had a parental incentive to catch it. 'You're back in London before they're even packing up!,' Pez would say, a manic glint in his sleep-deprived eyes. I don't see Pez as much as I'd like these days, but he can always rely on getting one bleary selfie on the last Monday of August.

trousers. Then I rushed back to the flat, scribbled apologetic notes to Alfie and M.W. Barber, grabbed my bags, pegged it to Waverley, and crashed into the 6am train on which I would leave Edinburgh for the final time that year. The maddest month of my life, the post-*Taskmaster* triple header, had been a dizzying dance from delirium to disappointment and back again, the yardstick barely able to process the success or failure of any venture before I lurched onto the next one. The autumn would continue this dance, but just as on my previous train south from Waverley, I had something more important than any of this waiting for me in London. No writing beret on the 6am this time: just an eyemask, some earplugs and a jumper between my head and the window, a corpse drooling into the new day. Six hours later I was at a soft play.

CHAPTER 8

Stop Making Sense

In Los Angeles, in 1984, David Byrne, lead singer of Talking Heads, disappeared from the stage during a show at the Pantages Theatre, before re-emerging in a comically oversized suit with which he would go on to carve his name in music and fashion history.

In London, in 2024, Ivo Graham, host of *Comedians' DJ Battles*, disappeared from the stage during a clubnight at the Village Underground, before re-emerging in a comically oversized suit with which he would go on to embarrass himself quite badly at a child's birthday party.

154 YARDSTICKS FOR FAILURE

It shames me, and really ought to shame my father as well, that I hadn't seen *Stop Making Sense*, often feted as the greatest concert film of all time, at any point in the first thirty-three years of my life. Alongside the more esoteric slices of Celtic folk and Dutch prog that soundtracked our family road trips, most mainstream rock 1961–present got a look in at some point too. They're even one of my dad's Desert Island Discs. If my father is ever cast away, and I hope he isn't as I don't think he'd thrive on the island,* one of the eight tracks he would like for company is 'Houses In Motion', off 1982's *The Name of This Band Is Talking Heads*. This live album now exists as something of a historical footnote to its successor, perhaps because it's audio only, and features neither the band's biggest hits nor its biggest suit. But it did feature in the Grahams' late-nineties Renault Espace in quite a big way, because that was the Talking Heads CD my dad owned, and that's how things worked in the olden times: adjacent slabs of a band's discography either seared into one's earliest memories or a

---

* I actually think that though he'd miss his favourite peoploids terribly, my dad would probably thrive on the island, especially if he had his twelve-string Chapman Stick bass as a luxury item, and probably the latest *Private Eye* annual as the book. The Grahams are exhausting extroverts and need rest forced upon them against their will! My dad used to live alone in the week a lot for work, and in 2005 I received a forty-five-minute accidental voicemail from him, a potential nightmare of a situation but which amounted to little more than Dad humming to himself as he whipped up another Michelin star beans on Marmite toast. I listened, out of a delighted curiosity, to the voicemail in its entirety, a feature-length reel of kitchen folio punctuated by my dad quite adorably exclaiming the names of his children to himself, using our names, as he would put it, 'for his encouragement.'

total mystery, depending on which of them came to hand in the shop that one fateful day in 19whenever.

But there still can't be many other Talking Heads fans who were so invested in Adrian Belew's seagull-guitar effects pedalling on 'Houses in Motion' that they'd want to listen to it with only real seagulls for company, and yet had never got round to watching *Stop Making Sense*, made by the same band (albeit without Belew) a couple of years later. It quite literally doesn't make sense. But my father will live and die in these outer crescents of the cultural Venn. He's walking a line! Get outta the way!

Anyway, I've been musically, if not financially, independent of my parents for more than half my life now, and so some of the responsibility for not seeking out *Stop Making Sense* has to be laid at my door too. In 2018, I did get to watch its naïve melodies in the flesh, treated by another of my benefactors, Josh Widdicombe,* to David Byrne's *American Utopia* at the Hammersmith Apollo. Josh and I have played this venue a combined fourteen times, thirteen of them Josh, but tonight its stage was graced not by some squeaking satirist but a living legend, jerking this way and that as he led another exquisitely choreographed and uniformed ensemble through the hits. I'd never seen anything like that before. Five years later, *Stop Making Sense* was re-released in 4K,

---

* Josh knows what's what: the man has a neon 'This Must Be the Place' sign in his home, and the song was the soundtrack to his and Rose's anecdote factory of a wedding in 2019. That is their story to tell, of course, and it is a tragedy, really, that the scorching Puglian carnage of their nuptials, officiated by some agnostic goon who forgot to print the vows for the ceremony, was one of the final chapters of their non-podcasted life BPH (Before Parenting Hell).

and though I still don't really know what that means in technical terms, I do know what it meant for me personally: that I would go to the cinema to watch it three times in eight months, and spend a considerable amount of money on my own custom costume in tribute. The film swept me off my feet, it changed the course of my year and maybe my life, and if I get dropped on a desert island, I want to take 'Burning Down the House' (*Stop Making Sense* version) with me. Sorry, Dad. Sorry, Adrian Belew.

My first *Stop Making Sense* was at the Hackney Picturehouse, east London, in October 2023. I went with my friends Orlando, Elliot and Rosie, and I wore a nice shirt, and I watched out, and I got what I was after, and I burst out of the cinema feeling so lucky to be in the creating game at all, especially after Edinburgh's debut of *Comedians' DJ Battles*, just a clubnight but one where I had got to try something new and surprising and silly, holding tight through some of the nastier weather of my adult life.

My second *Stop Making Sense* was at the Prince Charles Cinema, central London, in January 2024. I went with my brother, and my friends Alex and Luca, and I wore a vintage grey, but only standard size, suit, and I watched out, and I got what I was after, and I burst out of the cinema feeling so determined that at *Comedians' DJ Battles* in London, a few months later, we would play some songs from *Stop Making Sense*, and maybe I would dress up for that too, an homage to my heroes, close enough but not too far.

My third *Stop Making Sense* was back at the Hackney Picturehouse, east London, in June 2024. I hosted this screening with my friend Paul, and I wore my brand new big suit, and I watched out, and I got what I was after, and I burst out of the cinema feeling so excited to don the suit again at *Comedians' DJ Battles* in London, just a week later, so much preoccupation and preparation finally at fruition with me, on stage, an ordinary guy burning down the house.

The big suit ball had started rolling in March, when, after daydreaming of the stunt for weeks, I remembered someone who I suspected might be able to make these baggy fantasies a reality. Costume designer Patrick Jack had been a darling support to me throughout the *Taskmaster* studio records in autumn 2022, and without him we wouldn't have had our *Sgt. Pepper* outfits, the greatest clothing triumph of my life, and I'll say it, the greatest clothing coordination in the show's *history*. Maybe I could get by with a little more help from my friend? Patrick's responses to my emails were as joyously can-do as ever, although he was glad of having rather longer than forty-eight hours this time to build – and how *thrilling* it was when he started using the verb 'build' – the plasterzote structure that would lift the suit up off my chest and waist. He even remembered my measurements! By the time Patrick delivered the suit to my flat in May, its hulking frame hidden beneath a vast red drape, I was booked in to co-host the *Stop Making Sense* Hackney screening the following month. This latest trip to the Picturehouse would not just serve as part of the *Comedians' DJ Battles* promotion, but to soft-launch the suit in the comparative sobriety of a Sunday afternoon at the movies.

There was one particular moment that day that the surreal and literal enormity of what I had committed to was given an unexpectedly jolting bump of reality. As I stood nervously in the corridor outside Screen Two, listening out for my introduction to the stage, the tension of the antechamber was pierced by a shrieking guffaw familiar to anyone who's taken even a passing interest in comedy podcasts and panel shows over the last decade. Nish Kumar and James Acaster have been by many measurements my chums and colleagues for said decade, but they remain, especially when hunting in packs, the bigger boys from the year above. They were also spending their Sunday afternoon at the movies, and the sight of me in this suit, ear pressed to the screen door, a nervous man dressed as a confident man, was an unexpected and pretty uproarious gift as far as they were concerned. James hasn't laughed at me that much since I pranked myself on the *Off Menu* live stream. Nish hasn't laughed at me that much, ever. The embarrassment was compounded by my enquiry as to whether they were here to watch my (yes, 'my'!) *Stop Making Sense* screening. They were not. They were going to see *La Chimera* next door. That was the main course, this was a simply succulent surprise starter.

Though I had given the screening as much of a shout-out as I could on social media, there were, I'm sure, many regular Hackney Picturehouse patrons who were there merely to watch *Stop Making Sense,* with little to no interest in what newly radicalised David Byrne superfan Ivo Graham would have to say before the screening, and certainly with no suspicion that he was about to stumble, nay squeeze, through the door, shoulderpads first, in a suit that even Byrne himself doesn't put on until about three-quarters of the way through the film. The addition of audible guffaws from more famous comedians out of shot presumably only confused matters further, and wasn't completely resolved by my wheezing summary of the situation: that hello, everybody, I'm Ivo Graham, and yes this is my suit, I'll explain that in a minute, and yes, that was James Acaster and Nish Kumar you heard outside, but don't get too excited, they're going to *La Chimera*. I regained my composure over the course of the ten-minute Q&A, and I managed to, if nothing else, plant the seed I was most excited to plant: that at some point a few songs into the film, I was going to be so overwhelmed by the majesty and energy of the band that I would loudly say 'fuuuuck', and hope that I spoke for all of us in that moment. Twenty minutes later, as 'Burning Down the House' reached its dizzying crescendo, I loudly said 'fuuuuck', and people cheered, and an hour after that, I was parading around the Picturehouse café in my suit, and my friend Billie and her dad were taking it in turns to try on the jacket, and I was increasingly certain that, mere tribute as it may be, I, or rather plasterzote pioneer Patrick Jack, had created something very special. Next up: the clubnight.

In the five months in between the Prince Charles and the Picturehouse, Jan–June 2024, a monumental night of DJ Battling had been devised for the Village Underground, and I had become *obsessed* with it. I was determined that the biggest Fun I'd ever Organised would be a triumph, not just in recouping its many costs but in creating moments that everyone there would remember forever. It was the biggest focal point yet for my proud and problematic prioritisation of shared experience above all else, Tom's wisdom about it being life's greatest currency gripping and twisting ever harder in the theatre of my ambition.

Eight teams were booked, twenty Battlers in all, featuring most of the guests who had dominated the format most iconically in Edinburgh (Alison Spittle and Sikisa) or helped me devise it in the first place (Rhys James and Celya AB). I asked Will Andrews, the gentle giant of graphic design who would later do this book's cover, to prepare not just a poster with all participants' faces on, but eight individual posters too. These posters announced each team alongside their nominations for which song they would most like to bagsy for themselves, and which they would like to ban from being played at any point in the night. Goodbye 'Mr Brightside'! Goodbye 'Don't Stop Me Now'! Goodbye the newly omnipresent 'Murder On The Dancefloor! They're all huge songs, but as Phil Wang once tweeted in a devastating two-bowls-out-of-five review of Edinburgh noodle institution Red Box, 'In order for new gods to flourish, the old titans must die.'

I thought the shit-stirring iconoclasm of the latter, in posters drip-fed onto socials one at a time like a football club's latest signings,* would create such phenomenal buzz around the event that the Village Underground would sell out with ease. At our first site visit one cold January morning, I had gazed out at

---

* 'Are you ready for ANOTHER ONE?' Swindon Town's admins always tweet, giddy to be posting anything that isn't another defeat, as the new recruits are revealed in the last few days or hours of the transfer window. Dramatic EDM blasts from the speakers, drone shots zoom in on the crumbling County Ground, and signing-starved fans start readying their 'HMS Piss The League' memes, before the camera cuts to an injury-prone MK Dons loanee awkwardly lifting a red scarf in the centre circle. The difference is, I suppose, that I knew all the *DJ Battles* guests were going to absolutely rip it, whereas most Swindon signings either return prematurely to their parent clubs, become local hate figures, or both. Nonetheless, releasing the Battlers' names one by one gave me, undeniably, a deadline day buzz. The dream scenario would have been giving a media interview outside the Village Underground, leaning out the car window like Harry Redknapp, reassuring journalists that I was still confident of getting Leo Reich in before the window slammed shut.

STOP MAKING SENSE   161

the empty club, with no doubt in my mind that on the night of June 8th it would be full, with 700 heroes absolutely having it in this railway tunnel. But I was a bit too complacent, and a bit too slow off the mark with the posters, and a bit too distracted by all the other fluster of 2024 and five months of inaction and distraction later, with just days to go until the clubnight, the main perspiration was coming from how many tickets we still had to sell. But now I had my suit. In a brief wind of al fresco bravado after a podcast record, I asked Alex Kealy to film me as I strutted the streets of west London as David Byrne, banging on about the clubnight, either proudly holding or awkwardly averting the gaze of less preposterously proportioned passing pedestrians.

Alongside this gonzo promotional content, I had thrown everything at the night, personnel-wise. We had three producers, Luca and Katy and Isobel from Off The Kerb, working alongside the Village Underground's technical team. We had a photographer, a videographer, an actual DJ making sure things ran smoothly on laptops 1 and 2, and my friend Tom Chamberlain entering frenetic amounts of Battle data into PowerPoint on laptop 3. And then, in the backstage room called the Sauna, someone who, like Luca, had been at the other end of a thousand WhatsApps about this night in the months leading up to it. Running the backstage bar, with a selection of weapons-grade cocktails she had prepared at home, was my friend Elsa Beckmann, routinely acknowledged by anyone to have enjoyed her hospitality as the greatest party host in the game. It was unthinkable that she would not be there, at the biggest party I had ever hosted.

Elsa's fiancé Luke, himself a master chef who can be relied

upon to bless any sesh with a tray of something incredible,* was not able to join us from Manchester for this particular weekend, so I had Elsa staying at my flat solo, and we'd spent the afternoon of the party there, alternating between playing hide and seek with my daughter and pouring cocktails from fun bags to big jugs. Ooh er! At 6pm, I dropped my daughter back with her mum, and at 7pm, Elsa and I were pretty much ready to leave for Shoreditch. Here we go! We piled bags and bags of booze and confetti cannons into an Uber XL: our van loaded with weapons, packed up and ready to go. It was only as we pulled out of my street that I realised the big suit was still hanging upstairs. Never in my life have I been more grateful to remember something, just in the nick of time. Nothing is better than that! (Is it?)

Forty-five minutes later, we and the suit pulled up outside the Village Underground. Two hours later, it was showtime at the edge of the stage. Five hours after that, I put on the suit. Three hours after that, I was still wearing the suit, eating chips on a ring road many miles from my home, asking myself how did I get there.

Even in this blissful orgy of nostalgic detail I cannot go through every guest, every song, every moment, of *Comedians' DJ Battles*, a party that I took to describing both before and after the event as a 'game-changing clubnight', 'a pinnacle of my existence', and 'my wedding to myself'. But there are

---

* The 2am vegetable okonomiyaki Luke produced at my friends' Charlie and Chris's epic fireball of a wedding in July 2023 is up there with my favourite food memories of all time, largely for the conversion of a belching Bristolian called Barney, who enjoyed it so much that he refused to believe it wasn't meat, and insisted that he be escorted directly to the chef so he could shake his cabbage-chopping hand in person.

certain things that I am especially proud of, and certain people to whom I am especially grateful.

Music-wise, every guest smashed it. A few of the night's less debauched participants went home straight after their sets, and one team had even requested to be deliberately knocked out in the first round. Despicably cynical stuff. But no one fluffed their lines with the tunes. Sure, the 'X Men' (Josh Widdicombe, Matthew Crosby and Producer Vin of Radio X) arguably trolled the largely Gen Z crowd a little too festively by playing Wizzard's 'I Wish It Could Be Christmas Everyday', in June, with Christmas hats and all. But minutes later, Crosby was stage diving into the audience during 'I Believe in a Thing Called Love', and was this quite epic showmanship going to disrupt his teammates' hopes for an early bath? Were their opponents, tournament favourites Sikisa and Alison Spittle, running scared in the wings?

No, no, they were not. Sikisa and Spittle don't do running scared. That was the last we saw of the X Men, whereas their victors went all the way to the final, pipped to the trophy by Sophie Duker and Ania Magliano with a huge and only semi-ironic choice of 'Mambo Number 5' at 2am.

The Battlers already had plenty of weapons in their respective armouries: years of stage experience, including previous participation in this specific format, plus, of course, all the purposefully popular songs I had invited them to play. None of them needed any more help from me. But, despite this, one of the most memorable aspects of the night – and the idea that I was probably most proud of seeing through – was the fact that I had also quite literally armed my guests, insisting that more room in the night's creaking budget be found not just for confetti cannons but for some rather heavier artillery:

CO_2 guns. I had seen Marlborough-educated Coachella head-liner Fred Again using these in a video on Instagram, and the firepower had passed from one posh opportunist to another. Luca, her contributions to *DJ Battles* kaleidoscopic in their range and dedication, had travelled that week to Slough to pick up the guns and receive a full briefing which qualified her to oversee their use on the night. This qualification saved us hundreds of pounds in further personnel, but also meant that every fifteen minutes (once per team, during their last song) she would be yanked back into action from whatever fun she might tentatively be having, to make sure the drunk guests weren't about to quite literally shoot themselves or an audience member in the face.

Jamie Allerton was the first Battler of the evening to be entrusted with these munitions, and there was only one time he was ever going to fire them, during the chorus of his favourite song, Daniel Bedingfield's 'Gotta Get Thru This'. Every comic who handled the CO_2 guns over the course of the night relished the raw power invested in them by the guns, but some *really* had understood the assignment when it came to Narrative, and there is a video of Rajiv Karia letting rip, at the exact point My Chemical Romance's 'Welcome to the Black Parade' changes gear, that I watched approximately fifty times in the days after the Battles. People were making moments all right. I so wish Tom had been there, but he was, represented by so many of his friends and fellow Springsteen apprentices, whom I joined in a circle pit for the inevitable, unstoppable 'Dancing In The Dark'. Our guns were only for hire, but our memories were for life.

The Village Underground was nearly full at this point, and it needed to be, because alongside the night's other flourishes and fees, I had spent a considerable amount of our as-yet unre-couped cash on costumes. I had decided that I would save the Big Suit to wear during the *Stop Making Sense* medley of the final hour, but I wanted to go (metaphorically if not literally) big even before then. For this purpose, costume counsel Patrick Jack had sent me a link online to an aggressively lurid pink and orange two-piece, which I bought immediately before I could overthink it, and which I continue to wear and love so much to this day.

The other costumes were for for Luca, Isobel and Katy, the show's producers, their roving commission insisting (I did insist!) that they delegate and celebrate as much as possible, but which still did boil down to them doing pretty much every spare job going from the night's start to its end. Many of these were quite legitimate tasks that we had anticipated and pre-pared for in advance, and some were quite ridiculous tasks that we had not anticipated and prepared for in advance, like me buying a John Lewis lamp for the Talking Heads finale the day before the gig, and then bringing it to the Village Underground without a bulb. Can someone pop out into Shoreditch at 10pm to buy me a bayonet bulb, please?* My life is one long medley of *Taskmaster* tasks, and I can't wholeheartedly recommend getting swept up in it. Especially as I may try to thank you, or punish you further, with an outfit.

I hate to reiterate something I've had to stress a number of times in telling people about the night, but let me state once more on record: I don't get a *kick* out of dressing women.

---

* I am proud to say that I sorted the lamp issue myself by switching off and debulbing one of the more superfluous lights backstage! The only practical thing I did over the course of the whole night!

Quite the opposite. Until recently I found dressing myself hard enough. I have probably bought eight items of clothing for women, ever, in my life, and four of those have been politely acknowledged and then exchanged for store credit. Of the four that haven't, one is a pair of genuinely excellent (but also non-refundable) orange trousers I bought for my mum in Ghana, and three are the identical grey suits that I bought Luca, Isobel and Katy to wear at *Comedians' DJ Battles*. And even then, *only* after checking that they were all OK with the idea, putting them in a WhatsApp group with Patrick to brainstorm ideas, and absenting myself from the brainstorm with the promise to pick up the tab at the end. They went with grey gingham suits, and they looked fantastic, and they were so clearly identifiable as the ones in charge of the night, and they came onstage to dance to Talking Heads at the end, and we were grey-coded just like in the film, and the lamp's new bulb flickered gorgeously during 'This Must Be the Place', and my lord, I was proud of us during that moment. I never put any effort in for costume parties the first three decades of my life, and now, just as everyone else grows up, I'm deciding that big suits are the best,* and matching suits are even better.

A few minutes after 'This Must Be the Place', it was 4am, and we were done. By this point, the audience had undeniably whittled down, though the Sauna was still swelteringly full of people. The heaving guestlist of +1s had drunk our back-stage bar dry, and when the final settlement came in from the Village Underground, I could only laugh at the hefty charge we'd received for not hitting our minimum spend at the main

---

* There's a *Peep Show* quote that this calls to mind, but I cannot endorse the second half of it in a book.

bar. Elsa, who I'd barely seen all night as we ruled our respective roosts onstage and backstage, had supervised such a stunning subterranean speakeasy that many of her patrons hadn't needed to venture above ground at all.

But this was no time to be contemplating the losses incurred by the night's bountiful quantities of verdita tequila and CO2. Balance sheet be damned: *DJ Battles*'s London debut had been a triumph, an all-timer, and it wasn't over. Elsa and I had left my flat ready for an afterparty, should there be demand for one, and there was demand for one, by which I mean, I was shouting at the bug-eyed battalion of Battlers and bandwagon-jumpers in the Sauna to get out their phones and note down my postcode. I had at one point in the run-up contemplated booking a minibus to be waiting outside the Underground at 4am: I ruled this out as not just a business-expense bridge too far but such an egregious temptation of fate that it could only have resulted in me travelling home alone on an empty minibus. As it was, we could have filled it twice over, even if my manic invitational approach did lead to some whispered intrigues as to who exactly some of the strangers in my home were. Unfortunately, I was last to join these intrigues, as, with Elsa and my brother already sent ahead to open house, I accidentally booked a taxi not to my flat but to a street with the same name in Essex. A sobering splash of failure after a night of triumph. After being far too slow to notice this navigational nightmare, and being told by the driver that it was too late to change destination, I was chucked out at the next exit from the Essex road. My final public appearance in the big suit was calling the next cab outside a kebab shop in Wanstead at 5am, people on their way to work gawping at my dreams walking in broad daylight, my halloumi wrap falling apart in my hands.

Comedians' DJ Battles returned for four more glorious nights at the Fringe, and though the now garlic sauce-stained big suit didn't travel north, the kebab shop was not its last public appearance of the summer.

One July Saturday, the day of England's Euros quarter-final against Switzerland (kick-off 5pm), Edie and I had been invited to attend a fourth birthday party in Ascot. The four-year-old in question was a cheeky young Crisp called Alfie, and his Granny Karen had recently sent me a video of him giggling deliriously at a clip on her iPad. What clip? The clip of me in the big suit, three days before *DJ Battles*. Well, there was only one thing for it: I'd have to bring it to his birthday party. People have worn stupider things to Ascot.

Edie and I arrived at Granny Karen's house at 3pm, the suit under its red drape in the boot of my car, alongside child-size, non-plasterzoted suits for Edie and the birthday boy, in case there was the chance of a fully coordinated Dance Mode* moment, taking the number of grey suits I had purchased this financial quarter to six. However, the giddy abandon with which I had chucked this multi-generational dressing-up box into the Fabia on departure then rather crumbled when faced with the standard-issue pandemonium of a four-year-old's birthday party. The whole thing was a blur of whooping, screaming kids, most of whom I'd never met. There was also a professional entertainer hired by Alfie's parents: in the 'professional entertainment' field of making genuinely impressive balloon

---

* If you have a child between three and six and you haven't watched the 'Dance Mode' episode of *Bluey*, well, perhaps, you've got a more rigorous approach to screentime than I do, but I'd really recommend it. 'This seems to happen to us – a lot.'

animals, rather than my rather less applicable 'professional entertainment' field of navel-gazing stand-up, navel-gazing theatre, and needlessly complicated clubnights. I realised quite how much goodwill and good fortune would be required to pull off my attention-seeking Dance Mode moment at this party. It wasn't clear enough where I would put on my own suit, let alone bustle my daughter and the birthday boy into their own costume changes, in the wafer-thin sliver of time between balloon animals and tea. The plan was abandoned.

Unfortunately, I had told Alfie's Uncle Charlie about the suit in the boot. Charlie, who once convinced me in a Burford twin room that he was the CEO of a company called Sugar Box Productions, had now made it his personal mission to both seal and sweeten the deal of my outfit change. 'Ivo's brought a surprise!' Sugar Box was now saying to his sister, his brother-in-law, and several other guests, many of whom didn't know who I was, and might not even know who David Byrne was. Meanwhile, I had a new problem in my pocket, a flare-up on WhatsApp the like of which I've grown rather familiar with – if no better at swerving or soothing – over the last few years. It turned out there had been a misunderstanding with my daughter's maternal grandparents about when I was dropping her at their home that afternoon: not a crisis by some of the more global definitions of the word but one given a bit more nail-biting, hair-greying clout by the chequered history of these (usually mutual) misunderstandings and their consequences in the co-parenting and co-grandparenting trenches 2019–present. Though I would have been available and delighted to take my daughter home to mine for the night, I was of course also grateful to Granmuz and Granpops, whose generous and insistent clutches of the childcaring conch have facilitated all sorts of curricular and extracurricular excursions over the years, and would tonight allow me to relax with a non-session ale and enjoy what turned out to be England's best penalty shootout performance of modern times. But today, as far as they were concerned, their granddaughter was already meant to be at their home, rather than playing with a balloon giraffe forty-five minutes' drive away, with the candles on Alfie's cake yet to be lit, and an increasing number of party guests asking what my 'surprise' was going to be.

My mistake – on top of all of the other mistakes – was to have brought the big suit (under the drape) out of the boot of the car and onto the premises: stashed in the coat room of Granny Karen's house, but within reach of Sugar Box, who, to my horror, had gone to get it and was now presenting it to me just as the children were sitting down for tea, a brief window of comparative stillness at the party which he had not incorrectly identified as a good moment for me to Do My Dance. But I didn't want to Do My Dance. I wanted to shove a handful of triangular sandwiches into my pocket, make my apologies and whisk my daughter onto the M3, back to my impatient out-laws. 'I don't have time,' I pleaded, pathetically, to my friend, as other parents audibly started to speculate about what was under the drape. Sugar Box looked understandably baffled about why I was refusing to put on something I had brought, unprompted, to his nephew's party. 'Just the jacket, then?' I could hardly decline this most equitable of compromises. I whipped off the drape, put on the jacket, and, without the further context of any memory jogging, musical accompaniment, or matching trousers, waggled my arms hurriedly at the birthday boy. Alfie, his mouth full of sausage roll, looked at me so blankly that it was unthinkable this was the same child who had been whooping with joy at this suit on an iPad a few weeks ago. My own child, who I had also not briefed on my plans, looked at me with equal bafflement. I will embarrass her much more deeply over the next decade, I am sure, but this was a solid early addition to the mad-dad scrapbook. And on top of this, I was now proposing to take her home before the cake.

In *Stop Making Sense*, David Byrne disappears to put on the suit while the nine-strong Talking Heads, now led by Tina Weymouth, perform the Tom Tom Club's iconic, and extensively sampled, 'Genius of Love' in his absence. His reappearance, initially just as a giant silhouette on the back wall of the Pantages, is as perfectly executed as every other transition in the concert. As the band turn up the heat with 'Girlfriend Is Better', Byrne jerks and twitches through the early verses and choruses before exploring the full, rippling potential of the suit in the song's final third, the sweaty succession of judders and lunges that he aims first at his bandmates and then, thrillingly, at us. 'Stop making sense! Stop making sense making sense!' he bellows into the void, and then, in the film's defining image, he holds the mic direct to the camera, as if we the viewer, at the Hackney Picturehouse or the Prince Charles or the Hackney Picturehouse, might be able to make sense of it all for him. I truly believe it is one of the best performances, of anything, of all time.

I did not, of course, do full justice to the suit at *DJ Battles*, where I convulsed around in it for fifteen minutes to a merry, but diminishing, crowd, and didn't even play 'Girlfriend Is Better'. But no one can ever have done less justice to a David Byrne suit, or looked less natural in it, than my short waggle in the jacket at Alfie's birthday party, followed by a breathless garble of goodbyes and apologies and a mad grab of first my daughter's possessions, then my daughter herself. The final cruelty was the balloon giraffe bursting as I did up her seatbelt. Tears till Chertsey. And there I was, behind the wheel of a small automobile, radio commentary of the England-Switzerland first half largely drowned out by the consequences of my actions, wondering once more how I got here, and how I work this, and which of these large highways would get us home first.

Two months later, in September, I took Edie back to Ascot, for a quiet Sunday with Alfie, his parents Ed and Kate, his uncle and his granny. There was no one else there, and we had the one thing I so rarely allow myself: plenty of time. I packed all the suits, and we got changed into them after lunch, and we danced all afternoon, and the plan's triumph was as joyous as its failure had been excruciating, back in July. If someone asks, this is where I'll be. We go again.

CHAPTER 9

Propa Wallop

In a period of my life that has contained many of these comedy costumes, with wildly varying results, one of their most epic failures took place in April 2023, only a few hours after that year's most epic success. A few hours after representing my biological family at the marathon, I was representing my football family at the EFL Awards.

My two and a half decades supporting Swindon Town have brought many more failures than successes, and over the last few years I have waded ever deeper into the irate debates around the club and it's management. Who knows where this wading may lead? Lower-league football is an ugly business. The EFL Awards, however, are about as glitzy as lower-league football gets. When, in February 2023, I received an invitation to that year's awards, to be held at the Grosvenor House Hotel on Park Lane, I was thrilled. This would be my first evening back on the booze after I had succeeded or failed in my quest for Sub 3, the cheerleading cherry on the cake of a potentially classic day. I didn't anticipate the very specific way in which that cherry would be soured by bad luck and, to be fair, very bad decisions.

A few days prior to the Awards, getting more excited for this merry little coda to my marathon day, I had had an idea which I was absolutely certain (and this is huge talk from a perennially uncertain man) would be very funny. My team, Swindon Town, were going to be unrepresented at the ceremony, having endured a dismally underwhelming season (with worse yet to come) compared to our thrilling late surge to the League Two play-offs a year before. Perhaps the main talking point at the 2022 EFL Awards had been Swindon's cheeky talisman Harry McKirdy, included deservingly in the league-wide Team of the Season, flicking the Churchill Vs to the Awards' black tie dress code by turning up in white bucket hat and shades, plus a white T-shirt, white trainers, and no tie of any description. There could be nothing more logical: I would wear the same in 2023. McKirdy (now warming the bench at Hibernian) would not be at the Awards in person, but he would be there in spirit. I would take to the stage, fresh from the marathon, to present the 'EFL Club Employee Award' – it's no 'Goal of the Season', but I'm no Jeff Stelling – in my own bucket hat and shades, and the room would go almost as wild for the callback as the Swindon fans on the London Reds WhatsApp group, whose respect I feel I am yet to truly earn.

On Wednesday I texted the idea to the friends I knew would be at the EFL Awards: my +1, sitcom and crytocurrency's Tom Rosenthal, and the encyclopaedic hosts of elite lower-league podcast *Not The Top 20*. Their responses were positive, or perhaps they were just polite. That is the murky nether zone where my delusions thrive. On Thursday I ordered my shades and bucket hat off Amazon Prime, and on Friday, of course, they arrived. I would spend too much of my Edinburgh show that summer wrestling tediously with my Amazon Prime-related guilt, and needless to say, every product bought from any establishment other than Amazon is a victory, however tiny, for forward planning, for commercial competition, and for, fundamentally, the Resistance. However, I am ashamed to say that my own efforts for the Resistance continue to be undermined at every turn by the impulsive chaos of my day-to-day life.[*]

On Sunday, the seizing of my sub-3 dream in the marathon only emboldened my hubris that, for one day at least, I was Midas himself, and the sinking of two Neck Oils and a Guinness on a stomach only thinly lined with crisps didn't do much to dissuade me either. I said a triumphant goodbye to my family and then, suddenly panicking that I was now late for the Awards, I broke into a humiliating, hobbling, headache-inducing run to get home and get changed. Fortunately, the bonus feature of

---

[*] Yours may be the same. You may have bought this book off Amazon. I may even have told you, in some excruciatingly caveat-heavy social media post, to buy it off Amazon. It is what it is. In recent months and especially as of November 6th, 2024, the world's other zillionaire has been pulling some pretty chilling focus from Jeff. Who knows, by the time you are reading this, perhaps Jeff will have his own state department too. Some days it feels like we're all so totally fucked that having any principles at all is pointless! Just swim against the tide as much as you can, I guess! Good luck out there!

my definitively hilarious costume was that it did not take long
to put on. Without the speed bump of tying an actual black
tie, I got to the ceremony bang on 6:30 as requested, tucking
straight into my entrée with bucket hat and shades burning a
mischievous hole in my pocket.

At 9:15pm, Club Employee of the Season beckoned. The
awards (there were about fifty of them!) had dragged, and the
room could do with a bit of fresh energy. Bring on the bucket
hat! Of course, I wasn't yet wearing the bucket hat, I was
pacing on the spot next to the stage with hat and shades still
in pocket. I was going to go onstage wearing them, wait for
the ripples or even gales of laughter to die down, make a joke
about how host David 'Prutts' Prutton didn't pull his weight
in the Swindon relegation season 2010/11, casually drop in my
marathon time (ex-Man City midfielder Michael Brown had
already mentioned his), and dish out the gong. A solid advert
for me as funster and fan lest the EFL wanted to re-employ
me next season in an even more illustrious capacity than presenting Club Employee of the Season for no fee. I exchanged
a businesslike nod with Lee Hendrie. It was time.

I walked onto the stage to what must at best be described as
a mixed response. Of course, it was always going to be hard to
get an immediate and in any way accurate read of what such
a large, distracted and echoey room had made of my stunt
outfit, but if there were ripples of laughter there certainly
weren't gales. Later that evening, one steaming stranger in the
loos said I was the biggest wally he'd seen since Widdicombe
at Wembley. This wasn't a reference to any stand-up comedy
fail of Josh's, but rather his decision to turn up at the home of
football three weeks ago in a costume of his own, supporting
his beloved Plymouth against Bolton in the Papa Johns Trophy

final (pure EFL) dressed as a white-suited Spice Boy. This decision was brand-reinforcingly nostalgic and deliciously dapper, but it did make him look a bit of a bell when presenting next to plain-clothesed Boltonian Vernon Kay, and Josh was punished for his creamy confidence with Plymouth getting a 4–0 hammering. Meanwhile, my own punishment was seconds away.

In amongst my final marathon preparations (chowing down carbs, begging godparents for donations, forgetting to buy a Garmin watch), I had not taken any time to look up the full list of nominees for the EFL Club Employee of the Season Award. I only knew of one, an employee from Bristol City called Jerry Tocknell, because of a chance meeting that week with my City supporting friend Rich, who'd told me about Jerry, confirming that this guy is essentially the guy you go to if you need to buy or sell a Bristol City ticket at face value in the days leading up to the match. So it's Jerry the ticket man against two other nominees who presumably do similarly solid if unspectacular business for their clubs. Cheers, Rich! Bring on the awards!

At 9:20pm on Sunday, onstage at the Grosvenor House Hotel, I learned, along with the hundreds of footballers and football fans sat watching me, that Bristol City ticket re-distributor Jerry Tocknell had not won the EFL Club Employee Award.

The non-laughter at my arrival onstage was only made worse by David Prutton, who went in immediately with a sneering studs-upper about me 'definitely not getting the dress code!!!'. I clumsily tried to parry back with the Swindon 2011 relegation dig, but he'd already snatched the mic away from me, so I didn't get a chance to flaunt my marathon time, let alone crow at it being forty-nine minutes faster than Michael Brown's. 'Prutts' directed me quite firmly to open my golden envelope so that we could find out who's won (and, said his eyes, so that you can get off my stage in your bucket hat). I read out the name 'John Clarke, Burton Albion'.

John Clarke is a Burton Albion fan and season ticket holder of twelve years, now in his early twenties, who has had quadriplegic cerebral palsy his entire life, and who in 2022 joined the Burton Academy as a voluntary member of staff, supporting on and off field personnel of all ages in various aspects of club life. He couldn't be a more respect-worthy winner of EFL Club Employee of the Season, and I'd decided to show my respect by giving him that award in my bucket hat and shades.

I know that I don't get a free chuckle pass just because I raised £12,000 (not nearly as much as Michael Brown, annoyingly) earlier in the day for a disability charity. But it's probably still worth clunkily dropping in before we return to John Clarke of Burton Albion, who drove to the stage on a large motorised scooter not unlike my mother's Quickie. I wasn't close or incisive enough to see whether it was a fault with the scooter or with the EFL Awards' otherwise-untested ramp facility, but something went wrong and it took John an excruciatingly long time to get to the stage.

In June 2011, I performed as MC (and booked Joe Lycett, Rob Beckett and Seann Walsh for a combined £800: not bad!) for a gig in a disastrously unplayable bell tent at Oxford's Christchurch Ball (tickets £165: not good!). The lowest point of that evening's carnival of lows was a viewer (one of the six), this viewer also in a motorised scooter, trying to move away from the gig during my compèring, but their tyres getting stuck in the faux rustic coir matting of the bell tent's floor, and spinning loudly and distressingly into the silence. There was,

I see now with thirteen years' worth of hindsight, one saving grace to all this: I wasn't wearing a white bucket hat and shades.

At the EFL Awards, the last thing I had said before opening the card was that the winner was bound to be 'propa wallop'. This is something my ex-Swindon style icon McKirdy says on Instagram a lot, and back in the simple times of this all being a brilliant idea, I thought the use of his catchphrase would be the perfect topper, another delicious Easter egg for a room already stuffed with comedy chocolate. In the live unspooling reality of me actually doing all this, me saying the catchphrase was just another unfortunate and irrelevant footnote on a series of events that was now bigger than me and beyond my control. I read aloud the contents of the card and turned round to first lay eyes on the propa wallop Mr Clarke, stalling his scooter midway up the ramp for what may only have been ten seconds in real time, but each second containing its own agonising eternity as I wondered whether this was the moment to take off the bucket hat and shades. Or would that be worse? That would be worse, wouldn't it? Both were definitely bad.

I don't need to gild this problematic lily any further by telling you that my attempt to pass the award into John Clarke's lap, only to have it whisked away from me by his colleague, was a uniquely bad social interaction. The final blow was landed by Prutts, who caught me trying to sneak out of the presentation photo and took what I can only surmise as a sadistic pleasure in insisting that I stay in the frame. If only he'd displayed this creative zest and will to win in the relegation season of 2010/11, I ruefully observed to myself on the staircase later. The same decision about hat/shades removal had to be made, in a split second, for the photo. The same decision was made. The hat and shades stayed on. And then I got the hell off.

Astonishingly, despite the total failure of the enterprise, I decided to stick around for the afterparty, and cement my shame further with a dreadful attempt to chat to Vincent Kompany about a friend of a friend who used to go out with his compatriot, Adnan Januzaj. I then watched my posh podcaster pal buttonhole a hammered Wigan Athletic exec about player recruitment before we spilled onto the dancefloor at 2am, Papa Johns pizza in hand, as 'Mr Brightside' ushered in yet another caterwauling curfew. I returned home, endeavouring to learn a broad and chastening lesson about always thinking through every single possible consequence of my actions, even and especially if said action is a drunk costume-based stunt on the same day as a marathon. The bucket hat went to the back of a very speculative fancy dress drawer, and I wondered if I would be invited back to the Awards in 2024. I was not. But I did run the London Marathon again, this time in a team with Rosie Jones, raising money not just for the MS Society but for UP – The Adult Cerebral Palsy Movement. To the casual glancer, I may seem like an athlete and philanthropist having a great time with his friend. But I know who I really am: a bucket-hatted buffoon trying to sportswash his shame.

CHAPTER 10

CP Gone Mad

The increasingly inescapable inquiry as to what one can and can't say in comedy these days was, I'm proud to say, never a priority of this book. There's a constantly recruiting army of purple-faced bad faith merchants out there making more than enough noise about the things you supposedly can't say these days, when most of the people actually working in shock comedy, rather than in comedy shock, know that, for better and worse, you can still get away with quite a lot of things. If the joke's good enough, you'll be fine, and if you won enough BAFTAs in the noughties, the joke doesn't even have to be that good. I've never steered my scull too close to Cancel Island myself, but that's mainly because I'm not good enough at writing those kinds of jokes, and I didn't win any BAFTAs in the noughties. I won a Shakespeare Reading Prize and came fourteenth in a steeplechase.

And now here I am, getting older and bolder in my own middle age, sneaking in the most potentially edgelord-adjacent story of my book in between distractingly heroic stories about running marathons for the MS Society. I know I don't get a free pass just because I'm the gobby son of a wobbly mum. It's a blue badge, not a carte blanche. But I also think that at the right moment, a bit of comic relief about these topics can serve a positive purpose, and at my MS Society gigs, for example, I enjoy referring to my comedy career as being like MS, in that it 'gets on my mum's nerves'. This joke is almost as tight as the nine-letter team name that I gave to cerebral palsy's Rosie Jones and political correctness's Nish Kumar at *Comedians' DJ Battles* in June 2024. Ravers of Shoreditch, please welcome to the stage: CP Gone Mad.

Rosie and Nish pumping CO_2 into the crowd to 'Take On Me' was one of many highlights of that epic and expensive night in east London, but while Nish has been pushing Rosie around for hilarious photos on social media for many years now, and reprised this role villainously on the Village Underground stage, I was able to watch from the decks in the smug knowledge that I now had some mileage of my own on that front too. Rosie had kindly appeared at several of my MS Society fundraisers over the years, where I was proud to introduce her on more than one occasion as 'representing a rival disability'. I can't remember if I ever directly checked that introduction with Rosie or merely inferred her permission with all the entitled certainty of a privately-educated and able-bodied man, but I certainly felt more confident in the venture given Rosie's own well-established disregard for comedic boundaries, whether in specific conversations about disability or more general ones about, say, whether the host of a panel show should be able to sit on its guests' laps in 2024.*

In more recent interviews about our friendship I have felt confident enough to describe Rosie as 'rude', 'aggressive', and on one occasion even 'toxic', and while I hope to get many more chances to do so in the very best of faith, let me also say here, in the clearest of language and the most permanent of print: the woman is a comedy phenomenon and I am so lucky to be her friend, her colleague and, on two occasions so far at least, her engine. In the autumn of 2024, as I've watched deadline after deadline whooshing past on the first draft of this book, she has been bringing her big daddy energy to the latest series of *Taskmaster*, doing a damn sight better at the tasks than I did, and evidently charming Jack Dee a lot more than I did when I was stinking up the stage as his curry-wafting support act in 2018.† Even if it often feels like the race between inclusive society and extinct planet is being won quite horribly easily by the latter, I am proud to live in an era where some imbalances are being redressed (however much I might have once benefitted from all of those imbalances), and few cultural forces are as influential in that regard as *Taskmaster*. My own

---

* As in the very well-titled *Out of Order*, where she delicately navigated my shyness around my fellow panellists by bellowing at me, 'Look at the ladies, Ivo! Look at the ladies!'
† A story detailed first in my *Off Menu* episode, and then dragged up even more devastatingly in Jack's.

contribution to the discourse might have been little more than 'look, sometimes Eton doesn't work!', but I'm also very proud to have played a brief part in a show that has represented so many different bodies and brains so triumphantly over the last decade. Even if, in this case, it's representing a rival disability.

Rosie headlined the MS Society gig I helped to organise in November 2023, by many measurements a fantastic comedy night and fundraiser, but an only partial success by my own more demanding yardstick. The moving of this annual gig from the historic but only semi-accessible Comedy Store to the accessible but only semi-historic IndigO2, one of the perimeter venues of the former Millennium Dome, had taken the number of tickets we needed to sell from 400 to 2,400, and despite assembling a terrific line-up, we'd fallen more than a few hundred short, due to that lovely catch-all, 'a combination of factors'. Too many charity gigs? Not enough promotion? People just really hating the name 'IndigO2'? Whatever it was, we played the gig that night to a bustling ground floor, with next to nobody in the vast seating bloc upstairs. 'Don't mention the balcony!,' I'd hissed to the various acts side of stage, like Basil Fawlty, and in these frenetic attempts to control the narrative I broadly forgot to enjoy myself, express my gratitude to the many friends who'd come to perform at or watch the gig, or, most damningly, advertise the quite vast quantities of souvenir tote bags.*

At the end of the night, however, as most of the audience swarmed past the school night delusion of our 'VIP after-

---

* These tote bags were emblazoned with the words 'Some Nerve', another may I say lovely bit of business from yours truly, even if, in the same spirit of honesty, there are probably too many tote bags in the world now.

party' and straight onto the Jubilee Line, something happened that would change the course of my 2024, teeing up future fundraising that would more than compensate for an unfilled balcony and an unflogged box of totes. Fresh from her barnstorming headline set, Rosie came to meet my parents out front, the rival disabilities laying down their weapons once and for all. History doesn't quite recall whether what my dad did next was an idea I'd previously suggested to him, which he merely relayed without my authorisation, or something he dreamed up entirely in the moment. He is, after all, a lanky maverick. But names had barely been exchanged when he, with more brio than I'd shown in the entire evening, pointed at my mum and said to Rosie something along the lines of, 'He's done a half marathon with her, when's he going to do a full marathon with you?'

And the rest, as they say, is, history. Not immediately, of course: sure, the proposal got a gratifyingly positive response from Rosie, but it was moderated by my vibe-sapping insistences that 'you obviously don't have to commit now'. She went home, my family went home, and after fifteen minutes chatting to a retired Eurostar driver called Tony* in the VIP bar, I went home too. A few days later, I followed up with Rosie, and she was just as keen on the idea even without my father looming

---

* High Speed Tony, a man in his sixties with a heart of gold and a pocket full of privs, has come to approximately twenty of my shows in the last five years, most notably travelling from Gloucestershire to watch me do three consecutive tour shows in the Scottish Highlands in 2019, and upgrading my return ticket from Inverness to London so that I could join him in first class for eight hours. Tonight, Tony had brought his boyfriend, Neil! Lovely to meet you, Neil! What a VIP bar this is, eh? Do you want a heavily discounted tote bag?

expectantly over her shoulder. We met with her friend Aisling, who quickly became the brains of an operation of which Rosie was the beaming face and I was the undeniably shapely legs. We resolved that in spring 2024, we would do the same one and a half marathons together that the various combinations of Grahams did in spring 2023. We booked in for the Victoria Park half in March, and, thanks to the wranglings of a very patient communications manager called Lianne, we got a late access place for the London Marathon in April. I contacted Martin at Delichon about hiring another Delta Buggy. Two, in fact. Here we fucking go! The marathon in 2023 was my proudest day of the year. This was going to be more complicated. But you know what they say: if at first you don't succeed, fetch the yardstick. If at first you do succeed, change the yardstick.

On March 10th, 2024, Mothering Sunday, the Grahams arrived at Victoria Park, mere minutes before the start of the half marathon. The two Delta Buggies were loaded up in the back of my dad's green van, his pride and joy, the Air Force One of the small fleet of accessible vehicles he has bought, pimped and then upgraded over the last few years. I would be pushing Rosie in one of the buggies, and my brother would be making his pushing debut with my mum in the other. The weather was, alas, dreadful. It was far too wet to Wordle. But that was mitigated by the excitement of having two chairs on the road, both running side by side for the majority, my brother and I attempting multiple 'speed swaps', only one of which resulted in a wheel-scraping minor collision between the Buggies. We were joined by primetime hunks Joel Dommett and Ed Gamble, the latter on his birthday, and Danny, Ann and Holly from Off The Kerb. It was another brilliant run, captured in another brilliant team photo at the finish, even if by this point it really was shitting it down something crazy. Aisling took loads of footage, and she edited it into a campaign video which got shared online by, amongst other celebrities and mathematicians, Carol Vorderman. Donations started coming in. Lianne at the marathon asked if we'd like to fire the starting gun* for the elite wheelchair racers. Which was a lovely offer, even if that did confirm one thing: we weren't the wheelchair elite. Not this year.

The night before the marathon, Rosie, Aisling and I were all booked into a hotel in Greenwich, the best way of making sure we and the Delta Buggy made it to the start line together in the morning without, for example, me being late. The hotel was being used by several hundred other runners who had travelled to London specially for the marathon, so there was a hilarious tension to the breakfast, a full restaurant's worth of data on what dietary advice people were following on race morning: chia-sprinkled porridge as far as the eye could see, people shoving bananas into their pockets like stolen doubloons, and one lunatic in Lycra tucking into a full English with all the trimmings. The latter caught me double-taking as I passed his table, and, laughing, exclaimed, 'Why not, eh? Why not?' as he plunged his black pudding into his beans. It was one of the highlights of the whole day.

Not quite brave enough to follow my grease-guzzling new friend into the great digestive unknown, I rationed out my rolled oats with the rest of the robots, and then squeezed alongside the folded buggy into the back of Aisling's Peugeot 107. Half an hour later, we were in pre-race VIP, where Rosie

---

* This is a button, not a gun, although I could vouch for Rosie's reliability with a gun, having literally given her one at the clubnight.

was quickly becoming a one-woman selfie station while I took multiple trips to the loo and furtively asked *Ted Lasso*'s Phil Dunster if he had any spare energy gels. (He didn't, and that's fine.) Romesh and Joel were also doing the marathon, which was fun, so I said hello to them and we had an Off The Kerb group photo. Matt Hancock was also doing the marathon, which was not fun, so I didn't say hello to him, and instead thought of some scathing comebacks to have ready in case he asked me if *I* had any spare energy gels. 'Hey Matt, why don't you clap and hope a carer brings you one?' 'Hey Matt, why don't you give your mates a government contract to make you some?' 'Hey Matt, why don't you skip the marathon and then cry about winning it on television?' Matt Hancock did not ask me for spare energy gels.

The last few minutes before the race flew by: a pre-race chat with Gabby Logan, firing the starting gun for the wheelchair elite, and a few texts with Edie's mum, who was bringing our girl to her first marathon. Edie couldn't stay for the finish because of her swimming lesson: fair enough, we're all athletes, but it meant we'd have to catch them, or them catch us, en route. Rosie kindly agreed to take charge of the co-parenting comms during the marathon itself, but even with her help I wasn't sure if the plan would actually work. Suddenly, we were being ushered out of the tent and into the race, and of course I then realised I'd forgotten to stretch, a laughably major omission amidst the Dunster dives and the imaginary Matt-slams, but never mind that: straight into the melee.

The melee of the marathon is fantastic, don't get me wrong, it's just that London is the biggest marathon in the world, so it's also the biggest melee. Everyone spends at least the first few congested miles mainly watching they don't clip their neighbours' ankles, and on three wheels, you're a bit more aware of the potential consequences of such a clip for wheels and ankles alike. On a day when there were heroes as far as the eye could see and cheers as far as the ear could hear them, Rosie was the biggest and loudest energy of the lot, a megastar brandishing a megaphone which, as many people smilingly pointed out, she didn't really need. It was a privilege to watch her experience the marathon for the first time, and to experience the marathon through her.

I was involved in some of the panting chats and clumsy selfies along the way, but I was mainly focused quite furiously on the chair, never more than a few centimetres from potentially ending someone's race, diluting the communal euphoria of the atmos with my own rather harsher cries of 'watch out!' or just 'ANKLES!' I started to dread the water stations, where people (and I've been these people and will be again) would suddenly swerve sideways to get a bottle, down half of it, and then chuck it on the floor, to be tidied away at the race's end but only after most of them had gone under our wheels. I couldn't bear the thought of a puncture: I didn't have a repair kit and I wouldn't know how to use one even if I did. In a sneak preview of what disaster a puncture might entail, we went over a speed bump, and a suddenly non-amplified Rosie shouted 'fucking speed bumps!' as one of the batteries flew out of her megaphone onto the floor. We could not stop to pick it up, and we could not source another C Cell battery mid-race, despite putting out an appeal at mile 10 in an Insta live video with Harry Judd from McFly. Rosie was acoustic for the rest of the race, but her team spirit doubled to match, and I finally started to grin as the crowds finally started to thin. Every so often a clearing emerged on the outside of a big bend in the route, and I adored charging into these spaces, getting even the briefest taste of the buggy at top speed. We've *got* to start nearer the front next time.

Rosie and I completed the marathon in 3 hours and 36 minutes, a time which only one person in the world could have seen as a failure: the man writing this book, *Yardsticks For Failure*; the man telling anyone who'd listen about how it was the crowds not the chair that slowed us down. But we were so happy at the end, and we had so much to be happy for. There were no punctures and no collisions, I didn't hit the wall or tear one of my unstretched hamstrings, and Rosie was dispensing jokes and jelly babies with as much gusto at mile 26 as she was at mile 1. Most emotionally, for all my fears that something would go wrong, that they'd be in a different place and the comms would fail, we got to Canary Wharf and there they were, Edie and her mum. Slowing to a stop to give my girl a hug mid-race was of course one of the best moments of my life, even if I then turned around to see that I hadn't put any sort of brake on the Delta Buggy, so Rosie was just drifting merrily away into the melee. Running a stranger over while I was steering would have been awful, but running one over while I wasn't would probably have been even worse. I hugged my girl goodbye, wished her a happy swimming lesson, and ran off in pursuit of my runaway Jones.*

---

* The week that I wrote this sentence, I took my daughter to watch her mum complete a big neighbourhood 10k, and due to various factors, but the main one being my own sloppiness, we weren't there to see her come in at the finish. This isn't the book where I pick over the various co-parental balls dropped 2019–present, but I can't write up how special this marathon reunion was without holding my hand up to botching the return leg last week. We go again in 2025.

At the end of the race, we got a second chat with Gabby, and various other media interviews in which Rosie couldn't have been more brilliant and I couldn't have been more of a gibbering mess, occasionally mumbling fragments of banter like 'no nipple chafing this year!' and 'Harry Judd couldn't find our battery' like a broken toy belching out its catch-phrases at random. We got a hero's welcome from Aisling and the Off The Kerb team, took a photo of Rosie pushing me in the chair (caption: 'next year') which had smashed my Instagram Likes Personal Best within the hour, then went back to my parents' flat for another stunning buffet of crisps. Some things never change.

In 2025, two weeks before this book comes out, Rosie and I will, all being well, have done our second marathon together, this time in her sort-of home county of Yorkshire,* the Leeds Marathon, the Rob Burrow Marathon no less, following in the footsteps and tyre tracks of legends, pure Delta Buggy heritage. I'm going to say it now: if we get a good starting spot, we'll do it in 3h10. But I'm also going to say it now: none of that matters. Of course it doesn't. Just watch your ankles, everybody, and bring spare batteries. Team MS aren't feeling nervous at all, and team CP are going madder than ever.

---

* Rosie's from Bridlington in East Yorkshire, Leeds is in West! I know and respect my different Yorkshires!

I Love this?

In real life, the artist herself currently has very little passion for football, but despite this lack of experience she expertly captures what that passion might feel like.

CHAPTER 11

Leddersford Town

While I hope that running the Leeds Marathon with Rosie in 2025 will be my greatest ever triumph in her homeland, I don't have to think hard on what I would nominate for its Yorkshire yang, my greatest God's own county gaffe. This gaffe also took place in spring 2024, a period where despite an already heaving plate of deadlines and domestics, I continued to tempt myself into doomed dashes and questionable quests at every turn, snatching at new and entirely avoidable yardsticks for failure, so preoccupied with whether I could that I didn't stop to think if I should. One night in Huddersfield, I added to this heaving

194 YARDSTICKS FOR FAILURE

plate of faff with an actual heaving plate of food. And it was all because of one man.

In 2016, I went on a rustic retreat with Josh Widdicombe, Chris Scull, and Michael Marden, who shortly afterwards launched their nostalgic football podcast, *Quickly Kevin, Will He Score?*, and invited me on to dissect *Striker*, a detective novel apparently written by the manager Steve Bruce in the late 1990s. The recording would go on for one hour, maybe two, they said. A brief diversion into literary lampooning for the lads, something to lighten up the feed between their more reverent interviews with Mark Lawrenson and Matt Le Tissier. But much like Bruce's protagonist, the cunningly disguised football manager 'Steve Barnes', we had no idea what we were getting ourselves into. We would end up talking about *Striker!* for the best part of a decade.

It didn't take long to confirm what the *Quickly Kevin* boys had suspected: that *Striker!* was every bit as much of a goldmine as one might hope from a detective novel written by a football manager. It wasn't just the joyous lumpiness of Bruce's plots and phraseology but the very *notion* of it. Here we had one of the great no-frills centre-backs (and landlords) of the not-quite-modern era, carving out a few hours in 1999 in between training sessions and family shopping trips to dream up a parallel universe where he is no longer Bruce but Barnes, where he is no longer in Huddersfield but Leddersford, still doing the football managing but also, if you can let yourself dream with him for a second, *solving murders*. Or, if not solving them, then certainly getting embroiled pretty chaotically in the solving process, through plotlines so simultaneously intricate and idiotic that it's hard to tell where the hopelessness of Bruce ends and the hopelessness of Barnes begins. I am one of the people in the world most qualified to settle that debate, and yet, simultaneously, one of the least. I'm in too deep now. I hate this man, and I love him. I've spent far too much of my life in his tripe factory, but it's Michelin star tripe, and I've stuffed my face with it.

Unfortunately, in May 2024 I found myself moving from a metaphorical face-stuffing to a more literal one on Steve's behalf, in a quite astonishing slice of non-standard behaviour which was, like most of my slices of non-standard behaviour, entirely voluntary and avoidable. And yet it was also, like most of them, carried out in the sincere belief that this behaviour was not just an option but a duty, another great 'bit' to which I simply had to commit. Since 2016, *Quickly Kevin*'s brief jaunt into the semi-fictional footballing netherworld had become a permanent residency. The book review had become three book reviews, that single hour of podcasting had become about fifty. Barnes had become such a key figure in the Quicklyverse that their podcast subscription channel was named after his car, and such a key figure in my own blathering portfolio that I was now trying to recreate a meal from the book for a quite understandably baffled audience in Huddersfield.

And once more, as I furiously chopped cucumber sandwiches into triangles at the Lawrence Batley Theatre, I asked myself: how did I get here?

One of the regular features of my gigging life 2017–present has been getting pre-show tweets from men, and they are almost always men, saying things like 'Waiting for @ivograham in Exeter, hoping for plenty of Steve Barnes content', messages that make my heart sink a little in the green room of the Corn Exchange, knowing that I'm about to go out and waffle on about the recent developments/deteriorations in my personal life, with no mention of their and my beloved Jag-driving antihero. You can't please all of the people all of the time, of course, but I have certainly had moments onstage over the years when it's felt like I'm closer to pleasing none of the people than all of the people. On those nights, would it have been so hard to lob in even one reference to, say, 'old Bill Shakespeare', as Steve Barnes calls him, to ensure that at least one person in the audience goes home with a sense that their very reasonable demands have been met? Remember who pays your wages, boy!

In 2022, I bore this in mind on another front, grabbing a banana and yoghurt from Sainsbury's en route to my photo-shoot with Matt Stronge,* creating a *My Future, My Clutter* poster that doffed its cap quite directly and unambiguously to my *Off Menu* humiliation.† The show then started with a retelling of the sequel to this humiliation, the doxxing at the Doubletree, and as the titters spread around the room from the very first mention of the hotel, I experienced the onanistic rush one can get from simply reinforcing one's brand live onstage, telling a story of something that a good majority of the crowd would already have watched unfold, either on the original live stream or on YouTube.‡ Of course, there were narrative bene-

---

* This is a lie: Matt Stronge bought them for me, because I was late.

† Where James Acaster unleashed a hot jet of contempt for the simple culinary pleasures of the Graham hearth, resulting in, I suspect, many more hits for the episode than if I'd merely turned up for the podcast and picked a high-end pudding. Was that all part of my brilliant plan? That's between me and my trash family.

‡ And, to be honest, as much full-throttle shame as it contains, I must nonetheless steer anyone who hasn't watched the video to seek it out. It is probably the most anyone has ever laughed at me, and that is 'at' rather than 'with'.

fits to the retelling too. I was no longer freefalling live on the internet but looking back on the saga a year on, unable to regain any dignity from the incident but at least gilding the indignity with some of those lovely long sentences that anyone reading this book must have developed a Stockholm syndrome-esque affection for by now.

'I have an only semi-exaggerated and extremely potassium-heavy breakdown, and very little sleep before the following morning I am due to interview Dean Windass about his mental health on a pedalo, for the first episode of a travel show which is not recommissioned by the Dave channel.' Every night, I looked forward to this sentence, a steaming word-soup that I could proudly say contains not one exaggeration* of the story, and which I hoped would validate the retelling for both those who were there and those who weren't. Of course, the purist in me still objects. The fantasy scenario would be that with each new piece of my art (and yes, in the fantasy, it's art) I reinvent myself completely, like Bowie in the seventies, wrongfooting my fans and biographers at every turn. Alas, I am not Bowie in the seventies. I am not one of the most beloved pop stars and fashion icons of all time. I am a plummy-voiced podcaster with a few loud shirts, currently able to fill a large arts centre or a small theatre because I recently sat in a caravan instead of a shed on Channel 4.

Spring 2024 marked the final leg of the *Organised Fun* tour, the alternately exhilarating and excruciating death by a

---

* OK, fine, Dean Windass talked more about his mental health journey in the pre-pedalo bit of the interview! By the water I was mostly just getting him to name all of his Hull teammates from Wembley 2008! Art is a lie, nothing is real!

198 YARDSTICKS FOR FAILURE

thousand Top Trumps of my post-caravan era. The show's loose and desperate format had already provided the foundations for all sorts of bespoke hijinks, such as recreating Hugh Grant's *Love Actually* dance in Southampton, or kicking an ice cream tub into a man's face in Milford Haven. No hijinks, however, would be more bespoke than in west Yorkshire in May.

The *Quickly Kevin* podcast had announced that it would soon be saying 'Robbie Slater, see you later' to its listeners for the final time, and we were squeezing the final drops of milk from the teat with chapter-by-chapter Patreon episodes about *Defender!*, the last and baggiest book in the Barnes trilogy.* A week before our final episode of the podcast was broadcast,† I was doing my first ever tour show in Huddersfield, aka 'Leddersford', the very town where Bruce apparently penned the detective novels while manager in 1999, with enough references to driving (and occasionally skinny dipping) across the Pennines to leave little ambiguity as to the real-life geography of the stories. And now I was heading (fully clothed) to the

---

* Like *Paddington in Peru*, which delighted a tri-generational Graham audience at the cinema without ever hitting the heights of its predecessors, *Defender!* messed with a winning formula by relocating the action to South America and then staying there for too long. Our hero's attempts to track down his star player in Rio de Janeiro features some iconic moments ('Steffa Barnsa! Steffa Barnsa!'), but the narrative is so half-arsed as to make books one and two seem like airtight Grishams by comparison. This didn't stop me legging it up Christ the Redeemer on my own on New Year's Day 2020, a festive trip to visit cousins in Brazil temporarily abandoned to chase a bit more *Quickly* clout on the 'gram.

† Our last *Defender!* readalong, not the interview with Steve Bruce himself, a broth which I was logically but still unsentimentally not invited to come and spoil.

Pennines myself! The podcast was coming to an end and now I was doing a tour show in the very place most of the (Bill) Shakespearean hi-jinks were set! Some people might be emotionally disciplined enough not to be moved by a coincidence like this. I am not those people.

There was already one reference to Steve Bruce in the *Organised Fun* tour, included in a slideshow at the end of the set, a liberally tweaked version of the genuine Top Trumps set I had made in 2008 about which of the guests at my eighteenth birthday party had given a love bite to my seventeen-year-old sister. Crucially, Bruce (then forty-eight) had not been at my eighteenth birthday party in 2008, and, despite some of the dubious gender politics and occasional creaks of mid-life lusting in his books, there is nothing to suggest he would have been involved in any such shenanigans even had he been. But every night it was fun to linger just long enough on his picture in the slideshow to hear a couple of cackles in every room, the Jaguar XJ8 elite finally getting what they came for. In Huddersfield, however, they were going to get a lot more.

The week before my trip, in our latest episode on *Defender!*, we had cackled gleefully away at a scene where Barnes, investigating the alleged kidnap of his pivotal Brazilian centre-back, is called in to discuss the situation with his brandy-sipping club chairman, Sir Laurence Brook, and distracted from the quest by a ludicrously heavy platter of sandwiches and cold meats. In another just-about-traceable link between the stories and real life, Sir Laurence Brook is a substitute for Lawrence Batley, the Huddersfield-born entrepreneur and philanthropist who would still have been cash and carrying in town when Bruce was managing there. My tour show was in the Lawrence Batley Theatre! This just got better and better. 'Make sure you pour out a brandy for Sir Laurence,' Josh said, when I told him about this.

'At the very least,' I replied. At the very least.

Having spent most of the previous day crawling through bank holiday traffic back from the Machynlleth Festival, I decided to treat myself to trains and a hotel in Huddersfield, a noble grasp at self-care which did mean that I was enjoying Steve Barnes's favourite views through a train window rather than the windswept roads he holds so dear. But these views from the TransPennine Express, over the sheltered moorland that used to thrive on wool manufacture until forty or fifty years ago (sic), were a joy, and I reached my destination at 4:45pm, a quite astonishingly punctual arrival for an 8pm tour show by my standards. I took a selfie with the statue of Harold Wilson outside the station, daring to dream that Huddersfield's favourite son might be blessing this pilgrimage in the footsteps of another local legend. With the sun on my back and time on my hands, I headed to the Sainsbury's in the centre of town. The plan, if you can use that word for a series of deranged impulse calls piled on top of each other, was to get just a couple of items from the Sir Laurence platter. But this Sainsbury's was massive, and my ambitions swelled to fill it. Twenty minutes later, I was heading out of there with sandwiches, pork pies, chicken drumsticks, a wheel of Camembert, and two wooden chopping blocks on a two-for-one-deal. Twenty-five minutes later, I was heading back in because I'd forgotten the spreads. The comedic high point of the scene is Barnes daubing his pork pie liberally with mustard! I couldn't not have mustard! So I got mustard. And I got pickle. And I got piccalilli. It was going to be a hell of a daub.

It's safe to say that I was giddy with excitement by the time

I arrived at the beautiful Lawrence Batley Theatre. I gave the technical crew a manic speech, fairly polished by this point in the tour, about my lack of tour manager, support act or HDMI adaptor. Today's instructions, however, included the bonus detail that I had brought a vast amount of food with me, and that I was going to be bringing it onstage with me as part of the show, and was this OK, and would I be able to invite an audience member onstage to eat it, and would someone be able to film it, and oh shit I forgot the brandy, is there any chance I could get a couple of brandies? A man called Will said I could bring an audience member onstage, a man called Rob agreed to film, a man called Dominic confirmed the bar had brandy. 'Is Courvoisier OK?' I was gleeful to tell Dominic that Courvoisier was, indeed, OK. Soon I was back in my dressing room, adding Steve Barnes pages to the PowerPoint, and laying out the platters. Sir Laurence just eats cucumber sandwiches: now, obviously supermarkets don't sell those as part of their meal deals, but never fear: I'd bought plain cheese sandwiches and a cucumber. 'I've thought of everything!' I cackled to myself as I peeled the plastic cheese off the bread and replaced it with slices of cucumber. Everything apart from one crucial thing: where any of this would fit into the show.

At 8 o'clock, I took to the stage, buffet laid out next to the tech box. The show started in the traditional fashion: a meandering audience chat based on questions sent in via email prior to the show, a hardly revolutionary piece of user-generated content-harvesting but one which did tend to smooth my path towards the funniest or at least the chattiest audience members ahead of the games later on. On the tour shows where I didn't have a support, I really needed these bits to go well, not just to lay the Top Trump groundwork, but also to get to the 8:30 interval without eating into too much material. On this particular night, I was more relaxed: I could move through the content harvesting a bit more quickly, and then crack on with making Leddersford history. So it was quite a twist when the opening ten minutes instead yielded one of my favourite chats I've ever had onstage, with a man in the circle who claimed that he owned several pairs of fancy pants, enjoyed so much by his wife that he gave her a card. 'A business card?' No, came the immediate and perfect response, a 'pleasure card'. To confirm: a pleasure card his wife could play whenever she wants to see his pants.

'And then what happens?'

'I do a dance.'

Once more, like in Potters Bar, I was in the grateful but still dangerous position of being given such gleaming gold direct from the audience that I might not be able to improve on it, that I might alchemise it in the wrong direction. A good MC turns lead into gold, a bad one turns gold into lead. In crowdwork, as in life, one must know when to move on, for the sake of the other members of the audience, and their general reassurance that you do have a show.* But I spend a lot of my life not moving on. I lag, I lurk, I linger. I am one of the great lingerers. Usually you can sense in a room when a silent, increasingly impatient majority are willing you to move on, but here in Huddersfield, the chat with the couple I was now calling Mr and Mrs Fancypants was going so well that it genuinely felt the room would be sad when it was over. At one point, I started talking to someone else and he urged me to 'get back to the main narrative'. The main narrative! The main narrative was no longer Ivo Graham's *Organised Fun*.

---

* Although saying 'I do have a show' somewhere amidst the faff will, I find, buy you some time.

It was the breakout hit already christened 'Romance Night at Pants HQ'. Other audience members started chipping in with their questions. Was he wearing fancy pants now? He was not. (Perhaps a sensible answer, whether true or not.) Could Mrs Fancypants describe her favourite pair? 'Green with zebras, I think'. *I think?* Imagine being this emotionally invested in the pants and not knowing what's on them. Perhaps he's just dancing too fast.

We were half an hour in before I'd bidden an even temporary farewell to the main narrative. We could have called the interval then and there and people would have been floating to the bar on a cloud of fancy-panted joy. And that made things a bit tricky, from my pork pie platter-plotting perspective. I couldn't have known that such a perfect moment was going to fall into my lap, pantus ex machina: it's not the sort of thing you can ever count on. If I had known what a lot of mileage we were going to get out of one man's patterned undergarments, I might not have felt the need to spend £30 in Sainsbury's on meats and spreads at all. But I had spent that now, and I'd laid it out, and Dom had got the Courvoisier, and Rob was filming, and also the extra slides were already in the PowerPoint. I spent a lot of 2024 doing things I regretted because the extra slides were already in the PowerPoint.* No, I was going to go through with it. I was in Leddersford the week of the podcast ending. This was more than comedy, this was history. And there would be

---

* Hurriedly clicking through an unexplained series of slides about Steve Bruce and pork pies would have been its own homage to shows I've loved in the past by the likes of Jonny Sweet, who once did a whole Edinburgh hour rushing through the history of a decommissioned naval frigate, and Nick Mohammed, who used to 'accidentally' flash his audience with pictures of his bank statements.

204 YARDSTICKS FOR FAILURE

Quickly Kevin fans in the room who would shit their pants with excitement, fancy or otherwise!

As it turned out, there was one *Quickly Kevin* fan in the room, and he did not shit his pants with excitement, fancy or otherwise.

One of the things we'd most enjoyed microanalysing on the last podcast episode was how many people at my average tour show would have heard of Steve Barnes, and whether there could be even the most minute increase to this number in the home of the club he managed for two and a bit years and then fictionalised for the ages. The Leddersford trickle effect! Well, Steve *Bruce* was remembered, I knew that, because when I had popped his face on the screen during the pre-show tech rehearsal, one of the ushers, a smiley man in his fifties or sixties, started muttering, 'We don't like him round here.'

'Because he went to Crystal Palace?'

'Aye, dropped us, he did.'

So there were embers to be poked, but crucially, the embers of the real-life Steve Bruce's abdication from Huddersfield twenty-four years ago. The life, not the art. But what of the lol-tastic and surprisingly lucrative parallel universe where Steve Bruce is in fact *still* managing the team *and* solving crimes in the local area? There was no evidence whatsoever that the usher knew about the podcast. As far as he was concerned, I was just planning to do a brief bit of local if slightly dated material about someone who worked in the area a quarter of a century ago. So, penny for his thoughts and everyone else's when I said, as the final pants-based chortles subsided, 'I knew tonight was going to be special, given I'm back in the home of Steve Barnes', and clicked through to my photo of Steve Bruce on the screen. There's a world where the usher genuinely just thought I'd got his name wrong. There was certainly not the roar from the in-crowd that I'd expected, and that would have tipped off the rest that there was *some* sort of connection being made here. There were cautious, confused titters. RIP the main narrative.

'Give me a cheer if you've read the Steve Barnes books?' I pleaded into the void, like David Brent asking who's heard of Eric Hitchmough. I got one single cheer, from a man called Herbie, a name that I took a few goes to catch, denting my diminishing momentum further. This slowness on my part was due to (1) the rarity of the name and (2) the fact my Leddersford lynchpin was right up in the gods, really about as far as he possibly could be from the stage, which was especially sub-ideal because about ten seconds later I was inviting him to the stage to dine with me. This did, thankfully, get a few laughs, not because I had outlined the point of the exercise in any remotely convincing way, but because watching a comedian force-feed slices of pork pie to an audience member is, quite rightly, a rare occurrence in this or any theatre.

I told Herbie, who had already had dinner and was baulking at the wooden board of congealing meat in front of him, to 'daub the pork pie liberally with mustard', as Barnes does in *Defender!* chapter five. This added further confusion to Herbie's newly starring role, partly because he had not listened to this episode yet, and partly because I'd forgotten to bring cutlery. Herbie, to his immense credit, resolved this situation by deciding to use a ploughman's sandwich* as a knife. This only made it funnier when the hand of a technician then appeared through

---

* This was right at the height of ploughmania on the Elis James & John Robins show, making this show the podcast injoke crossover event of the century.

the curtain, holding a knife aloft like a Kirklees Excalibur, approximately half a second after Herbie had plunged his sandwich into the Colman's. The technician could barely have got the knife quicker, but it wasn't quick enough. The pork pie was already being liberally daubed.

The good people of Huddersfield still didn't have a clue what was going on, but the DIY daubing got a big laugh, encouraging me to then bring out the Courvoisier and ask Herbie if he wanted ice with it. Through a mouthful of pie, he said that he would. Ha! He'd fallen straight into my trap! I clicked the PowerPoint on to a zoomed-in page where Barnes notes his chairman is 'always complaining about the modern fad of ice in brandy'. You fool, Herbie! You've disrespected Sir Laurence in his own theatre! It is amazing that I still had the gall to treat this as some kind of 'gotcha': my brilliant ambush of an unsuspecting podcast casual who hadn't listened to the latest episode and was currently wincing quite badly at the mustard overdose he had daubed himself into under duress. We clinked and downed our room-temperature brandies, Herbie returned to his seat, and the interval was called at 8:55.

The second half proceeded much less controversially: I mean, sure, I broke the mic stand and spent far too long speculating on the life expectancy of Sir Patrick Stewart, but the latter was *sort of* prompted by another audience member, and Will from the venue confirmed that the base of the mic stand had been coming loose a bit recently.* Content-wise, I did do 'the show', eventually, and the Top Trumps finale was fun, even

---

* Here's how I'd sum up my nervous energy onstage: I won't grip and twist the mic stand forcefully enough to break it if it's new, but if it's already wobbling, I'll finish the job, no trouble.

if the *madness* of bringing audience members onto the stage had rather been gazumped by the events of the first half. Sure, we'll play Top Trumps with you, the volunteers consented, with nervous glances at the leftovers congealing in the wings: just don't make us plunge a chicken drumstick into a jar of piccalilli. And I didn't. I wrapped up the show, thanked Herbie and the Fancypantses again, and plugged my 2025 week-long residency of 'Romance Night At Pants HQ'. I stuck on the *Weakest Link* video and left the stage to return to a dressing room that absolutely honked of pickle and Camembert. What a night.

The recurring pattern of my life has been making things more complicated than they need to be: a clubnight with a slideshow, an awards do with a bucket hat, a marathon with a wheelchair, a child with two homes. Some of these twists turn out to be upgrades. Some of them are amongst the proudest achievements of my life. Some – and you can probably add 'stand-up show with a buffet' to the latter – are just a bloody mess. And later this month was a weekend that I really didn't want to bloody mess up.

schooll
days

The artist, herself a schoollgirl, paints an idyllic portrait
of the playground camaraderie that the boarding houses of
her forefathers would have swiftly stamped out.

CHAPTER 12

The Book of Keals

I didn't want this book, which lest we forget is not called 'Eton Mess', to feature too much reminiscing about School, but a few of the more palatable poshos from my past have come to play a predictably prominent part in my present. My most palatable and most prominent is Alex Kealy, and he pierced his foot on a spike for me in Machynlleth, and he met me with crisps at the end of the marathon, and we host a music podcast together, and he offers me such a huge and wide-ranging amount of support in my life, and now in 2024 I had to organise a huge and wide-ranging stag weekend for him. We're going to need a tad more background, even if it involves a tad more tailcoat.

January 2004: my first encounter with Alex, in a literally and spiritually chilly classroom in SL4, where he is interrupting our maths teacher, the late great Mr Rose, to ask if he can tell 'the ultimate joke'. I have just returned from Sydney, with the very faintest of Aussie tans and twangs, and started as I meant to go on, by arriving at the school a term late. My long-term social strategy amounts to little more than keeping my head down and making no impact whatsoever until university. I will make errors of my own on this front, namely entering and winning the Shakespeare Reading Prize later in the term, my yellow-stockinged zeal as Malvolio delighting my English teacher and sponsor, the late great Mr Welsh, but probably doing more harm than good with the boys my own age. On this frosty day a few weeks prior, Alex's quest for the 'ultimate joke' is being met with similar derision, and Mr Rose is managing the situation as best he can. 'We're not here to tell jokes, Alex,' he says. 'We're here to study maths.' Well, the joke was on him, because twenty years later, what would Alex turn out to be? That's right, a professional maths tutor.*

June 2006: though the ultimate joke continues to elude us, the seeds are planted for future jokes and adjacent blather, when Alex and I share our first live music gig, The Strokes

---

* This switcheroo was one of the early successes of my then quite disastrously long and unfocused – sound familiar? – best man speech for Alex. Truthfully, I don't remember if Mr Rose really did say those exact words, but, also truthfully, Alex asking to tell the 'ultimate joke' is pretty much my first memory of my time at Eton. Like the song in Tenacious D's 'Tribute', we never did learn what the ultimate joke was, although, for me, it's probably Alex's almost sexily cerebral routine about the film *Interstellar*.

(supported by The Raconteurs and Gogol Bordello) at Hyde Park's O2 Wireless Festival. We are now in the same tutor group at school, and our long walks to Mr Evans's house in Willowbrook give us ample time to discuss which are the most disposable songs on the undeniably baggy third Strokes album, and for that matter the hilariously baggy ninth Red Hot Chili Peppers album.* Could these two dweebs possibly imagine that one day a hundred and twenty people would be willing to pay £3.80 a month to listen to these chats? (NB: that subscription service has since been abandoned.)

October 2008: the dirty elitist conveyor belt carries me, as night follows day, to Oxford University, where I do my first stand-up gig that December, in the upstairs room of the Turl Street Kitchen. I don't make a second of eye contact with the audience for the duration of my five-minute set, and MC Tom Goodliffe advises me afterwards that my material might be a tad 'Varsity ski trip heavy' for non-Oxford gigs, but none-theless: the fuse is lit. A year later, after a tolerant gap year in America, Alex joins me under the dreaming spires and he too starts doing stand-up comedy. We both shamble our way through the same awkward gigs in college bars and balls. Our parents begin to fear for our futures.

June 2012: Alex and I graduate and move to London, where we spend the next decade of our lives doing gigs, watching gigs, and supporting ourselves financially through maths tutoring (him) and voiceovers for pet flea treatments (me). We become old pals in a new world, discovering the comedy scene together while bonded by the gilded cage of our shared history, even as politicians from those shared establishments lay waste to Britain's

* 'Killing Lies' and 'Readymade'.

public services and international standing. Alex becomes a prolific user of microblogging website Twitter (now X).

February 2021: Alex starts chatting to journalist Mhairi Beveridge on said microblogging website about the comparative hotness of various CNN news anchors. There have been more romantic and epic meetings between future spouses in history and literature, sure, but we are in the midst of a national lockdown. The meeting is, if nothing else, the greatest possible validation of Alex's borderline toxic addiction to Twitter, American politics, and tweeting about American politics. The starcrossed lovers/ stripecrossed losers slide into each other's DMs, and soon are meeting up for a socially distanced walk on Hampstead Heath. This is their first date. There will be many more dates to come over the years, only some of them accompanied by a needy third wheel who has taken to calling himself 'Dupree'.

March 2023: the first episode of *Gig Pigs* is released. This 'incredibly arduous' (*Guardian*) and comically unprofitable music podcast format has mixed consequences for our romantic fortunes, but Alex's are going from strength to strength, and Mhairi tells a very classy story about an adult nappy in an early episode about the Arctic Monkeys.

May 2023: A month after clagging me with crisps after the marathon, Alex proposes (successfully) to Mhairi on the Amalfi Coast. I knew he was going to do this, and, truthfully, Mhairi knew he was going to too. As Alex has himself noted in yet another of his annoyingly well-honed if tantalisingly non-viral stand-up Instagram reels, proposals should not be a surprise. Despite the lack of jeopardy, I am so very delighted for my friends. I am thousands of miles south of Amalfi, on a rather more bro-mantic trip to Ghana with various members of indie band Foxes and Hedgehogs, whose song 'Ojai' is the *Gig Pigs* theme tune. We down our Star Lagers in their honour, and I wonder if and when Alex will ask me to be his best man.

Mere days later in May 2023: Alex asks me to be his best man. Change of tense. Mega chapter of faff incoming. Here we go.

Being Alex's best man was a privilege which flattered me so very deeply, and a responsibility that crushed me so very predictably. Preparing for it – chaotically and against a series of rapidly onrushing deadlines – dominated the first half of my 2024. And talking about it – chaotically and against a series of rapidly onrushing deadlines – would dominate much of the second half as well.

I had organised one stag before, for my friend Ted Crisps in June 2018, but the stag was, at his request, just a single day in London (like the olden times!), and I was sharing best man responsibilities with our friend Charlie, and even then I managed to quite spectacularly mess up one major bit of it. Having left it too late to secure any larger vessels, I had booked us a trip down the Grand Union canal on a twelve-person barge, despite being a party of thirteen, with the terms and conditions of the booking quite explicitly stating the inflexibility of the boat's maximum capacity. I had merely hoped, cynically and arse-coveringly, that someone would drop out before the stag, or that the bakerishness of our dozen would go unchecked by the ship's captain. Neither of these things happened, and it was a deep and burning shame to admit this snafu* to my much more organised friend Mr Crisps. I've told this story pretty

---

* The stand-up about this incident was my first public use of the word 'snafu', and almost certainly where Alex Kealy pilfered it from, while on tour with me no less! No honour amongst thieves! *Dinner?*

extensively in stand-up (and later on *Would I Lie to You?*) since then, my only poetic licence being to say that my punishment was spending the whole canal trip walking parallel to the boat on the cycle path, whereas in truth we all took turns, and I didn't even go first, though I did go longest. We then did a quiz about the stag in Regent's Park, got hammered at Paradise by Kensal Green, and the following morning I learned I was going to be a father. What a world.

At the early stage of planning Alex's stag – solo, and with no strong steer from him about where he wanted to go – all I had to do to start the ball rolling was get the list of proposed staggers from Alex, and use a needlessly complicated online poll to find out when they were all free. The wedding was on June 15th. The stag was booked in for mid-May, on the one weekend nearly everybody could attend, and I barely gave it another thought for the remainder of the calendar year 2023.

In January 2024, the central question of Where To Stag was still unresolved, as I continued to see-saw between the two main categories of 'bouji European citybreak' and 'board games on country estate'. These options were still bouncing round my head at the end of January, when I took a forty-eight-hour trip to Ireland for tour dates in Limerick and Dublin. Despite being one of the most disorganised comedians and people in the country, I don't usually travel with a tour manager; however, these were my first ever tour dates in Ireland, and though this was not my first Emerald adventure, my confidence had recently been knocked by a disastrous attempt to do a Cork accent under duress on BBC Radio 5 Live. As such, I was accompanied for this trip by Luca Dunne, producer of pretty much everything I did in 2023 and 2024 but also, crucially, from Ireland. Her delicate and expanding tour managing role included, but was not limited to: hunting down pubs that served Beamish,* visiting the sleepy village of Broadford just because it has a Waterboys song named after it, and asking very confused audience members in Dolan's if they wanted to buy T-shirts with Diane from *The Traitors* on them. And that was just day one.

On day two, Luca's patience with these wild goose chases was rewarded with a road trip to her home town of Bray, a golden afternoon I cannot allow myself to reminisce about for too long here. However, the trip did lay the foundations for more reminiscing elsewhere, once we'd finished our toasties at the Harbour Bar and set off back along the cliff road towards Dublin. As we stopped to look out over the water to Dalkey Island, the sea air in my nostrils, the DART train chugging along the coast beneath us, and the punning potential of 'Dalkealy'† forming in my mind, the decision was made. It was city and it was country, it was near and it was far, it was old and it was new. It was beautiful. *This* was where we would stag.

In February the destination was revealed to the group (if not Alex himself) and I booked twelve Aer Lingus return flights to Dublin. The destination was now locked in. Light the beacons, whisper it quietly to your wives and children, Ivo Graham Has Made A Decision. For now.

Unfortunately, by April, no accommodation had yet been booked to accompany those flights. I was so confident in the

---

* Not just a *superior* porter, a hipster feather in my cap to separate myself from the rest of the stout louts, but a little joke for my Swindon Town WhatsApp group, the London Reds, as Swindon slid past the dreaded '(Ken) Beamish Line' to our worst ever league position.

† Answer Smash!

rich touristic potential of the Dalkey/Bray area that I didn't even do a cursory search for rental houses back in January, and now I was searching, with just a few weeks to the stag, and of course there weren't any. What were my options? Well, clearly: (1) secure alternative accommodation by the sea, or (2) secure accommodation elsewhere in the Dublin area. Needless to say, I chose neither of these options, and spent much of April considering abandoning the Irish stag idea entirely. This was a paralysis of quite ludicrous proportions, the whole weekend's fate in the hands of a man with a disastrous aversion to commitment, a man who cannot make decisions or stick with them once they've been made, a man who can give himself a nervous breakdown merely deciding whether to drive or get a train to Potters Bar. I am not proud to be that man. And I so wanted to be proud of this stag.

When it became clear that there were no empty twelve-person houses in Dalkey or Bray, I went into full-velocity, choice-paralysis panic mode. We could spread the group across multiple smaller Airbnbs, sure, or book into a hotel, like the Royal Marine in Dun Laoghaire, just a short walk from the Forty Foot swimming spot, which I'd already earmarked as one of our primary destinations on the stag, because of its role in the TV show *Bad Sisters*, which Alex loves. But only now that having a big house to ourselves was impossible had procuring said house become my most urgent and unbending priority for the stag. Of *course* we all had to be together! For big breakfasts and bigger board games! We wouldn't definitely be playing Settlers of Catan on the stag, but we should have the option! All under one roof gaming! I was suddenly looking at big houses not just further away in Ireland, but also back in England, torturing myself with the tennis court we could have had in Hertfordshire, or the hot tub in Hampshire, and the two or three staggers who couldn't make it to Dublin but might have been able to join us if we'd gone somewhere closer to London. Was it too late to pivot to the Home Counties? Without informing the group of any of these late machinations, I was now emailing Aer Lingus about their refund policy, learning that it was your classic 'credit not cash' situation, and contemplating whether I wanted to spend the next decade of my life working through two grand's worth of Aer Lingus credit from a cancelled stag.

I did not want to do this. Back to the Irish accommodation drawing board.

As well as Luca, trapped in the tortuous tennis match of my process but unable to speed it to any sort of conclusion, the one stag participant to pierce my force field of evasion and denial was Edinburgh Comedy Award winner and Irishman-by-marriage Ahir Shah.* Ahir did not try to hide, or certainly did not succeed in hiding, his dismay when he learned that we were still without accommodation a month out from the stag, and urged me to book us rooms at the Royal Marine in Dun Laoghaire. There were still some lovely rooms at the Royal Marine. Unfortunately, by the time I returned to the Royal Marine's website after another fortnight mulling the relocation of the entire stag, those rooms were gone too. Options were collapsing around us. The best two remaining

---

* Ahir, who had been inquiring since January as to how much the stag might be deafening the doorsteps of his Dalkey-dwelling in-laws, is a man of elegance and efficiency who both books his Edinburgh trains and writes his Edinburgh shows a damn sight earlier than I do. I'm not the first comic to pay my insecure respects to him in a footnote. It's probably time to stop now.

were a twelve-person Airbnb in Glasnevin, north Dublin, or some apartment hotels in the city centre. After more furious assessments of these options' pros and cons, and in the midst of a mad day in Norwich in which I walked half a mile down the central reservation of a ring road just to get out of my head, I booked the Airbnb. It was sorted.

It was sorted for about two hours.

Our Airbnb host, Stephen, accepted the booking and then sent me a lengthy document called 'quiet time after 9pm'. This stagna carta of litigiousness warned of a 'night manager who will be present on the grounds from 9pm to 6am for the duration of your stay'. I enjoyed a brief reverie imagining this as some late epilogue to BBC1's *The Night Manager* (2013), where Tom Hiddleston returns from his high-octane Egyptian adventures for this rather more modest peacekeeping assignment in north Dublin.* Unfortunately, whether the night manager was to be Hiddleston or a local bruiser with rather less certainty in their own brilliance, I didn't like the sound of this extra surveillance. Even if we weren't likely to be the laddiest of stags, and we'd probably hope to be out after 9pm on both nights anyway, I felt immediately quite embarrassed by the thought of revealing the Ts & Cs of the booking to my beta-male charges, who might enjoy spending some of their friend's stag in silence for mindfulness purposes, but ideally not under duress.

So I sent Stephen a very delicately worded cancellation email

---

* As well as our party containing multiple self-hating poshos who had – like Hugh Laurie – gone to the same school as Hiddleston, it would also have been a thrill to introduce the Loki Charmer to Phil Wang, who tore him and his multivitamins advert to shreds in the viral hit of 2019, a truly delicious lampoon of a truly undelicious breakfast.

explaining our reluctance to be night managed, and I booked us into the apartment hotels. These were essentially just double rooms, it turned out: minimal communal space, no table big enough for board games, let alone the Encona-spattered scrambled egg symposiums that Alex loves assembling, and to which he'd surely expect to have access on his stag. I looked again at the big garden table in the listing for Stephen's Airbnb, and pictured it piled high with scrambled eggs, the full gang breaking bread around it, together, in any of the fifteen hours of daylight we weren't being night managed. I cancelled the apartment hotels and crawled pleadingly back into Stephen's DMs. That was it. That had to be it. We had our location and our accommodation. Now what were we actually going to do on the stag?

This is what we did do on the stag.

On Thursday 16th May, Alex spent his pre-stag night at my home, after joining me that evening for my tour show at the Alexandra Palace Theatre. Climbing the hill to play that magnificent peeling Palace, next door to the barn where we'd watched so many great gigs over the years, was a proud milestone indeed, my buzz only slightly harshed by an audience member who asked, in the pre-show email questionnaire, 'how long do you think you can keep this up for?' This blade cut deep in what was then a particularly manic state of pre-stag fluster: I had spent the last couple of days preparing and purchasing various stag props, and the last of these were brought to the gig by Dave the T-shirt Man, a comedy fan from Hertfordshire whom I arguably commissioned too much custom clothing from in 2024.

The following morning, Friday 17th, Alex and I woke at my flat, him after a solid six hours' sleep, me after rather less, having sat up into the night printing itineraries and quiz sheets in a whirring production line that I hoped wouldn't be audible from the spare room. Alex put on the 'My name is Alex and this is my stag' custom T-shirt, which, I'd decided, he was obliged to wear for as much of the weekend as possible, and I put on the 'This man is Alex and this is his stag' T-shirt, which, I'd decided, would be rotated around the rest of the group over the course of the weekend, in an if I may say *ingenious* solution to the dilemma of whether to bring stag T-shirts for everyone or no one. The T-shirt handovers, and other lotteries, were to be settled by random draws of the 'Alex's Stag Do' Top Trumps cards, which I began handing out as we started to pick up personnel at Paddington. Unfortunately, this backfired immediately: I had dreamed of keeping our destination a secret from Alex until at least Heathrow, but sometime circa Acton Main Line, he exclaimed 'ooh, Dublin!', because one of the categories on the cards was 'previous visits to Dublin'. I fell to my knees in mock/real agony on the Elizabeth Line. It wouldn't trouble the 'top 10 regrets of the stag' rundown that I would lament to hundreds of people a day at the Fringe in August, but it was still a shame to have my best laid plans once more undone by my own Trumps.

By the time we were through security at Heathrow and splitting the first G of the weekend* in the pub at the departure

---

* Even in the six months since the stag, I have seen more and more angry online discourse about, essentially, English twats obsessed with trying to 'split the G', i.e. drink the exact amount with their first swig of Guinness that the black line then perfectly cuts through the letters on the glass. I can completely see why people would hate their bar queues being held up by long pours for long bores, culturally appropriating Sassenach pricks who mainly love the challenge because they aren't even laddy enough to down a whole pint. Even though we were these men, all weekend, I hope there is enough Irish appreciation elsewhere in this chapter to put us at least at the more bearable end of the G-splitting spectrum.

gate, there was another regret for the list, albeit a funny one. I have long been intimidated by Alex's not just subscription to, but ability to actually read and recall information from, the *London Review of Books* magazine. I had put these intellectual insecurities to one side with another not inexpensive commitment to the bit: visiting the LRB's Bloomsbury headquarters the previous day to pick up a copy of the latest edition for every member of the stag do. I was prepared for winces from staggers who didn't want any last-minute disruption of their packing with a literary journal they hadn't requested. What I hadn't anticipated was that not just Alex but three other staggers would have already brought their own copy. Twelve men travelled to Dublin with sixteen LRBs between them. How much noise could these boffins really be expected to make after 9pm?

Several hours and several articles later, we were speeding towards Glasnevin in a fleet of Ubers. Unfortunately, the man driving my sub-group, after a non problematic start to our chat, then leant into such an extended riff about a local Chinese restaurant that I apologised patronisingly and profusely to Phil Wang afterwards.* And the apologies sadly didn't end there: proud as I had been when I pre-booked the grocery order earlier in the week, we opened the Airbnb's doors to a note saying that the driver had beaten us there, found no one in, and taken the groceries back to

---

* Arguably Phil might have been less fazed by the original incident than by my decision to recount it every night in my Fringe show, and if that is the case, Phil, and you're reading this, then I apologise, and also, thanks for reading my book! Let me compensate further by really very strongly recommending, to any readers who haven't got it already, Phil's own musings on microaggressions, stag bravado, and other topics in his book *Sidesplitter*, the final line of which made me get far more emotional than I was expecting from a story about frequent flyer points.

Supervalu Swords Pavilions. Luckily, I was assertive/pitiful enough on the phone to Supervalu that our driver was turned around, and soon burgers were sizzling on the barbecue, and we were sitting down to eat, one group at one table, the first communal ambition of the stag realised. At 8:59pm, I ushered everyone out of the house with rapidly escalating urgency, and at 2am, I was shushing us back in, after pints at the Gravediggers and the Bernard Shaw, and gyros and chips at Yeeros. The carbs would serve us well. We had a big aquatic Saturday to prepare for.

The next morning, as one of Alex's great loves – a big breakfast – was coming together in the kitchen, another of them – a beautiful train journey – was disappearing from the agenda upstairs, with the disastrous discovery that the DART to Dalkey was closed for engineering work. Alone in my room, Admin HQ, while the rest of the gang scrambled and sautéed obliviously downstairs, I cursed my rotten luck, but I was not going to be defeated by this. I was the best man, and I would get my men to the sea. I called a minibus company and managed to broker a deal with a driver called John, a deal brokered by agreeing to pay the exact sum he proposed.* John arrived at the house half an hour later and drove us to Dun Laoghaire with gratifyingly few restaurant based riffs, at least as far as we heard. Admittedly we were quite immersed in a game of *Traitors*, masterminded remotely, in the Claudia role, by absent stagger Richard Hanrahan. Traitors, Trumps, and trivia: it was perhaps not the biggest feat of imagination for me to have moulded so much of this weekend from the same ingredients as my *Organised Fun* show, a show which had itself had such

---

* Another tweak of the 'tache' to Old Wang here, and his fantastic riffs about haggling on *Taskmaster* Series 7.

mixed fortunes over the past nine months. And it still felt like the jury was very much out on this particular Fun.

Another chasm between expectation and reality yawned mockingly at me when we arrived at the Forty Foot swimming spot, looking on this grey May Saturday rather less cinematically inviting than *Bad Sisters* might have advertised it. It was very grey and it was very cold. There were only a few people in the water and most of them were shouting 'feck'. A lot of the group immediately announced they would not be swimming, which was not the worst news, as I had just realised that I had left half the towels back at the Airbnb. We had so many more LRBs than towels. But you can't dry yourself on the LRB: you absorb it, not the other way around.

I was part of a hardy quintet that braved the waves regardless, but our bravery didn't last long, and Alex was shivering so much when we got out that the whole thing started to feel less like a group bonding activity and more like a stag prank, a quick blast of hypothermia for bants. I'd have loved to offer him a second towel, if there had been one to offer. Instead, we took shelter in the nearby James Joyce museum: this was not on my itinerary, but it was heated and free to enter and as such the group were suddenly fucking keen to learn as much as they could about James Joyce. One of our hosts offered us a private viewing of some of the rooms upstairs, where Joyce had stayed in 1904.* The group accepted gratefully, while I, the

---

* My distractions on the day itself mean that pretty much everything I know on this topic has been learned while writing this book, rather than in the James Joyce museum itself. This includes the lovely coincidence that *Ulysses* is set – and Bloomsday therefore celebrated – on the 16th of June, the day after Alex and Mhairi were due to get married! Portals of discovery under our nose the whole time!

lone keeper of the day's timetable, winced, knowing that this was going to make us late for kayaking. The kayaking was in half an hour, and if we wanted to get our lift there, driver John needed to go in the next five minutes, because he had another job afterwards. I didn't want to upset a man who we needed to drive us back to Dublin that evening and had thus far been both punctual and politically correct. I confided my anxiety in my friend Greg, one of the most infectiously cheerful men I have ever met, who had already been a very soothing presence in my private breakdowns about night guards and cancelled trains. Greg asked if there was any world in which we just *didn't go kayaking.*

This was a revelatory proposal to me. The kayaking had been the focal point of the whole stag weekend, the group bonding activity with an iconic destination at the end of it, the very island I looked out at when I was standing on the cliff road in January dreaming this whole thing up. It was one of just two activities that I had actually made a downpayment for in advance of the stag. A local watersports operator called Pavel had already accepted a hundred-euro deposit. Pavel was expecting us. The last few months of stag 'planning' had been an exhausting series of U-turns. What the stag needed is the same thing my *life* needs, more than anything else: the mental clarity and commitment to pick a path and stick to it.

And yet. And yet. I thought about how cold Alex looked after the swim, and how much he'd winced when I'd mentioned kayaking later, and how we only had half the towels and they were all already damp, and how happy everyone was right now in the comparative furnace of the James Joyce museum, and how if we cancelled the kayaking, we could just spend the afternoon walking round beautiful Dalkey and going to pubs.

Suddenly no plan ever seemed so glorious as not going kayaking.

Unfortunately, cancelling the kayaking meant sending Pavel the quite brazenly last-minute text that we would not be joining him owing to a 'medical emergency'. This was a bit of an exaggeration on the truth: that the stag was cold for a bit and that we had run out of towels. Pavel was less concerned with our fictional emergency and more with the non-fictional loss of his earnings. He had already received a deposit, but this was a small fraction of the kayaking motherlode to come. You might say that these deposits, calculated on an elegant economy of mutual interest, both ensure prospective kayakers take their bookings seriously *and* also insure the kayak operators against any major losses if they don't. Pavel didn't say any of this. Pavel just said, 'I need to pay my men.'

I didn't know whether Pavel was bringing up his 'men' to make me feel guilty or make me feel scared. Luckily, I didn't have to choose: I was more than capable of feeling both at the same time. It's very easy to wheel out the phrase 'panic attack' in moments like this, and arguably, if I was having an actual panic attack in this moment, I would have appeared to the friends and strangers around me like someone having a panic attack, rather than merely one of the less James Joyce-inclined patrons of the James Joyce museum, the portrait of the group leader as a young man mostly on his phone. But there was certainly panic attack energy bubbling up inside me at this moment, as I remembered that I had provided Pavel with all of our names – and wetsuit sizes! – earlier in the week. This crime had a paper trail. If relations soured then the stag's five working stand-up comedians would be doing all future Dublin gigs with a target on their pre-measured backs. This seemed like one of those situations where it was probably best to pay the men. The first deposit would be taken out of the group kitty, the second would be from me alone. I texted Pavel to say I'd transferred another hundred euros, still fearing that this wouldn't be enough, that he would demand more, that this was the start of my lifetime on the run from a thwarted watersports operator. Pavel replied, 'thank you'. This was our final correspondence.

In our group photo on top of the Martello tower, you can see, amidst the general camaraderie of the twelve now fully dried Joyce enthusiasts, the particular glint in my eye, a man who has been through a quiet wringer of his own making, now with freedom in his soul and cans in his bag.* We swigged those cans as we walked to Dalkey, where we now had a joyous stretch of afternoon to sit in Flanagan's pub and play the board game 'Codenames', which I had personalised† at 3am the night before we left for Dublin. The giddy optimism of our post-Joyce era was then blessed by increasingly clement

---

* I am rarely drunk, but I love being tipsy, and I love cans. Guinness! Guinness! Jagerbombs! Guinness!

† Personalised by replacing all the 'character' cards with pictures of Alex, Mhairi, and Alex's parents, and all the 'word' cards with words relevant to Alex's life and work: STROKES, INTERSTELLAR, CHORTLE, AMALFI, DUPREE. We even played a bonus game on the walk where everyone got five of these word cards each, and had to 'get rid of them' by getting someone else to innocuously say one of your words. This game was a huge success, by which I mean that multiple people claimed it had ruined all attempts at actual conversation, and even I found myself cursing it hours later, when I thought my friend Tom Moyser was genuinely interested in my boarding school trauma, but he actually just needed to get rid of his last card by getting someone to say 'Eton'. And it's not the hardest word to tease out of me.

weather, soon so hot, in fact, that as soon as the group was stationed at the pub, I was now, inevitably, lamenting that we were indoors, and not larking about in the sun on that finest of vessels: the kayak.

I wasn't mad enough to get back in touch with Pavel, but there was another option. After my extensive pre-stag research of potential activities, I was surely now one of the world's leading experts in, amongst other things, the Dalkey pleasureboating industry. The island wasn't only accessible by kayak: there was also Ken the Ferryman and his motorboat. None of the work, all of the glory. We still had an hour until our dinner reservation at the Dalkey Duck. A call to Ken couldn't hurt. I went for a frenzied pace around the block, the maverick commander eyeing up another side-quest, and called Ken to ask about his ferry. Ken's reply was agonisingly tempting. If we could get to the harbour by 6pm, he said, the boat was ours. 6pm was in fifteen minutes. The harbour was ten minutes' walk away. This was dramatic stuff. But despite all of the evidence accrued thus far, in our twenty-four hours in Ireland, in the six months I had been supposedly planning the stag, in the thirty-three years of my life up to this point, I still reckoned it was a good idea to try and fit this in. I told Ken that we'd see him soon, and I charged back into the pub. The Codenames had been going brilliantly, but it had to end, immediately.

While the confused group tidied up the game, I ran down the road to the supermarket, a side-quest to the side-quest, to get more snacks, more cans, and cash for Ken. We were now fully equipped. But there was a final, ludicrous, obstacle still awaiting me. I arrived back at Flanagan's, with ten minutes of Ken's ferrying window remaining to us, only to find the group giggling with delight outside the pub, repeating a sentence I had not expected, a twist that had not featured in any of my pre-stag risk assessments. That sentence?

'Paul Rudd's in there.'

'Paul Rudd's in there?'

'Paul Rudd's in there.'

'Hollywood actor Paul Rudd, star of *Ant-Man* and *Anchorman*, the seventh Friend, his name a byword for eternal agelessness, is in there?'

'Hollywood actor Paul Rudd, star of *Ant-Man* and *Anchorman*, the seventh Friend, his name a byword for eternal agelessness, is *in there*.'

This is not how the conversation actually played out: I have included the mini-bio for the benefit of any Rudd-light readers. In reality, I took the news impatiently in my stride: of course, I would have liked to know why he was there, what cancelled watersports fiasco of his own had led Rudd to Flanagan's on this particular May Saturday, and yes, if we'd had more time I'd probably have wanted to show him the Codenames, but right now Rudd was a speed bump, an A-list celebrity in a pub stopping me getting some D-list celebrities onto a boat. Obviously I escorted Alex over to him for a photo, but it was a hurried affair, as evidenced by my minorly regrettable (but still regrettable) failure to take Alex's jacket off so that his stag T-shirt was fully exposed. Rudd might have winced at the tee, and even without it, he probably found the whole thing a sub-ideal addition to his Saturday afternoon. As I lined Rudd up next to Alex for the picture, I told him that we were actually comedians, and friends with his recent co-stars, James Acaster and Aisling Bea. I conveyed all this information in a very calm and measured way, which was why Rudd felt the need to reply, 'I believe you. Take the photo.' But he didn't need to worry. I'd already taken it. These cool cats had a ferry to catch.

The group were giddy with post-Rudd energy as I frog-marched them down to Coliemore Harbour. What a brilliantly unexpected addition to the highlights reel: a highlight, in fact, that would be pretty much the main talking point in the various debriefs over the coming weeks. 'Hey, the stag looked fun! Did you really meet Paul Rudd?' In my Fringe show later that year, I painted myself as quite embittered by this turn of events, a weekend of obsessively plotted and re-plotted itineraries that would mainly be remembered for an entirely coincidental encounter with an off-duty Ant. This was not true, of course: I was thrilled by the stardust sprinkled on proceedings, and the suggestion from a couple of staggers that I had somehow *summoned* Rudd by my stag-wrangling energy alone, an act of divine providence to reward the hard yards put in elsewhere. Do I believe such higher power was involved? It's not for me to say. 'Great leaders make their own luck,' to quote the title of an AS Level history essay I was commended for in 2007. But the true providence was in what awaited us next.

We arrived at the harbour on pretty much the dot of 6, and what a sight awaited us there: the sun beating down on the lush hills of Dalkey Island, separated from us by a hundred metres of shimmering sea, so far and yet so near. The boat was docked and ready to go. We all had to put on life vests, which was both safe and fun. Speeding across the water, and then climbing to the top of the island, playing Max Richter and 'Bloodbuzz Ohio' off my portable speaker, felt absolutely transcendent. The weather could not have been better. The location could not have been better. The company could not have been better. What could possibly harsh this high?

Only a furious kayaking instructor waiting for us back at the harbour.

As we motored back to the mainland, I saw some kayaks there that I had not spotted when we were leaving, and instinctively shrank into my life vest in fear. *Could* this be Pavel? Would it be so very mad for him and his men, stood down for the afternoon at half an hour's notice, to have paddled a kilometre up the coast to check that the James Joyce jilters hadn't taken their business elsewhere? What would they make of my 'medical emergency' turning out to be nothing more than the desire to drink four pints, meet Paul Rudd, and get to the same island as before at a fraction of the cost and effort?

Luckily, we were spared this showdown. There were no men waiting by the kayaks, and my betrayal went unpunished. We ate like kings at the Dalkey Duck, and then coach driver John met us at the restaurant and delighted us all the way back with a sensational series of stories about getting sunburned at Live Aid, soundtracked on my portable speaker by the various bands he was telling us about. At one point John mentioned Dire Straits and I skipped not just to 'Money for Nothing', but the good bit of 'Money for Nothing', so quickly that John said, 'Jeez you're fast!', and yes, this was another strong contender for high point of the weekend.

Our trip ended the next day in a suitably pretentious fashion for a bunch of LRB-subscribing lads and dads on tour: a trip to the 'Book of Kells Experience' at Trinity College. We pensively stroked our hungover chins at this twelve-hundred-year-old manuscript, then moved to the college lawns to inspect its rather newer counterpart, my freshly-printed Book of Keals, full of pictures and quizzes and tributes to the stag. 'Is that why we came to the Book of

Kells,' pretty much everyone asked, 'so you could also do a Book of Keals?' Yes, obviously. I had been desperate to pack this weekend with not just as many puns as possible but as much friendship as possible, to show my gratitude to this man who has been such a resolute support to me for so long. And the 'Book of Keals' was itself very much indebted to another best friend, and all the dedication with which Tom used to chronicle and venerate his friendships. Tom would have been proud of my printing, even if he'd have done it earlier than 3am on Stag Eve. And I was proud of it too. A fitting souvenir for a phenomenal trip. A credit to Alex and the gang of G-splitting legends he had assembled for said trip. A credit to Ireland, its beauty and its charm and its patience. But also a credit to the four months of obsession since January: a series of lonely, inefficient stress headaches which could have been so easily shared or avoided, but had still got us here, to an iconic weekend jam-packed with moments and memories. We didn't even disturb the night guard. I was giving myself the full five points for this one.

I would probably give myself less than five for the wedding itself, a heavenly day on the Mull of Kintyre which I spent far too much of fretting, alone, about a stunt for the church. One of mine and Alex's happiest and stupidest running jokes involves buying each other Krispy Kremes, since an end-of-tour 'donut draft' at Woolley Edge service station in March 2019, where we picked up a Mixed Dozen at midnight and clogged our arteries gleefully into the night by eating six each between Leeds and London. Recent twists on the formula like Alex's post-marathon 'crisps in a Krispy Kreme box' had raised the subversion stakes higher. Now I was about to boldly donut where no man had ever donutted before: the altar. Would it be funny to produce two ring donuts when Reverend Lyn Peden asked me, as best man, to produce the rings? Yes, of course. Should I stop to get those ring donuts before getting my train to Scotland? Yes, of course. Did stopping to get them make me miss that train to Scotland. Yes, of course.

Even in this vast index of travel rearrangements that I call life, the day before Alex and Mhairi's wedding was a particularly insane one. I arrived at Euston at 9:58 for a 10am train, just in time to hammer on its already locked doors, beg the guard to let me on as he blew the whistle, and smother a howl of rage into my suit carrier when he refused. So far, so normal. But I then realised that the next train at 11 would not get me to Glasgow in time for the tiny plane to Campbeltown, so I made the perfectly natural decision to instead dash to Luton Airport and ask if they could let me onto a sold-out flight to Glasgow in ninety minutes. Obviously it was no longer possible to book the flight online, because it was sold out, but everything's always OK if you just go to the airport, right? Pure *Love Actually* logic, and outside the Curtis-verse, pure insanity. The flight remained sold out and I was humiliatingly rejected, just as Thomas Sangster should have been. I hung my head in embarrassment and made way for the person behind me in the queue, and the person I will now always associate with this idiotic day: ex-Wales and Swindon footballer Hal Robson-Kanu. Eight years previously, Robson-Kanu scored maybe the greatest goal in his country's history at Euro 2016, and though he'd since retired, and Wales hadn't even qualified for this year's tournament, Hal could still take comfort in having something I could only dream of: a valid boarding pass for an easyJet flight. He glided past me like the Belgian defenders he sent for stoemp and saucisse back in Lille, and

I scowled enviously at his wife and children, before returning to Euston to start again.

The first hour of the 12pm train north was spent biting multiple bullets of textual shame: messaging Alex and Mhairi to say I was going to miss the rehearsal, texting the Campbeltown connection crew to say I wouldn't be joining them on the plane, and texting the larger wedding WhatsApp group to ask if anyone was driving from Glasgow that evening. (Thanks again, Georgia and Ben!) As the eye-rolling and cry-laughing emojis poured in, I stared mournfully at the donuts that had got me into this mess, willing myself not to eat them, and wondering, for the millionth and never the last time, whether my life was going to be like this forever. *How long do you think you can keep this up for?* Alas, no time to dwell, as yet more damningly, I now simply had to turn to the next item on the agenda: my speech. I had had an 'Alex speech ideas' document on my computer since January, in the same folder as the equally unedited 'Alex stag ideas' document. Now it was time to thrash it out. Yet another commission against the clock, squeezed into a sweat-soaked sprint to Scotland.

I don't think the other (vastly more punctual and involved) members of the wedding party had expected me to be much cop on the table laying or flower arranging fronts,* but I was still a criminally absent party from most of the group admin on the wedding morning. I was locked in my room, scribbling cue cards for the speech, and trying to gaffa tape Krispy Kreme boxes into the inside of my tailcoat. The latter was a

---

* Mhairi's sisters Nina, Katy and Izzy basically did all of this, and me namechecking them here is not the same as writing the thank-you letters I've been meaning to send for months.

non-starter: even if the tape did hold, there was no subtlety whatsoever to the double-breasted bulge of the boxes. I ended up hiding the donuts behind the altar before the ceremony, a solid manoeuvre but running the risk that even if no one else spotted them (which they didn't), I would be distracted from all other ushering duties by my obsession with guarding the altar (which I was). Suddenly, the congregation was seated, the organ was playing, and the bride was walking up the aisle, for this emotionally anticipated and impeccably arranged wedding ceremony that I had not only not rehearsed but was actively planning to disrupt. Hymn, reading, hymn, reading, Kremes.

As is increasingly the way these days, there are few parts of Alex and Mhairi's wedding that weren't filmed in glorious high definition, so I've been able to watch back, through my fingers, the long-awaited moment in church where I present the 'rings'. The bride, groom and Reverend laugh, in various states of disbelief, and Alex immediately and correctly asks, 'Is this why you were late?' Of course, I was so keen to prove that I did still have the *real* rings too that I didn't even take a moment to share the stunt with the room, scurrying the donuts back behind the altar like I'd been forced into this blasphemous horseplay against my will, rather than prioritising it above all else to great financial and reputational cost. I spent much of the drinks reception afterwards being asked, 'What was that thing you held up at the altar?' So much planning and yet so little. I should have held the boxes up for everyone to see! I should have maybe taken one of the donuts out of the box! Next time?! But alas, there is no 'next time' for 'presenting a bride and groom with ring donuts in a church'. Another of those one-stop shops on the learning curve of life.

My missed train was called out deliciously by Mhairi in her

speech that evening, and Alex has edited the footage so it cuts to me when she does so, 'hello darkness my old friend' playing over the top as I grimace into my lentil wellington. Her speech was poised and perfect. Her father's speech was proud and perfect. Her husband's speech had been subject to some of the same last-minute mania as my own, but Alex was not far off perfect either, the gig of his life on the day of his life. And mine? Well, mine lasted for twenty-three minutes. I hadn't decided which bits on the 'speech ideas' doc were most important, so I basically just did all of it, grabbing memories at random, setting up callbacks I failed to come back to, giving the congregation whiplash with the speed I veered between topics: early memories from boarding school interspersed with excerpts from Fringe reviews, the happy couple's extended families equally baffled by my references to the Red Hot Chili Peppers and the Iraq War. I didn't realise at the time I'd gone on for twenty-three minutes, but it was the number everyone was quoting during the delayed ceilidh afterwards. It's all on video. Well, two videos. The videographer had had to change memory cards halfway through.

Being the best possible best man for Alex and Mhairi had been one of my main goals for 2024, and even if I'd lobbed more krispy grenades into proceedings than even they might have expected, the only real fallout had, as ever, been the stresses I'd caused myself along the way. The stag had ended up great, the speech was lengthy with laughter and love, and I'd only minorly debased myself in a house of God. There was only so much disruption I could cause to their day, an iconic wedding that was so much bigger and better organised than me. I waved Kintyre goodbye through the window of the tiny plane on the Monday morning, and readied myself for the next chaotic chapter.

Nods *here* to rainbows, witchcraft and love both romantic
and platonic, in a multi faceted piece which elegantly avoids
any singular definition of 'friendship'.

CHAPTER 13

All My Friends

On the very day Alex and Mhairi were putting a glazed ring on it in Scotland, another triumph of love and admin was getting underway at literally the other end of the country. Nine heroes in matching Lycra were setting off from Land's End, and they were heading this way. (It's the only way you can head from Land's End. That's the whole point.) A fortnight later, those heroes would be long past Kintyre, hurtling towards John O'Groats, feet on the pedals of history.

Most of that fortnight is not my tale to tell. I've trampled over a few other people's tales in this book, sure, but I'm particularly wary in this case, because I am very hopeful one of the nine heroes, or all of them together, will write it up into their own book, a book with the same dedication as this one, and dedicated with the heft of hundreds of miles rather than hundreds of tangents. That dedication is to our friend Tom.

In May 2023, I, and many others, received this tantalising and moving invitation from Will, one of Tom's oldest and best friends, via WhatsApp:

Back in pre Covid 2020, Tom, Louis, Debz and I were going to cycle from Lands End to John O' Groats in June, and we were all set – with the exception of not having done enough training. Tom saw it as a chance to get to know our own land, and worried that his three competitive friends would miss picturesque village greens in their quest to set good times on Strava segments. Next year we'd like to make the odyssey in his honour. It seems like a great excuse to do something centred around him, and we hope to make it a mass-participation event of his friends and family.

I had thirteen months' notice for this chunky save-the-date, fifteen days over two weeks and three weekends to keep free in June 2024, should I have any aspiration to the full thousand-mile Land's End to John O'Groats, aka LEJOG. I ought to have been putty in Will's paws: we'd just spent five days in Ghana together, my first non-working holiday in years, and one of the most vivid and liberated weeks of my life. I've loved Will since meeting him in my first term at university, where he captained the college rugby team to Cuppers triumph,* made swift manoeuvres to secure the affections of his future wife Penelope, and enlivened our various undergraduate adventures

---

* My role? Organising the custom T-shirts that we wore to watch them.

not just with his own roguish energy but that of his friends from school. But I've grown to love him, and those friends, so much more in the last two years.

I didn't hang out with anyone from school very much while at university, carefully swerving the Bullingdon Club on account of my principles, but also admittedly on account of never being invited to join. Will, on the other hand, was pre-armed with some of his best ledz from King's Wimbledon. These were not Buller boys, I should stress, literally or spiritually: thrusting chaps, sure, and a force to be reckoned with at critical mass, but also, on an individual level, some of the most disarmingly sage men I have ever been to court with.* There was Louis with us at Univ, Debz down the road at Magdalen, and, over the bridge at St Hilda's was Tom, a hardworking, hard-playing historian, already part of Hilda's heritage as part of the college's first ever generation of male students. Tom became a huge part of my life over the next four years, and then, through the Hoffman Project (amongst the other thrills and spills of our twenties) a huge part of the next ten, too. Will, his housemate for much of this time, was subjected to many of the Hoffmans, and these were special afternoons on the sofas of Lexham Mews: hearts in mouths for *Mission: Impossible III*, pillows on laps for *The Getaway*. Meanwhile, Tom and our friend Jess started going out in 2013, and got engaged in 2019, and married in 2021, and then in 2022 we were all back together in another church, St Bride's on Fleet Street, and Jess was delivering the most devastating address, and nothing would ever be quite the same again.

Will and Penelope's home in Tooting has become another

---

* Never an actual court, I must stress, though I was requisitioned to play judge in multiple late-night tribunals at Will's stag in 2016.

of my safest sanctuaries over the last few years: host to umpteen birthday parties and playdates around our kids, dinners together after the kids have gone to bed, and, in May 2023, the *Succession* finale in their front room. But the house has also served a truly brutal purpose, a purpose it was never meant to serve, but for which I am still so grateful: it has been one of the main places I have grieved Tom. It has been ever since that day in September 2022, the day when I got the call and drove straight there, to share shaking embraces with Will and Penelope, them a couple of hours ahead of me, shellshocked but already directing the comms, Will assuming the role of group leader, which he has played ever since.

Tom was not at the house for their daughter's last two birthdays, despite being her godfather. Tom was not there for the *Succession* finale, despite being the most eloquent TV critic amongst us. But Tom is there every day, on their walls and in their thoughts and in their plans. And my, what a plan was coming together for June 2024.

The last two years have been full of Tom: occasions and traditions springing up in his name, groups of us coming to huddle around the hot flame of his memory over picnics and punts and poetry nights. Will had been in charge of organising Tom's stag for October 2022, already a strange post-wedding affair owing to the vagaries of lockdown, now an untimely event on the most epically cruel of scales. It was perhaps sensibly decided that we would not pursue the full three-dayer in Canterbury as originally intended, but also that the event would not be cancelled completely: in fact, quite the opposite. Five weeks after losing our friend, eighteen of us spent a Saturday in Hampstead toasting his friendship over and over again, a hefty pub lunch earned with a swim and rewarded with as many pints as the catharsis demanded. We've done it twice since on the same autumn weekend; Will has presided over small but symbolic tweaks to the formula,* and the annual momentum shows no sign of slowing down. Sure, to the untrained eye it may look like a bunch of mostly married men clinging to the one 'stag' they can still get away with, but amidst the locker room lapses the event remains the purest story of friendship

---

* As a man on a constant quest to close the loop on my own regrets, I have been well served by the consistency of the stag formula so far. In October 2023, I arrived at the Parliament Hill lido too late to secure one of the precious 'sauna wristbands' handed out once an hour to those punctual enough to claim them, but decided, in a damning indictment of my deep-set social entitlement, to follow my shivering friends out of the pool and into the sauna regardless. Five minutes later, a gendarme arrived to throw me and a few other illegals out, an incident which caused me a small shame at the time but which was far more powerful when brought up six months later, voting in the London mayoral elections at my local church, when I was 'recognised' by the polling officer, not from one of my various tele-vised snafus but from the October 2023 sauna ejection. Returning to the lido a year later and getting a sauna wristband therefore became a hugely significant personal #goal, and I'm embarrassed to say that despite the sincerity of that goal, I still very nearly failed. But I did not fail, and what a long-awaited thrill it was to legally cross that threshold for the first time, before then realising I was still committing the (comparatively smaller) crime of not bringing a towel to sit on. Some long mourners respect the sauna etiquette more than others, and this probably also includes me laughing too loudly at a story Ollie told over the coals about Tom's behaviour on his own stag (Budapest 2017). I'd like to use this paragraph to apologise to my sweaty but silent neighbours from that day, just as I apologised to the polling officer twice in 2024 (mayoral elections and then again at the general), but I suppose it's also worth warning that if you're a regular patron of that lido, and that sauna, the 10am slot on the mid-October Saturday is always likely to endure a few breaches of the peace.

and legacy I know, an eternal credit to the man being remembered and those gathering to remember him. People won't be able to make it every year, especially with the current churn of children amongst the group (three were born in the very week of the 2024 stag, one of them named Tom), but what a great comfort it is to know that it will be back next year, that it will always be there, and that our friend will always be there in it.

For me, the highlight of 2024's stag came out of a contribution from one absent friend, our Australian correspondent Middulz (sic), who texted in from Sydney with a letter Tom had once written him about their teenage *Lord of the Rings* quotathons. The letter emphasised Tom's certainty that they would never forget those long days and deep cuts, so deep that they considered 'You shall not pass!' almost beneath them, a basic bitch bit of Tolkien regurgitation compared to, say, Gareth being able to do the whole of Pippin's Song from memory on the 93 bus. As I read this letter aloud, eyes turned to Gareth at the end of the table, who looked around to make sure we were ready, cleared his throat to check that *he* was, and then sang the song, surely his first rendition in over a decade, word-perfect from memory, the room in rapt silence. A waiter poked his head round the door and withdrew it immediately. Fly, you fool.

Meanwhile, I of course had other cinematic conventions to curate. On February 2nd, 2023, the ninth anniversary of Philip Seymour Hoffman's death, five months after Tom's, I organised a big-screen Hoffman viewing. This was the coup that Tom and I had always daydreamed about pulling off some time in the future, without any sense of how horrifying that future was. I booked the beautiful Castle Cinema in Hackney, hire charge generously waived by its proprietors, and chose *The Talented Mr. Ripley*, Tom's favourite film from the Project, not Hoffman's biggest role but maybe his most iconic, and in a film which no one could quibble with for pure entertainment value. Unfortunately, the actually quite queasy nature of the 'entertainment', as well as the distance of the north-east London cinema from most of the congregation's south-west London homes, conspired to make this not, in fact, a great cathartic moment, but one of the most anxious evenings of my life.

Forty of us gathered in the Castle bar that Thursday night, the first time such a Tom-centred mass had been together since the funeral, an emotional reunion but an initially triumphant one. The Castle had only been able to give us the 9pm screening, and by the time we'd all dribbled in, and I'd finished my wobbly welcome with a few readings from Tom's hilarious and devastating Hoffman journal, we didn't get started until close to 9:30. *The Talented Mr. Ripley* is two-and-a-quarter hours long. Still, as the Italian sunshine beat down on Matt, Jude and Gwyneth's beautiful nineties faces, no one was worrying about that yet. And when Phil himself rolled across the piazza in the hypnotically slimy introduction I'd primed everyone for, a few people in the Castle cheered.

Unfortunately, these cheers didn't last for long, as we entered *Ripley*'s blood-spattered psychodrama of a second act, and I started to panic, during the first of the film's two main bludgeonings, that making everyone watch these scenes, on an evening organised to commemorate a tragedy of our own, was one of the most insensitive things I had ever done, a story that would be hilarious if it wasn't so horrible. As the clock struck eleven, with Damon's dastardly deeds still in full flow, people started to stream out of the cinema: some of these early exits – young parents and professionals who would be in a pretty pickle if they missed the last overground – had warned me that they wouldn't make it to the end, but it was still hard not to draw a line between the mass exodus and the potentially traumatising content that I had lined up for this grisly séance. At one point, Penelope left just to go to the bathroom, and I rushed out after her, desperate to voice even for a few seconds the panic that I'd been cooking up for the last two hours. My friend was impeccably tactful as ever, reassuring me that people didn't see it like that, wouldn't see it like that: it's a great film, Ivo, a classic film, you even checked with Jess and with Tom's parents that they were OK with the choice, it's just so lovely all to be here together, you've done so well, it's not weird. I was so grateful to her in this moment: I hugged her and we returned to the screening, just in time for Ripley's final murder, suffocating his lover over the end credits, the lover breathing the final words of the film: 'Tom . . . Tom . . . Tom . . .'

I had watched *The Talented Mr. Ripley* as part of the Project in 2015, and again in quarantine with my housemate Caz in 2021: a triumph both times. Surely my memory was clear enough to green-light it for this screening without a third viewing? Well, here's one of the more wildly specific lessons from this book, to any poor soul for whom it might be relevant: if you're trying to remember a film's potential triggers ahead of a trauma-adjacent screening, there really is no substitute for watching the film again with the screening in mind. Don't trigger-scan from memory. Because it really would have been great to remember that Mr Ripley's name was Tom.

My breathless post-film apologies to those who had stayed the course were batted away with even more hurried good-byes: the Overground was gone, but people might still be able to get the last Northern Line. Whether the night had been a triumph or a disaster or anywhere in between, it was over, and I resolved to do better with next year's film night. Surely I would.

On February 2nd, 2024, we were at the Prince Charles Cinema, barely a month after I'd watched *Stop Making Sense* there in my standard-size suit. This year I had decided that this tribute to a tribute should take in *Capote*, the film for which Phil won his Oscar, on the ten-year-anniversary of his passing. And though Hoffman's Capote, like Hoffman's Freddie Miles, is a masterclass, and the film, like *The Talented Mr. Ripley*, is a classic, it is also, like *The Talented Mr. Ripley*, chock-full of death. The deaths aren't as visceral, or as stressful, and everyone watching was a year on in their process, but nonetheless: this was another *heavy* film. Most Hoffman films are heavy! I made more apologies. To organise one memorial showing of an unpleasantly violent film may be cast as a misfortune; to organise two looks like insanity. On February 2nd, 2025, a Sunday, we will watch *The Big Lebowski*, the stoner comedy about bowling and drinking White Russians, and it will be laughter that ties the room together, even if people still cry.*

Amidst these shambleses at my end, Will was continuing to steer his own ghost ship† with his usual clarity of vision. Throughout the second half of 2023, cycle updates were starting to pop up on the LEJOG WhatsApp group: training rides around Richmond Park, routeplanning dinners poring over Strava, the announcement of more friends committing to the

---

* 'Strong men also cry, Mr Lebowski. Strong men also cry.' This was the first line of Tom's journal entry about this film.

† This is obviously a horribly morbid expression, but I hoped that Will would enjoy the nod to our favourite Suffolk ale, a market leader in both the 4.5% and 0.5% ABVs.

'end to end'. And yet, despite the clear benefits to being on Will's shoulder for anything,* especially this commemoration of our friend, I had never really considered there being any chance of me doing the full cycle. By autumn 2023, the three weekends of June 2024 covered by the LEJOG had also been earmarked for Alex and Mhairi's wedding (in Scotland, while the cyclists set off from Cornwall), my uncle and aunt's 60th birthday party (in Oxfordshire, while the cyclists passed the halfway point in the Lake District), and Glastonbury (in Somerset, while the cyclists sped through the Highlands towards the finish). I was a not insignificant player at the first two events, and though I might have had a slight chance of influencing the date of those events if I'd made enough noise back in May, it was now far too late, and I was expected at both. As for Glastonbury, I couldn't be a much less significant player there, but I do love it, and I have been lucky enough to weasel my way in every year since 2014, and it's always the best weekend of the year, and I'm not sure they were ever going to move that one because of my cycle ride, however emotional the backstory.

With all those dates in the diary, and a certain rising anxiety about how much of summer 2024 I was going to be co-parentally AWOL for, I barely considered that I would be joining the

---

* Travelling in Will's effervescent but efficient slipstream on our trip to Ghana – where he drunk the most drinks and made the most jokes, while also keeping a full diary of the trip, and looking after my passport and money with his own during all transfers – made me feel like such a useless passenger that I did a bit about it in my *Organised Fun* show, clumsily melded with other stories as I sped us towards the Trumping finale. I still think there's a good bit in 'Don't you hate it when your friend is so grown up you start to call him Daddy?', but I didn't do it, or Will, justice in that show. I hope you feel I'm doing it justice here, my friend!

cyclists for more than the mini-stint proposed to all casuals in Will's mission statement. A shame to be pulled in these various directions, but not a crime. And also, elephant in the room: not a cyclist. I'm a runner, sure, a worshipper in the same church, but a separate, rather lonelier altar. I didn't have a bike. I was not technically or physically or ideologically equipped to take on one of *the* great cycle rides. Perhaps I could come aboard for a day somewhere around Shropshire.

In June 2024, I came aboard for a day somewhere around Shropshire. And it was such a perfect day that I spent most of the summer regretting that I hadn't done more.

I'd kept vague tabs on the countdown to the cycle in the preceding weeks, and embraced Will, Jess and co all the more gratefully at the London *DJ Battles* on June 8th, knowing that they had come out to dance on legs they really ought to be saving for the epic challenge in store. The following Saturday, as the LEJOG WhatsApp group started to ping with pictures of them pushing off at Land's End, I muted it, deep in my pre-speech tizz at Alex and Mhairi's wedding. It was only in the following day's post-speech tizz at Alex and Mhairi's wedding, as I made my limp, hungover contributions to the tidying of the marquee and avoided eye contact with anyone who might mention my twenty-three-minute running time, that I caught up with the WhatsApps. I saw that as well as the momentous pictures of the gang, in the fearless flight of their first foray, Will had written up the most stunning review of the day. This literary epic, that he must have barely had time to scribble before bed in Fowey's Galleon Inn, was already the toast of the many family and friends who were on the group, with more being added by the hour. That evening on the Mull of Kintyre, the wedding leftovers ordered takeaway pizza and watched England scrape past Serbia, and just before I tucked down to bed, the LEJOG day 2 review pinged in, of equally impressive length and scope, a new scribe (Debz) for a new leg (Fowey to Moretonhampstead). This cycle ride already felt truly epic. And in three days, I would be rocking up to join it.

Though the exact Strava routes were being thrashed out amongst the nine End-to-Enders on their more exclusive WhatsApp group, Will had kept the extended community updated with fitness tips and packing hacks for months, so it was with some embarrassment that I reached the eve of my own single-day cycle, Clun to Nantwich, sixty miles across two counties, with not a single training ride done and not a single piece of equipment bought. I had no bike, and when I flagged this to Will, at the criminally casual notice of a week before their departure, he had pointed me towards a solution that my slapdash approach simply did not deserve, a sweet ride weighed down only by its emotional symbolism. Tom's parents, John and Kate, would be driving the length of the country in a van alongside (not literally alongside) the riders, carrying bikes on which they would join for a couple of the less brutal legs, but which would remain largely in the van, for emergencies and, indeed, for opportunists like me. The bike they lent me was Tom's own bike, the one that would have done this cycle had the boys been able to take it on in 2020. As I say: heavy with emotional symbolism. But also, undeniably, light in design and practically weightless in terms of my own admin. I just had to get the train to Craven Arms in Shropshire and the bike would be waiting for me there. So on the Wednesday morning I dropped my daughter at school, popped to Decathlon for a helmet and some padded shorts, and got on the train. It couldn't have been much easier. I probably didn't even need to go to Decathlon. John would have lent me his helmet too. Though he might not have lent me his padded shorts. Those shorts do some ugly work.

As the train sped towards Craven Arms in glorious sunshine, that familiar feeling returned, the recurring sensation of a life in which I am so lucky to get to do exciting things but so chaotic that I often don't remember to get excited (or prepared) until said things are practically upon me. I was joining the cycle! The WhatsApp group was its own runaway train now, the daily conch passed from cyclist to cyclist with no drop in quality, the whole story a great unspooling drama with nine key players and a vast cast of cameos, feasted upon by the friends, family, and cameos-in-waiting who now numbered over a hundred people on the group. And my cameo was inbound!

Tom's parents and Uncle Rob were waiting for me at Craven Arms with the bike: we shared a glorious hug, I did a couple of laps of the station platform to show I knew how to use the gears that Tom so famously spurned, and then we parted ways. I would see them again in Nantwich the following evening, but I had a day's cycling to get there, and for now, just a healthy twilight training ride to meet the End-to-Enders for dinner in Clun, nine miles away. The weather was so stunning. The scenery was so beautiful. And the bike was so sleek! I *could* get used to this! I laughed and whooped to myself as I pedalled towards my friends, pausing in a lay-by to take a WhatsApp video call from my daughter, who couldn't understand the full emotional significance of this cycle, even my small part in it, but did enjoy pointing out that my helmet still had its label hanging out the side. I'm grateful all the time to my daughter just for the sheer unprecedented love and joy she brings into my life, but it's been weird in the last year or two to sometimes have real tangible gratitude towards this now terrifyingly grown-up child too: pointing out some beans I've left burning on the hob, or reminding me of a fellow parent's name at sports day. It would have given the End-to-Enders a lot of pleasure if I'd rocked up in Clun with a Decathlon label on my helmet, but I was too proud to out myself as being quite that much of an amateur, so I bade my girl goodbye, ripped out the label and continued on my way.

Will's laughing embrace in the street outside the White Horse in Clun was the sweetest greeting and followed by many more. I joined the End-to-Enders for drinks and dinner at the pub, and bore witness to their now well-established daily tradition of a new cyclist in turn presenting the agenda for the next day. Tonight's came from Joe Smith, one of Tom's dear Hilda's Joes, briefing us on the need for a prompt 7:30am departure if we were to make it to Nantwich, via stops in Shrewsbury and Market Drayton, and possibly a sighting of Ditherington Flaxmill, in time for England's 5pm kick-off against Denmark. Then, as most of the group peeled off to bed, Will and I and Joe Rice, the other of Tom's dear Hilda's Joes, took a moonlit walk up the hill to Clun Castle. Will pausing to read us Housman's 'A Shropshire Lad' amongst the castle ruins, the county rippling out beneath us in the darkness, was a moment of such pure tranquillity I can still taste it if I close my eyes.

At 7:30 the next morning we were off. Anthony, our host at Clun Farmhouse, set us on our way with bacon and eggs, and I was urged by my more road-hardened colleagues that there really was no limit on how much fuel I should get in the tank. Eating and greeting had been reported as two of the main themes of the cycle, and after a steady morning up and down the Shropshire Hills, mainly spent talking about my *DJ*

Battles suits to a very generously interested Jess in her 'salon' at the back of the peloton, we were awaited by an avalanche of carbs and more of Tom's family at the Orchard Café outside Shrewsbury Cathedral. After leaving them, the city, and the Flaxmill in our dust, a few more hours of sunshine took us to the Joules brewery in Market Drayton, where we hunted for ornamental mice in their backroom while sinking our first pints of the day. Then it was a step up in pace for the final leg to Nantwich, where, as we sped up the Shrewbridge Road into town at 4:15, forty-five minutes before England and Denmark kicked off, I remarked to Will, the most enthusiastic impulse swimmer I know, that this had been a disappointingly dry day on that front. He shrugged this off with the ease of a man who knew he has ten days of increasingly majestic lakes and lochs ahead of him: I, on the other hand, only had this day. As my FOMO petered into silence, however, a sign appeared ahead of us on a mini roundabout: 'Swimming pool'. Ten minutes later, Will, Debz and I were bombing into the Nantwich Brine Pool. Half an hour later, we were taking our seats at the Crown Hotel in time for the anthems. There was no air on this perfect afternoon. At least until England's dismal draw with the Danes.

A cloud of rather more unswervable FOMO started to loom overhead after the final whistle, as we were joined for dinner by many more cyclists, tucking in a day early for the Lake District weekend, and I sat with the group in the town square to watch Tom's childhood neighbour Jonny run the group through the route to Slaidburn that I would play no part in. I tried to keep the party going back at the Crown, hyping up Spain v Italy and trying to persuade Jonny to take part in a competition of who could make a Magnum ice cream last the longest, but these cyclists had five days of fatigue to my one, and ten days remaining to my nought. I was the last man standing in the hotel bar, as Jonny texted me from his room to say that he was sorry but he was going to finish his Magnum now. I celebrated my victory, alone, and went to bed, part exhausted from the biggest cycle ride I had ever done, but more by the longing to have done so much more.

The sadness of waving the gang off after breakfast was allayed at least by getting a long M6 of the soul with my friend Ciara, a drive that laid the groundwork for a perfect day in August when I would bring Edie round to her house to learn Vanessa Carlton's 'A Thousand Miles' on the piano. On this day in June, Ciara dropped me back in London, where I headed straight to school pick-up and took my young pianist to watch *Inside Out 2*, where we were introduced to uncomfortably on-the-nose new characters like Embarrassment, Ennui, and Nostalgia. I didn't need to stare into quite such a high-res mirror of my own fragilities when, despite this, our first trip to the cinema,* being a landmark parental moment, my mind was already wandering to a hostel in Slaidburn. But she loved the film, and she was still talking about it as I put her to bed, and the next day I dropped her with her mum, and then it was time to go to my uncle and aunt's 60th birthday party.

The end-of-day report from the Lake District that evening could have been torture. A huge gang of LEJOG part-timers had Avantied north and climbed aboard for the most beautiful vistas so far, joined by even more supporters for a thirty-six-strong dinner in Windermere. Luckily, I was saved from too much yearning by how special my uncle and aunt's festival was: sure,

---

* Unless you count '*Peppa's Cinema Party*', which I am not, no matter how grateful I was for it at the time.

by some measurements just a load of rahs in chinos glamping for bants, but from my rather more biased standpoint, maybe our happiest ever night as a nuclear and extended family. Pure wedding vibes: bell tents gleaming in the distance as we came over the hill, cocktails at sunset, a genuinely moving Shania-infused* speech from my uncle to my aunt, sets by actual professional singers and bands, and then the most wholesome of multi-generational raves. Cousins of all ages were pied-pipered to the dancefloor by my seventy-three-year-old aunt Bridget, who gave it pure #limbs till curfew and then confided in me on our way back to the tents that 21st-century house music isn't a patch on the disco she used to play at her clubnights back in the day. Take that, David Guetta! Shout out to *your* family!

In the morning, people ate croissants and drank coffee and I hosted a quiz, of course, and soon it was time to go home. I was elated as I drove away, thinking of a particular point during a band called Girl Ray where I was with my brother and sister and parents, right in the middle of it, eight legs and four wheels in a circle, all together maybe for the first time ever on a dancefloor and absolutely *having* it, my dad exclaiming, 'Listen to that fantastic bassline!' and my brother saying, 'Is this a moment? It feels like a moment!' The party had been a triumph. I was so lucky to have been there. But could I rest on these lucky laurels? No, I was now going to go home and continue to wrestle with whether I could pop on my Decathlon helmet to surprise the cyclists in Scotland. No one lives like you do.

---

* 'You're Still the One', crucially, rather than 'Man! I Feel Like a Woman', the latter a song which has soundtracked some of my favourite dances with my little girl, but might not have been so moving in this context.

Alas, parenting and podcasting meant I was not able to jump on a train to leap out of a lay-by in Loch Lomond, and so, on the Friday morning, as the End-to-Enders left Inverness, I was setting off, straight from the school drop, to the south-west instead. My destination was the Glastonbury Festival, another peak of human achievement that I'd been able to piggyback on without doing the work, unless you count a ten-minute set in the 'Poetry & Words' tent (renamed 'Mavericks' after dark) as work. My Mavericks set was at 1am on the Saturday, the time most people least want to do or watch stand-up comedy, but still: not a bad exchange rate for a free ticket and being able to drive your Skoda Fabia straight into the middle of Theatre and Circus camping. Riding shotgun in the Fabia was Chris Scull, host of *Quickly Kevin* and now the new *Let's Be Having You* podcast, intent on spending the entirety of the weekend (let's be) having it. Glastonbury over the years has played host to some of the most romantic and depraved moments of my life, and while those are best given a wide berth here for all sorts of reasons, Chris is one the still points of this turning field, a champion of the collective experience who just wants to get to our favourite tree at the Pyramid, plant his flag* and bellow 'more photos more memories' until his voice or bowels give out. There are more intrepid ways to do Glastonbury than setting up camp by the Pyramid, sure, but it's worked out pretty well for us over the years. This Friday night in 2024, we enjoyed a collective experience there so transcendent that I ended up spending much of my summer

---

* At Glastonbury 2019, Chris brought a Wayne Lineker tweet to Glastonbury on his flag, a triumph only topped when he bumped into Gary and got a photo with him under it.

trying to relive it. The soundtrack to that moment: the band LCD Soundsystem.

If you're not familiar with LCD Soundsystem – and I've by now harvested some pretty damning data as to how much of my audience aren't – they are a New York dance-punk band, heirs to the Talking Heads throne, who released three very beloved albums in the late noughties and then disbanded. Their leader, James Murphy, was an old guy in poptown even when they were starting out, a 'hobbled veteran of the disk-shop inquisition', and a hugely aspirational figure for anyone like me trying to be cool, *in a self-aware way*, into their middle age. All the wryness and weariness of Murphy's long run-up to was poured into 2005 debut single, record-collection resumé 'Losing My Edge', and then into 2007's nostalgic lament 'All My Friends', where he sings lines like 'I wouldn't trade one stupid decision / for another five years of life' over a single hammering piano chord. In a crowded catalogue of bangers and ballads, this song quickly became the band's most beloved. Then Murphy called time on the band in 2011, the ultimate 'quit while you're ahead', and exquisite torture for fans like me who'd never got to see them live. At least we had our endless rewatches of their farewell concert at Madison Square Garden.* In the most powerful shot of that film, during a spine-tingling 'All My Friends', the camera cuts to people in the crowd, destroyed

---

* I loved this film so much I insisted on a post-coital screening of it the night I lost my virginity, to a Vogue-smoking Czech exchange student who had expressed some interest in LCD but very much not this much. The film lasted over three hours, and the relationship not much longer than that. Promi te, Barbora!

by the drama of it all, crying at the line 'this could be the last time', because it was.

I spent the next five years trying to get with the plan, and then, to the joy of many LCD fans, and the chagrin of a few others,* it turned out that Madison Square Garden wasn't the last time. In 2016, with an honest if overlong (no judgement here) open letter about how he wanted to honour his decision, but how he also missed *his* friends, Murphy announced the return of the band for a series of gigs that summer. I went to the first I could, a 1am set at Primavera Sound in Barcelona, and any of my internal wrestles about the U-turn were silenced pretty quickly by the ferocious and emotional assault of the band's performance. It's still to this day my favourite gig of all time.

A month later, I saw LCD again, headlining Glastonbury's second stage on the Sunday night, bringing down the curtain on one of the more politically charged weekends in its history. In 2016 we were weighed down not just by the thickness of the mud on our boots but also of the Brexit result that came in on the Friday morning: a bunch of mashed luvvies insulated from its worst consequences, sure, but still allowed a few chemically imbalanced wobbles about what this grim result meant for our country and our future. Luckily, Brexit's been a resounding success, but we didn't know that then, and we wept serotonin-deficient tears when PJ Harvey read

---

* Some people had spent a lot of money on getting to the farewell gig, it turned out! And some people just really liked it as an ending! People debated their delight or dismay at the reunion over pages and pages of online messageboards, and I read so many of those pages.

'No Man Is an Island'* in between her songs about the First World War, and then LCD came out and told us what would make us feel better. Over the coming years, I saw the band three times more, one of them hammered the night before a *Taskmaster* filming day, a stupid decision that I wouldn't trade for another five points from Greg. The songs hit both harder and softer every time I saw them: the weapons-grade yesterlust of 'All My Friends' was more potent with every passing year, but the 'this could be the last time' line now had its own ironic frisson. Had it lost its edge? Had I?

Cut to Friday in the same field in 2024, and despite being in my favourite place, in the sunshine, wearing trainers for the fourth Glastonbury in a row,† I was distracted. My mind was wandering to forbidden memories from previous festivals, and to the cyclists closing in on John O'Groats, on Valhalla, on an emotional climax more potent than any synthetic summit in Somerset. I was still giddy to be at Glastonbury, desperate to pitch Chris's two-man tent as quickly as possible and get in amongst it, but I was not thinking straight: this no more evident when despite the demonstrably perfect conditions laid out for them (sunset at the Pyramid surrounded by All or at least Some of My Friends!), I uttered the criminally ungrateful line, 'Do we really need to watch LCD again?' Luckily, this sacrilege was dismissed out of hand by Chris, and a few hours

---

* I was very moved by the poem, but I won't ever be able to separate it from one of my dad's favourite bits of maybe his most-quoted film, *About a Boy*, when it's a question on *Who Wants to Be a Millionaire?* and Hugh Grant, a 'bloody Ibiza' of an island, declares proudly to his empty flat that it was written not by John Donne but Jon Bon Jovi.

† The stats don't lie! No wet Glastonbury since Brexit! The sunlit uplands we were promised!

later, we were there, in position with our friend Briggs, the ageless laughing cow of Glastonbury past present and future, watching PJ Harvey playing the slot before LCD just as we had in 2016. Time is a flat circle.

In a throng of friends* gathered under our traditional 'meeting point' tree, this crescendo is really built around three men. Two of those weren't even there, but all of them, as I have rued while awkwardly trying to shout them out on stage over the last year, have the same name.

The first of those was my friend Tom, the Tom to whom this book is dedicated, the Tom for whom the cyclists were cycling, the Tom with whom I never did Glastonbury, never really discussed LCD Soundsystem, but who would have found so much to enjoy in their wisdom and wit if I'd steered him their way. And even if his eternal soul was 600 miles north at this moment, riding the bike not the beats, he was still there with me, so many lyrics applicable to him, and so many brutally off-limits. How can you lament ageing with someone who didn't get to age? What stupid decisions wouldn't we trade for another five years with him?

The second, a Glastonbury regular but missing this year's edition for the birth of his child, was Tom Parry, lord of misrule in Fringe stalwarts Pappy's, themselves no strangers to a fake farewell. Tom, a force of nature permanently wearing either a yellow T-shirt or no shirt at all, is legendary for his love of

---

* A triumphant collision of various different crews, but which ought really to have included Charlie 'Sugar Box' Warner, Will 'first off the stag barge' Hitchins, and most criminally, Mancunian stylophonist Michael, legendary for deadpanning 'which one's this?' to our friend Dan as the band went into 'All My Friends' at Primavera.

festivals and their moments. These moments are usually elevated (literally) by his willingness, nay insistence, that the rest of the crew take turns to get hauled up onto his hulking shoulders, or those of his similarly natured and named brother, Tim Parry. I wouldn't call my sons Tom and Tim, but I'm glad their parents did, and if you're at Glastonbury with the Parrys, you know that at some point, you're going up.

The Tom who *was* there was my childhood friend Tom 'the young' Lambert, an actor, advocate and heir to the glimmering world, whose body you will know if you watched *Coming Clean* at the King's Head Theatre, and whose face you will know if you follow me on Twitter. For twelve years my profile picture has been the two of us at Swindon Town, piling onto the pitch after pounding Port Vale for promotion in 2012. We've enjoyed many more such ecstasies at games and gigs over the years, though increasingly more at the rockings than the Robins. This would be our most ecstatic.

'Dance Yrself Clean' is probably LCD Soundsystem's second best-loved song, mainly for the moment three minutes in that its slow, teasing build explodes into life in a way that might frighten you if you weren't expecting it. But I'm always expecting it. I've seen it six times now, and the second time, Glastonbury 2016, I was on Tom Parry's shoulders, and the sixth time, Glastonbury 2024, Tom Lambert was on my shoulders, the circle of life, passing the torch between the friends that always make me feel good. As the earth quaked to the greatest drop in music, I gave my present company a three-sixty-degree spin, as you always should when you're lifting friends at festivals, so he could take in the full furl of the field, fifty thousand other people peaking in paradise. And then the band went straight into 'All My Friends', and we set our controls for the heart of the sun. In what madness did I want to be anywhere else but here?

Next day, after another game-changing Glastonbury night where Dua dazzled us, Fontaines floored us and I realised in the nosediving temperatures of the NYC Downlow queue (unsuccessful) that I'd forgotten to bring a sleeping bag, I was back at my favourite tree. As I'd told anyone who'd listen, I would be sticking to this spot all day,* watching Cyndi Lauper, then Keane, then Michael Kiwanuka, then Little Simz, then Coldplay. It is worth noting that there are over a hundred other stages, musical and otherwise, on Worthy Farm, and it doesn't get more 'on the beaten track' than ten straight hours at the Pyramid. But after a Glastonbury 2023 where I'd spread myself too thin and then severed all comms by accidentally dancing on my phone under a giant spider, I was keen to be more careful this year, forgotten sleeping bag aside: clear plans with no deviations, single consistent meeting points, and a phone that on Saturday afternoon was going to transport me, however briefly, to a sight even more moving than Keane playing 'Somewhere Only We Know' to the biggest crowd of their career. Because while the politest port addicts† of the mid-noughties were taking the tawny

---

* I hand-drew a map of the spot for bone-dry musical comedian Huge Davies, who claimed in Edinburgh six weeks later that he'd come to find me by the tree and I hadn't been there. 'I took a picture to prove it,' he said. 'Look!' Huge then proceeded to show me a photograph in which I am clearly visible, wearing a deafeningly loud Ghanaian two-piece and clearly chewing the ears off my neighbours, right under my beloved tree. I don't think it would be an exaggeration to call this moment the highlight of that year's Fringe.

† A vicious rumour spread by Serge from Kasabian!

Tories to John Lewis nirvana, I was on WhatsApp, watching nine heroes closing in on destiny.

In came the updates: Altnaharra. Bettyhill. Thurso. And then there it was: John O'Groats. Pictures of the gang at the finish line, corks popping, tears streaming. Thousands of words of debrief to come, but for now, just one final, devastating picture: Tom's bike, resting on the 'Land's End 874m' road sign, its journey complete. This could be the end of everything.

31.10.24

A slice of everyday human drama, 'Lots of People at the Doctor', which in autumn 2024 travelled the nation in the Grand Designs pre-show PowerPoint, frequently receiving more compliments than the show itself. The artist has left some ambiguity as to what some of the People's exact ailments are: a sensitive reminder that not all disabilities are visible.

CHAPTER 14

Grand Designs

'Tournament football was a late-blooming passion of Tom's,'
our friend Debz had written in the LEJOG diary, on the day
that the cyclists watched England v Serbia in Dartmoor's Union
Inn. 'It satisfied his craving for narrative, and offered reams of
rushed copy for his sub-editor's eye to scan.' England's progress
through Euro 2024 would provide buckets of extra narrative
for a summer that was already creaking with it at my end.
It would also provide the brittle backbone of an Edinburgh
Fringe show that could definitely be described as rushed copy
in need of a sub-editor. That Fringe was now just weeks away.

After the high emotion of watching John O'Groats on my phone, Saturday at Glastonbury concluded with the coronation of Little Simz, the roast-dinner reliability of Coldplay, and of course, my hoarse whisper of a 'gig' in the Mavericks tent. By Sunday, the more sport-orientated festivalgoers were turning their minds to another off-site date with destiny, if by 'date with destiny' you mean: second-round match against Slovakia. As an actually quite dangerous number of cowgirls and sk8er bois kettled themselves across the site from Shania Twain to Avril Lavigne, those with sufficient signal were towncrying the team news to their fellow travellers. A couple of bars were rumoured to be screening it, as was, hilariously, Louis Tomlinson from One Direction, on a TV set up next to his tent. But I was blocking the game out entirely, my dogged loyalty to the Pyramid Stage keeping me there post-Shania to watch Janelle Monáe, the Renaissance woman of modern funk and soul, on this occasion left with a pretty meagre main-stage crowd by the competing draws of Southgate and Lavigne. I was so close to the front for Janelle that I popped up on the iPlayer coverage, grey-haired and grinning like a dad at a school play: I couldn't be refreshing for score updates now, not with the Electric Lady mere metres away. I didn't want to be *that* guy in this moment, even with England tipping on the tightrope of defeat. You can rock or you can leave!

England scraped through in extra time, and I celebrated by venturing, finally, off my Pyramid patch to go and rave away the last hours of the weekend, watching French electronic wizards Justice with my brother and the rave squad. A few hours later, I was back in London, back in the real world, wiping the mud off Chris's tent and looking ahead to Saturday's quarter-final. Just like in 2021, Gareth's group stage gruel was grinding grubbily towards glory, all the closer when all five heroes hit the spot against the Swiss, in a penalty shootout I watched with my old housemates in Putney, my daughter back with her grand-parents, my big suit outside in the car. England were now just one game from the final. Football was rumoured, once more, to be coming home. But, for the next match at least, I would not be at home to receive it.

Alongside the other interweaving plotlines of spring-summer 2024, I had been writing and recording *Obsessions*, the Radio 4 show that I was very proud to take over from Joe Lycett and which, I'd be a fool not to mention, is still available to listen to on BBC Sounds. Producer Gwyn Davies, if not Cardiff's favourite son then certainly Llandaff's favourite laff, had been very stoic about Wales's absence from this Euros, but it was with an understandably sadistic twinkle that he warned me early in the tournament that should England win their group and progress to the semi-finals, I would be missing most of the match for a radio record on the wrong side of the Severn Bridge. The prophecy was fulfilled, and the record could not be moved. The light entertainment radio show must go on. By the time we'd wrapped and Raya at the Glee had lowered the club's projector screen, there were only a few minutes left of England versus the Netherlands, still poised at 1–1. A good chunk of the radio audience had stuck around for the football, many of them presumably hoping for more egg on my English face after the humiliations I'd already endured trying to pronounce 'cacennau' and 'Bannau Brycheiniog'. In fact, Ollie Watkins struck in the dying gasps of normal time, and Gareth's modest Marxists were through to another final. At that moment in London, the Killers celebrated the win by playing 'Mr Brightside' to an ecstatic O2 Arena. At that moment in Cardiff, I celebrated the win by cueing 'Three Lions' to a groaning Glee Club. The role of giddy Englishman behind enemy lines was one I would reprise extensively later in the summer.

I did, however, watch the last match of the tournament on home soil, the definitive home soil of my parents' house, surrounded by family, on another date that had had 'Euros final?' pencilled next to it for weeks, without much expectation that England would actually be in it. The rather more concrete plan was another big birthday, this one for Ginna, my dad's elder sister; my aunt who glues the various strands of the Graham extended family together; my aunt who is the gold standard for kindness and consideration to all who know her; my aunt who has kept the homes and legacies of her parents and grandparents alive at home and abroad; my aunt who in 2019 was awarded an OBE for services to renewable energy; my aunt who is herself a force of endlessly renewable energy; my aunt who has spent too much time in the Royal Marsden recently; my aunt who has had me (and many other nephews, nieces and friends) taken onto her office's temp roster over the years; my aunt who has had me (and many other nephews, nieces and friends)* lodging in her spare room over the years; my aunt who has come to watch so many of my shows despite being surely quite embarrassed by much of their content; my aunt who has given me so many thoughtful presents I never properly thanked her for; my aunt who has turned a blind eye

---

* The longest-serving tenant being not me but my brother and his snake, Kazzy, a fantastically on-brand Bristol uni purchase who is still going strong a decade later, on a steady diet of one frozen mouse per week. Many aunts would not love having their nephew's snake living in their house. My aunt is, I must reiterate, a special woman.

to so many of my hangovers and latenesses; my aunt who has listened to so many of my rambling stories about long drives to weird gigs and told me to make sure to write it all down. Well, here we are, Ginna, I hope you feel most of it was worth writing. My aunt is a titan, and in 2024 she turned seventy, and my parents hosted a big lunch for seventy of her friends. Glasses were raised to the birthday girl, and we gave out the 'Ginna's first seventy years' books we had produced, to which every guest had contributed their own tribute of varying length, and then at the end of the day the twenty or so remaining family members and guests crowded into the living room to see if the cake could get its ultimate cherry. My aunt was twelve when we won the World Cup: was fifty-eight years of hurt[*] about to be laid to rest?

You know the answer to this question, of course, but it's no crime to remember just how tantalising that potential glory felt as the final approached. A real narrative was coalescing around this England team by now, Moments FC, an embarrassment of individual riches that tortured us with their collective lack of thrust, before pulling another rabbit out of the hat in the nick of time. Sure, all those rabbits had been pulled against opponents we were expected to beat, whereas Spain were measurably the best team in the tournament by far, but still: it's just one match. Maybe one rabbit might be enough. As the days ticked down till the final, every fan had their own choice to make as to where, and with whom, they would be, for this potential

---

[*] As Alex Kealy once tweeted to solid numbers, for all the genuine poetry of 'Three Lions', it's surely mad to suggest that the 'hurt' would have begun immediately in 1966. Could the laurels not have been rested on for even a year?

moment of national ecstasy and anarchy* unprecedented in
most of our lifetimes.†

As someone who famously hates these or any choices, it was
quite a relief to be in Wiltshire for the final, in the bosom of my
family, and the only real issue was the revelation at the end of
the birthday lunch that my brother, and my cousins, Will and
Paddy, were all planning on heading back to watch it separately
in London. My favourite of my brother's Glastonbury battle
cries is the concept of the 'galáctico signing', popularised by
Real Madrid president Florentino Pérez, now gloriously appro-
priated by Ludo to celebrate, say, his friend Holly joining him
for a 4am assault on Shangri-La. Ludo himself is always my
ultimate galáctico signing,‡ and I was pretty aghast to learn that
he and our cousins were planning to leave this, the very garden
in which we'd played our barefoot four-a-side epics since we

---

* A buzz-killing note here to say that, however many nods to my own
minor hooliganism this chapter includes, the scenes from Wembley in 2021
in particular ought to shame us as a nation.

† Of course, this is just one form of mass national ecstasy, and let's doff
caps to a few other sporting victories while we're here: World Cup wins in
rugby and cricket, Euros triumph for the Lionesses just two years before,
Andy Murray winning Wimbledon, Super Saturday in London 2012 amidst
other British Olympic and Paralympic triumphs, and club-level odysseys
like Leicester winning the Premier League in 2016, or Swindon winning
League Two in 2012, that warmed the cockles of every neutral in the land.
But nonetheless, this – the England national men's football team winning a
major international tournament – remains, to quote my father's favourite
line from *Pulp Fiction*, the Big Kahuna Burger.

‡ At Glastonbury 2024, I was so melodramatically appalled at Ludo for
not joining us at the tree for LCD that I first defaced and then binned a
bedsheet he'd asked me to bring him from London: a decision that was pretty
morally dubious even before the temperatures nosedived after midnight.

were kids, to watch the football in London with no doubt dear but for these purposes utterly irrelevant non-family-members.

I turned up the heat with a devastating blend of blackmail and bribery. What wouldn't it mean to Ginna to have us all there with her for the evening too? This was a cynical citation of an aunt who, for all her goodwilled garden goalkeeping back in the day, would have to be called football-agnostic at best. But nonetheless: the full quadrant of nephews should absolutely stay for this, the last bit of her birthday, and I'd give them all a lift back to London the second the match finished. If England lost, they'd still be in bed by midnight. If we won, the party would just be getting started. I had a flare in my flat* and I would not be afraid to put it up my arse.

Unfortunately, though Cole Palmer did produce one more rabbit for us, allowing me to tell everyone, yet again, how I'd actually seen him play live against Swindon in the FA Cup, this tedious anecdote and all other positive murmurs were silenced swiftly afterwards by Mikel Oyarzabal, and my arse went unflared for another year. It was a cheery enough cousinly roadtrip back to London, but the Fabia was flat with that familiar feeling, the despicable nearness and farness of what might have been. And now, for me, the resignation that there was no remaining excuse not to be getting ready for Edinburgh.

The imminence of August as comedy 'exam season', albeit an exam season where most of the examinees are out getting shitfaced every night, means that June and July, though full of

---

* The flare was a leftover from a photoshoot years ago, which, with me having failed to foresee its potential for 'Dance Yrself Clean' 2024, may emerge for a similar drop at Glastonbury 2025, or perhaps fulfil its rectal destiny under Thomas Tuchel in 2026.

fun, are rarely without their gnawing sense of dread, the dread of feeling the weeks and the work-in-progresses ticking down till you're back on that train. The Glastonbury comedown is doubly bad because, oh shit, that's June gone now. And the World Cup/Euros? Well, you shouldn't really let yourself get too consumed by them, but yes, if England have made it to the quarters, then the semis, then the final, well of course that's going to occupy nearly all of your waking thoughts too. But then, suddenly, bang, England haven't won the tournament, you were mad to think that they might, and it's now two weeks until Edinburgh.

With the evergreen delusion of a man who refuses to learn from his mistakes, and to be fair, the financial motives of a man with more legal bills than he expected to be paying in his mid-thirties, I had signed up for an even more high-stakes version of 2023's three-headed monster Fringe: bigger stand-up in a bigger venue, plus a fully-fledged run of the theatre show, and four more clubnights. The temptation to build on the promise of the latter two ventures, *Carousel* and *Comedians' DJ Battles*, was hard to resist: the greater anxiety was about turning round a new, and good, stand-up hour after the (a) mixed reviews and (b) general emotional experience of *Organised Fun* in 2023. The latter was the most shambolic show of my career, performed to the biggest crowds of my career, and there's no world where that isn't just a bit of a missed opportunity. The *Taskmaster* hordes had swarmed excitedly aboard only to be greeted with something far messier than even my messiest tasks: messier than my feisty French duck, messier than my six bananas on the jelly, messier than the balloon animal I tried to craft with hands coated in Vaseline. I was ashamed by the failure of *Organised Fun* (and yes, failure is subjective, but I am using the *Guardian* as a yardstick), and I was nervous about heading back north and it happening again. But I love the Fringe, and I wanted to do the other shows, and on a crucial Zoom in January, my agent Flo teased me with a fatally seductive blend of economic and emotional logic. Ryan at the Pleasance had proposed that I do a full month in the Grand, and Flo said that after a decade working my way up the greasy prepositional pole of the Pleasance, from Beside to Beneath and Beyond, playing to 700 punters a night in the Grand (less on weekdays admittedly) would be like 'completing Edinburgh'. What a rush! Sign me up.

Ideally, a stand-up show to be performed in the Grand, rescuing said stand-up's critical and commercial standing after the kicking received by its predecessor, would be the sole or at least primary focus of the months leading up to it, but, if you've even skim-read the couple hundred pages preceding this, then you'll know that wasn't the case. The preceding months were instead spent touring *Organised Fun*, work-in-progressing *Carousel*, booking and promoting *Comedians' DJ Battles*, writing and recording *Ivo Graham's Obsessions*, running the marathon with Rosie, planning Alex Kealy's stag, and writing this book. In the optimistic previous timeline where this book was released to the world in September 2024, its final draft was due in June. In late May, I sent Luca, producer and sounding board for every aspect of this demented juggle, a message detailing my three big fears for the summer: '(a) I don't learn *Carousel* in time (b) the book gets delayed (c) *Grand Designs* is shit'.

I did learn *Carousel* in time, but the book was delayed. One of the three fears realised, one averted. Be great to avert the third. Come on, *Grand Designs*.

Grand Designs the title was, like all Fringe titles, locked in six months before the Fringe, long before the show had any sort of shape, and based on the one thing I did know about it: that it was going to performed in the Grand. It wouldn't necessarily be based around the TV show *Grand Designs*, of which I'd only ever watched one episode, the north Devon lighthouse lunacy which dear Tom had recommended me in lockdown as 'a tragedy of Shakespearean proportions'. He would have enjoyed me referencing that in this show. But the wider themes of the episode and the show in general – of people building or sometimes not quite building family homes, of people biting off more than they could chew, of people staring down the gulf between their expectations and their reality – would surely fit themselves neatly around whatever autobiographical overshare I would end up dribbling out that summer.

If I'd been organised enough to lay down a team sheet of even just potential topics at any point between January and June, Gareth Southgate would have been on that sheet from the start. Six months before he bore/bored an expectant nation all the way to another final, Gareth inspired one of my first Grand(ish) Designs of 2024, when I went in January to watch *Dear England*, the play about his tenure written by my namesake (but not relative) James Graham. I went with my friend Thea, who wasn't too clued-up on the international performance of the England men's team 2018–2022, and had underestimated how much of the play, barring the odd Liz Truss cameo, would be concentrated solely on this topic. Thea has spent most of her adult life campaigning for the safeguarding of vulnerable women and girls in Africa, so hasn't had much time to participate in the mass biennial grumps about whether Trent Alexander-Arnold is wasted in midfield. Time to be brought rapidly up to speed in the West End.

Thea's confusion was compounded when I met her and her brother at dinner and took off my coat to reveal a waistcoat, a Southgate-infused lovely gesture that I thought would be shared by many a neighbour at the Prince Edward Theatre. Alas, when we arrived, mine was the only waistcoat in sight, and I looked and felt like a prick for most of the evening, especially as my late ticket purchase had meant that I was sitting alone. Two and a half hours is a long time to be mateless in a waistcoat. The play did a fine job recreating the shootout with Colombia in 2018, but my mind wandered to the BBC montage that had captured that in two minutes.[*] The play did a fine job summing up the political tensions that the team were navigating in 2021, but my mind wandered to the Tyrone Mings tweet[†] that had captured that in 280 characters. The play did a fine job getting us all to sing 'Sweet Caroline' at the end, but my mind wandered to the Neil Diamond original, and its innocent half century in the non-sporting sun before it got hijacked by every goon with a gram or a gilet.

'I did enjoy it,' Thea stressed, as we fought our way through the hands touching hands and out into Soho to debrief. 'But it really was all about football, wasn't it?' It was a verdict that was difficult to argue with. Alas, any reservations of my own were evidently cast aside some time between then and August,

* Intercut with old heartaches to the glorious and on-the-nose soundtrack of the National's 'England'. If you haven't seen it, do yourself a favour.
† 'You don't get to stoke the fire at the beginning of the tournament by labelling our anti-racism message as 'Gesture Politics' & then pretend to be disgusted when the very thing we're campaigning against happens.' Go off king! In stark contrast to a surely pre-scheduled Harry Maguire tweet the day after the final, encouraging disconsolate fans to pick up a free taco at Taco Bell.

when I elected to spend a month doing a show that was also all about football, a sloppy summer of stand-up about Southgate in Scotland.

Admittedly, it doesn't get much less 'behind enemy lines' for an Englishman than the Edinburgh Fringe, where my Brideshead to Braveheart ratio was broadly on brand in the Grand, and I still tried to placate any locals with a lengthy ode to my favourite Scottish footballer, Dundonian Simon Ferry, who had bossed the Swindon midfield in the dizzying anecdote factory of the Paolo Di Canio years. The PR for *Grand Designs* had promised pure stand-up with 'no ball games, no blind alleys, no backstage printers this year' but once more, as Rabbie Burns nearly wrote, the best laid blurbs of mice and men had gone awry in July. I hadn't written a tight new hour of stand-up, but I had purchased a remote control for my PowerPoint, so I could strut about the stage like a motivational speaker, clicking the audience through pictures of footballers they could already have pictured in their minds, or hadn't cared about in the first place. At least no one was being forced to speed-eat a Meal Deal.

The show was not entirely about the Euros: it also covered various other events that took place in those frenetic final weeks pre-Fringe, such as Alex and Mhairi's wedding, LCD Soundsystem at Glastonbury, and the general election. For all the various ways in which Keir Starmer had ground the hope and the joy out of his victory before it was even confirmed, it was still heartening to welcome the first non-Conservative government since my train duvet heyday of 2010, and it allowed me, a Known Posho, a solid opening joke about how most of my best friends had been made unemployed on July 5th. Then, after a Venn diagram about soggy Garibaldis that appalled several family friends,* I bade the politics farewell and moved on to the football, crowbar in hand as I turned my focus to 'another recently unemployed man'. Next up: twenty minutes on the freshly-resigned Southgate, and his plucky heroes who almost brought it home.

As I veered from the England-heavy but semi-topical Euro 2024 content, into the England-heavy and definitively non-topical World Cup 98 content, I pleadingly emphasised that these stories weren't about football, they were about memories and moments, moments that cultural figures far bigger than me had tried to insert themselves into. 'Did anyone see the Killers cheering on England this summer?' I clicked through to a picture of the Killers the band, but only after a very fleeting and very cheeky slide showing some serial killers from history. The latter earned me a stern advisory text from my dad on the night he came to the show, but the serial killers stayed in the PowerPoint. What larks I was having with my clicker! Apart from when the clicker's batteries were playing up, of course, and I would jump one slide too far by accident, a doubly problematic mistake as, with my back to the screen, I'd be the last person in the room to realise I'd done that. The internet is full of 'no context' accounts which revel in the surrealism of punchlines without setups, but it's still by most metrics not ideal to be talking about Ollie Watkins scoring against Holland, while accidentally projecting a picture of Harold Shipman.

---

* This Venn – which featured Giuseppe Garibaldi quipping 'Risorgimento? More like Jizorgimento!' before cutting to a picture of some terrified biscuits – justified the projector hire fee cost on its own as far as I was concerned.

From the 'big moments' of the Euros, I moved, via a quick picture of Kevin McCloud baulking at some hubris on *Grand Designs*, to big moments at music gigs, and then that fat chapter of best laid plans from earlier in the summer, the big moments I'd tried to create at Alex's stag and wedding.* Then, for the show's finale, I would attempt to create another moment, going big in the Grand, calling an LCD Soundsystem fan onstage to let off confetti cannons at the exact moment 'Dance Yrself Clean' dropped, with a background video timed to show, in perfect pre-juxtaposed unison, two English goals,† one Scottish goal,‡ and George McFly punching Biff in *Back to the Future*. What a sensory overload! Yes indeed. When it worked.

On a few nights of the run, with a crowd on board for all the football stuff, the themes of the show properly explained, and a hardcore LCD fan bouncing with excitement next to me onstage, this finale went as well in real life as it did in my head. On so many others, it did not, for lack of any of the above, or some failure in my own timing that meant that the confetti cannons didn't go off in sync with the song, or didn't go off in sync with the background video, or didn't go off at all. On tour, where I got to play some very beautiful theatres

---

* It was nice talking about my best friend in the show, and plugging his own show at the end, but I was, in a way, compensating for a shambolic best man speech by doing twenty more of them at the Fringe, and then multiple more on an autumn tour where Alex was usually the support act, a laughably claustrophobic schedule of Posh Man 1, Posh Man 2, interval, then Posh Man 1 talking *about* Posh Man 2.

† Saka v Switzerland and Watkins against Holland, nudging out Bellingham and Palmer by a whisker.

‡ The consolation against Germany, not even from a Scottish boot but an Antonio Rüdiger own goal!

with some very faulty HDMI connections, there were even more ghosts in the machine, alongside the rotating cast of individual errors I brought with me in my ongoing refusal to either sort out or sack off this moveable farce of a finale.

On the final night of the tour, in Swansea, I'd replaced the Scottish goal in the final video with a Welsh one: my Luton Airport nemesis, Hal Robson-Kanu, slaying the Belgians in 2016. I hoped this would go some way to earning the forgiveness of another non-English crowd forced to listen to memories of a Euros that, in Wales's case, they didn't even take part in. Alas, an audience that had been gratifyingly loud up until this point went dismally quiet when I went in search of an LCD fan, so I had to rope in a non-believer, a cheery chap called Mike who'd kick-started a merry first-half riff about me releasing my own erotic calendar.

As I tried to talk Mike, my lusty co-pilot for this, the final minute of the whole tour, through the incoming 'drop' in a song he'd never heard before, my countdown timer died in his hands, and in my agonising realisation that I'd ignored a 'low battery' warning earlier in the evening, I then failed to switch on the goals video at the right time either. I, the most disorganised comic in the game, had spent the summer trying to sync up a needlessly complicated and largely non-comedic mix of video, audio and pyro, and it had never been less in sync than tonight. Once more, I could take some solace in the thought that I'd given people the true Ivo Graham experience, the *Taskmaster* failure failing at a task. There were so many more laughs in Swansea, as Mike fired his confetti cannon almost apologetically into the void, than there were on the nights the 'Dance Yrself Clean' drop actually worked. 'It was a failure,' Alex said bluntly as he drove us back away from the

Taliesin Centre, tactfully allowing me first pick of the Krispy Kremes. 'But it was a noble failure.' Does the yardstick have separate measurements for that?

For all the noble failure of *Grand Designs*, a show whose title became apter with every fluffed finale, it was still an improvement on *Organised Fun*, and I tried to remember to enjoy performing it every day, especially in Edinburgh, knowing that I might never do a Fringe month in such a billowing basketball court of a venue again. This was an opportunity to be relished, even if I had elected to spend much of said opportunity asking my audiences things like, 'Who remembers why Glenn Hoddle lost his job as England manager in 1999?'* It was, all in all, another Fringe that I could look back at with real pride: *Carousel* got the best press of my career, and *Comedians' DJ Battles* went from strength to strength, even if I was still no closer to actual DJing. 'This is dead air, Ivo!' an audience member shouted at one point, into the horrible silence of me failing to successfully cue a track on Spotify.

The most painful ghost of 2023, the one I got a whole theatre show out of, was laid to rest when Edie's mum brought her to stay for three nights in the final week, and our afternoons with Alfie and his kids, at the flat and in the Pleasance crafts tent, gave a gratifying glow to a healing month for Ignom Towers. My parents and brother had both visited earlier in the month, and then, two days before my own departure, the full-family set was completed when I welcomed my sister to town, coming north to support on the strict reassurance that

---

* There was, if I may say so, a very good joke off the back of this, though if you didn't like my jokes about getting on my mum's nerves in the 'CP Gone Mad' chapter, you probably wouldn't like this one.

none of this month's shows were about her getting a love bite from an anonymous savage in 2008.

Georgia is the most thoughtful, the most sensible and most punctual of the Graham siblings, but she's also by most of your standard metrics the coolest, and I was excited and nervous to have her with me in Edinburgh, packing three shows into a twenty-four-hour visit. On the Saturday night, she was in for *Grand Designs*, the best it had gone all run, and then had the full no-air experience of being frogmarched straight from the venue to nightclub La Belle Angele, where the final *DJ Battles* was due to open in half an hour. She was onstage and backstage with me till the early hours as I danced myself clean in my orange and purple suit, before having her hangover clattered with our family history in the final *Carousel* at lunchtime the next day. 'Ivo Graham invites you to Laugh, Cry and Dance', the posters around town had proclaimed, and I was so pleased to get the triple thumbs-up from a sister who has watched me do plenty of all three over the years.* Georgia then had an enviably straightforward Sunday afternoon train home, whereas I would once more be pelting to the platform at 6am the next morning. There was no clubnight to host on the Sunday, at least, so I could have gone to bed at a reasonable hour after *Grand Designs* that evening.

I did not, of course, not go to bed at a reasonable hour. I did not go to bed at all. The Edinburgh Fringe is itself a dizzying carousel of all the things in one's life that have changed, and

---

* Earlier in the summer, in a sublime comedy roast en route to our uncle and aunt's 60th, Georgia had summed up my entire personality as 'Pro Plus, regret, and Barry Can't Swim', a laser-guided trifecta which had done nothing to diminish my dependence on any of the three, this of all months.

all the things that have remained exactly the same. So many things had changed, especially since 2022, that night almost exactly two years ago when I had stumbled down those same streets with Tom. But amidst all of those changes, from loss and lament to laughter and Lycra, my bedtimes, or lack of them, had stayed the same. However much I want certain things in my life to settle and slow down, I still love little more than chasing the night and the moment, thinking of the friend I loved, who loved it too.

CHAPTER 15

The Boss

Any hopes that the 2024 Fringe would see me become a master of all my various domains and Designs were of course deluded, but my theatre piece *Carousel* was the proudest I have ever been of a show. I felt proud of the topics I had grappled with in the script, a script that then benefitted, unlike most of my other shows, from a full year of writing and honing, with beefed-up production from Luca, and gorgeous directorial finish from pink-haired rules monster Matt Hassall. The show was good, and it was tight, and it was reliable: the latter word in particular not one that could be applied to many other things in my life. Over the course of the month, even as *Carousel*'s early afternoon timeslot was ravaged by ever accumulating hangovers and sleep deprivation, the show went exactly as planned pretty much every time, barring one day where I left one of the props in my dressing room, and another where I had to start a section again because I'd got the lines in the wrong order and inadvertently claimed that my grandmother had sent me an email from beyond the grave. (She found them hard enough to send when she was alive.)

But despite *Carousel*'s smooth running and gratifying press, it was and remains an awkward show to celebrate too whole-heartedly. On the one hand, its distillation of these most recent and delicate years of my life – the ongoing domestic challenges, the attempts to escape my head through running and raving, the loss of Tom – is the most honest and concise I have ever been on those topics. On the other hand, most of those blasts from the past are still unpleasant in my present, and sitting with them for an hour in a Portakabin was easier some days at the Fringe than others. Obsession with stasis rather than progress, with what I'd lost rather than what I had, continued to be the self-sabotaging story of my life offstage as well as on. My most-played song of the year, Fontaines DC's 'A Hero's Death' (Soulwax remix), was, by the end of 2024, another classic with an asterisk, its lyrics a series of mantras for life that I was still largely failing to heed, its opening line of 'Don't get stuck in the past' mocking me even as I copy pasted it into another *DJ Battles* PowerPoint. Many of the shows I have done over the past few years have been half-written: *Carousel* was, by contrast, a fully written show about half-resolved issues. How does that show up on the yardstick? In *Taskmaster*, I had made an epic, cousin Jasper-approved performance out of coming last. I'm usually very happy for that to be my role. But self-deprecation is a dangerous basket to put all your eggs in when life is providing its own jabs behind the scenes.

As I've disappeared further down these introspective rabbit holes, I've thought so much about my friend Tom, and not just in the minute of every *Carousel* show apportioned to silently holding my favourite photo of us, while the Waterboys' brutally poignant accordion and piano piece 'The Trip to Broadford' plays over the top. The photo, of us laughing in our final-year student house with our friends, Will and Louis, was uploaded to Facebook in summer 2012 with the 'Hipstamatic' filter, which lent a smudgy, tea-stained fuzz of instant nostalgia to all of our pre-graduation snaps in the couple of months it was popular: Tom and I loved this filter, and laughed at what a desperate, iPhone-assisted cliché of final-year Oxford students we were, artificially blurring our grinning twenty-one-year-old faces on Magdalen Tower or Christchurch Meadow to fast-track these photos' passage to the museums of our own youth. 'Those were the days,' we'd muse melodramatically to ourselves, as if in some nursing room armchair, while we examined a picture that was taken mere hours ago, and speculated how many Likes it would get. We joked about being mournful middle-aged men poring over these photos, as if our pasts were all we had. Now I'm a mournful middle-aged man, and Tom's past is all we have, and I pore over this photo every night.

If Tom was still with us, I might not be doing this solo theatre show at all. Perhaps I would still have filled a laugh-light hour with my other emotional wallows, but those other wallows are always quietly damned in my mind for being wilful refusals to move on, a strong show from a weak brain. Unlike the show's other regrets, most of them messes of my own making, the loss of Tom stands in its own category, a cosmic cruelty beyond all comprehension. And it is the one bit of my past that I feel not just proud, but duty-bound, to preserve and to share. However much I may be filtering it through my own pretentious prism (and making people pay for the privilege), I am glad to be doing my bit, alongside the army of others who love him and miss him, in burnishing Tom's legend, and making sure the story of his life and energy and wit never gathers too much dust in the archives.

In September 2024, we all gathered on Wimbledon Common to mark two years without Tom, and as Jess unveiled a new bench commemorating her husband, she shared a quote* about people having two deaths, the first when their breath leaves their body and the second when their name leaves other people's lips. On those terms, I'm confident that Tom will live longer than most of us. If you ever pass the bench on the Common, do sit for a moment with him. It's the one with the Philip Larkin line, the famous and delicate conclusion of *An Arundel Tomb*: 'What will survive of us is love.' Tom studied the poem for his International Baccalaureate, vigorously debated the 'almost-instinct almost true' in and out of

---

* Versions of this quote are attributed to everyone from the Ancient Egyptians to Hemingway and Banksy, but it was credited by Jess to our friend Joanna Lambert, a plate-spinning supermum with a quite legendary prowess in providing hot meals, wise counsel and station lifts to her children, her friends' children, her children's friends, and a menagerie of animals into the bargain.

class, and later made a pilgrimage with Jess to Chichester Cathedral to see the stone fidelity of the Tomb in person. I didn't know any of this until Jess told me: it is one of the many topics I will forever never have shared with him. And yet now I have. A poem Tom loved is now bound up in his legacy. The final line on its own simplifies the hesitancy of *An Arundel Tomb*:* there is an irony that this poem, that Larkin claimed mixed feelings about, was then read at Larkin's own memorial service, and its conclusion inscribed on his stone in Westminster Abbey. This Wimbledon bench now bears Larkin's words in tribute to another poetic soul, a student and a victim of the bitter irony of life and death. Some readers cannot separate Larkin from his bitterness. But Tom was rousing, and romantic, and silly, and sincere. He believed in the almost-instinct almost true. Ironies fade. Love lives forever.

The various seeds of passion that Tom planted in his life will bear eternal fruit for his friends, and I feel so lucky to have had more than one experience in the last couple of years where I felt him definitively by my side. In July 2023, I ran the full gamut

---

* Despite doing a literature degree myself, and sending producer Alex Gilman mad with my efforts to shoehorn a Larkin reference into the Hull episode of *British as Folk* in 2021, writing and revising this paragraph has probably been the most intensely I've ever thought about Larkin's or anyone's poems. Alongside wanting to do justice to Tom and to Jess, I hope I've also done even hurried justice here to *An Arundel Tomb*. For anyone wishing to dive deeper themselves, I particularly enjoyed various pieces online linking Larkin's misgivings with W.H. Auden's denunciation of his own work ('we must love one another or die', from *September 1, 1939*) as 'trash'. Will I be furiously turning on my own book after it has come out? Will I be hawking copies of the heavily edited paperback *Yardsticks For Failure* to an empty tent at the Hay festival in 2026, claiming it as the only 'true' version, before clearing up any remaining debate in a self-published sequel?

of emotions at the Bruce Springsteen gig I went to watch in Hyde Park, a gig he had booked us tickets for a year before, and which I was now going to watch with his parents and Jess, a gap next to us where a very tall man would have stood, eagerly telling us about what and who we were watching, about Steven Van Zandt's role in *The Sopranos*, or Max Weinberg's on *Late Night with Conan O'Brien*. The day before that Springsteen gig in 2023, I had been in Glasgow, filming *The Weakest Link*, which was itself a surreal time-travel of an experience. Can you bear one more drive in the Delorean?

Back in summer 2009, a week before my first-year university exams, I had travelled to Pinewood Studios to be roundly humiliated by Anne Robinson on the original version of *The Weakest Link*. Any Etonian hubris about waltzing through one of the easier teatime quizzes, and taking a couple of grand home to put behind the college bar, had been knocked on the head in a third-round exit which saw me bomb in both brains and banter. And this distraction did more damage elsewhere. Having spent more time as a fresher applying for quiz shows than actually working on my degree, my focus more on *Pointless** than Pushkin, I bungled my first-year exams to the extent that I was quite lucky to be welcomed back for

---

* I actually applied for a then-unbroadcast *Pointless* in 2009 with none other than Alex Kealy, who did all the application admin on my behalf (hmmm), and described me in said application, which I've just re-read, as 'terribly disorganised but with a bizarre talent for fitting in a ton of activities'. Our gawky friendship failed to make it past the 'chemistry test' we travelled to London for, a disappointing verdict and an ominous one for future podcasting adventures, but luckily, very little came of the TV show anyway.

second year at all.* Whimpering out of *The Weakest Link* in the third round and scraping through Prelims with a pass: get you a man who can do neither! The end of exams that June, however, was followed by a glorious final weekend of term, where I left no stereotypical stone unturned by spending one white-tie ball partying with my friend Orlando and another kissing my friend Clementine. I could have happily spent the Sunday sleeping off this forty-eight hours of highfalutin filth, but instead I was roused from my bed by Tom, who had bought us tickets to watch Bruce Springsteen in London that evening. I was a fan of Springsteen, but not as much as Tom was, and I was definitely unappreciative enough to be quietly regretting saying yes to the plan, as my hangover chased me up the M40. Youth is wasted on the young.

---

* A footnote here for the Russianist class of 2008, the Baltika Boys (and girl) whom I almost immediately fell some way behind as I had my undergraduate head turned by the needy glamour of the student comedy scene. I did not show nearly enough respect to our tutor, the late great Mike Nicholson, a true legend of the game for both the depths of his knowledge and the guitar-wielding mischief of his drinks parties. Dr Nicholson had so much wisdom to share, so many stories about his friends the Solzhenitsyns and beyond, but he had to spend most of our tutorials wincing at me reading bet-hedging, word count-chasing essays that I'd Pro Plussed to completion mere minutes before I arrived at his office. In the summer of 2009, he sent me a stern email about my Prelims marks, but continued to patiently indulge the only marginal improvement in performance thereafter, before generously coming to watch my final comedy show in 2012, a comedy show in which he'd agreed to have one of his termly reports quoted on the poster. Alongside 'one of the best young comedians around' – *Time Out*, that poster read 'frustrating glimpses of wasted potential' – Dr Michael Nicolson, Praelector in Russian. One final toast to the great man: спасибо, извините, and за здоровье!

A few hours later, though, the insane ingratitude of my pre-gig pessimism had been blown apart by the Boss. The then-fifty-nine-year-old Bruce and his E Street Band delivered a three-hour rock odyssey, just a day after treating the treehuggers of the Pyramid to the same in Glastonbury's Saturday night headline slot. The high point of the Hyde Park gig, about midway through the set, was an extended version of 'Racing in the Street', from 1978's *Darkness on the Edge of Town*, a gorgeous piano ballad itself a hymn to Springsteen's own dissolute youth. Look up on YouTube the version we saw that day, I urge you, and give yourself over to all nine minutes of it, from Bruce's bruised verses to the magnificent and epic outro, pianist Roy 'The Professor' Bittan dancing gracefully and longingly around the song's central chords, seventy thousand shut-down strangers and hot-rod angels staring in wonder, with barely a phone in the air, as the sun sets over Hyde Park. Summer was here and the time was right, and Tom stood in raptures next to me throughout. A few years later he would use the expression 'stepping into the sound' to describe a night watching the (also quite extended-outro-prone) American rock band The War on Drugs, and this was my first time watching him take that step. 'We were so lucky to have seen "Racing in the Street"!', Tom raved to me again as we made our way out of the park. The song hadn't even been on the band's setlist: Bruce had pulled a sign out of the crowd requesting it. And at sunset too?! What sweet destiny for us to have witnessed!

In 2009, a week after being humiliated by Anne Robinson on *The Weakest Link*, I watched Springsteen in Hyde Park with Tom by my side. In 2023, a day after being humiliated by Romesh Ranganathan on *The Weakest Link*, I watched Springsteen in Hyde Park without Tom by my side. Some destinies are sweeter than others.

I hadn't been bold enough to think that I was going to win *The Weakest Link* the second time around. In 2009, I might have been a spotty virgin with a Thomas the Tank Engine duvet, but I was barely a year out of Eton, and its proclamations of world domination were still ringing in my ears. By 2023, I had spent a full adult decade watching Old Etonians making arses of themselves in British public life, and I was one of them. My general knowledge is severely lacking in pretty much every field other than music and football. I was almost certainly going to leave the studio with more egg on my face. But surely I could make it further than the third round this time?

Obviously I got knocked out in the third round again. Just perfect. What spectacular commitment to the bit from me, if by 'commitment to the bit', you mean: not being able to remember the words 'vertebrae' or 'Bermuda' and being correctly voted off as the mathematically Weakest Link. Romesh was rather gentler to his stand-up stablemate than Anne was to that quivering boy fourteen years yonder, but he was still unable to contain all of his contempt for my collapse. *Coronation Street* star and *I'm A Celebrity* . . . winner Helen Flanagan generously pulled focus by saying that the white cliffs of Dover were made of cheese, not chalk, but she sashayed off set with a smile regardless, her path back to the green room not so haunted by the footprints of her past as mine. And the next day there were more footprints waiting for me back in London.

As I walked down the Bayswater Road towards Hyde Park's Cumberland Gate that hot Thursday afternoon, Jess and Tom's parents already waiting for me on the other side of the fence, I thought anxiously about what the emotional ratios of the day would be: whether the whole thing would feel sad, or merely some of it, whether Bruce's battery of anthems would prove at least distracting or, to use the word that has dominated the last couple of years for us all, 'cathartic'. There was one song, however, that I knew would ruin me. I didn't know whether I even wanted 'Racing in the Street', whether the song should stay as a perfect memory of a golden moment with Tom, whether hearing it again, here, without him, would be its own avenue of pain. But it was an avenue I wasn't exactly trying to avoid: under my arm on the Bayswater Road was a sign, reading 'Racing in the Street – like 2009'.

Alas, the last decade and a half has seen not just a sharp decline in gig-going etiquette but also an even sharper incline in the inflation and segregation of attending said gigs at all. Tom and I might have been on the standard-entry price point as students in 2009, but so was nearly everybody else. Now, those standard-entry tickets were separated from Bruce by fifty metres' worth of Gold Circle VIPs. I couldn't begrudge those VIPs too much. How could I? My childhood was one long and lonely gold circle. It's just a bit of a shame at gigs. I was running late, of course, but Jess had got to Hyde Park as soon as gates opened, and back in the day, this might have given her a chance of getting to the barrier, of getting a hug or a high-five* from the Boss himself as he wandered into the crowd. And if I'd been on the barrier with her, I might have been able to give him my 'Racing in the Street' sign. Now, there was a metal fence and a whole self-satisfied stratum of society between Bruce and my sign. But it didn't matter. We still had a fantastic position at the gig. And it wasn't like I'd bought the tickets anyway. How could Tom have known, on release day a year earlier, the chilling context of why I'd want to be further

* If not the full Courtney Cox!

forward at the gig, while he watched the show from his own VIP tier: with us, without us, behind us, beyond us?

For better or worse, Bruce didn't play 'Racing in the Street' in 2023. (None of the cash-flashing Gold Circlers had evidently brought their own cardboard sign, or thought to make one out of some discarded Veuve Clicquot packaging, or a carefully rearranged charcuterie board.) But there were some real wallops elsewhere, of course. A rousing first hour of the gig, from 'No Surrender' to 'Working on the Highway', had delivered on the 'distraction' front, and buoyed by the tipsy, early-evening cheer of it all, I'd gone to the bar to get a round in. As I inched back through my fellow non-Gold-Circle losers towards Jess, John, and Kate, distracted momentarily by the search for their bobbing heads in the crowd,* I suddenly realised that Bruce was telling a story, a rather longer pre-song intro than one usually gets, at least until the encore. He is, of course, a master storyteller, in poetry and prose, so much deeper than the litany of American-dream clichés his work is sometimes sneeringly reduced to. And now, though he still might look and sound fantastic for a septuagenarian, the peppiest pensioner in the game, Bruce is a long way from his oldest stories, a real-life Hipstamatic filter coating the 1950s childhood he recounts as if it were last week. Bruce has famously lost some of his closest E Street bandmates: organist Danny Federici in 2008, and towering saxophonist Clarence Clemons in 2011, two years after Tom and I saw the Boss and the Big Man on stage

---

* This is no time for 'Ivo's festival-hacks' – a book I hope to publish separately in the future – but I received multiple compliments at this gig and others about the utility of my yellow 'Hearts of Oak' baseball cap, a beacon in the crowd for those looking for me or just using me as a meeting point.

292 YARDSTICKS FOR FAILURE

together in this very park. And now Bruce was remembering his first teenage band, the Castiles, and reflecting that George, his final remaining fellow Castile, had passed away recently. 'At fifteen it's all tomorrows, it's all hellos,' Bruce rasped. 'At seventy-three, it's a lot more goodbyes. Makes you realise how important living right now is.'

I had, to my shame, not listened much to the new Springsteen album, or clocked from even just its song titles – 'Last Man Standing', 'Ghosts', 'I'll See You in My Dreams' – that this was Bruce, more than ever, in his own grieving chapter. In Hyde Park, he let his grief for George and the Castiles hang in the air for a moment, and then played a pin-drop solo version of 'Last Man Standing'. Even the Gold Circle pricks knew to chomp their quails' eggs a bit more quietly to this one. I froze a metre or two behind Tom's wife and parents as they held each other and cried, bonded forever by a goodbye the horror of which I couldn't imagine, while Bruce called out to his friends somewhere round the river bend. It was a terrible time to be rocking up with four pints.

I did, eventually, get to share this moment with the group, when 'Last Man Standing' finished, and there was a brief second to join the huddle before Bruce blasted us into emotional outer space with 'Backstreets', a sort of inverse 'Racing in the Street' where the song this time *starts* with a minute of solo piano, a Roy Bittan special so beloved that one critic famously proclaimed it should be the prelude to the Iliad. Tom loved that quote. 'Backstreets' is so epic, and also, in its latter stages, so loud and pompous, where 'Last Man Standing' was hushed and desperate. 'HIIIII-ding on the backstreets!' Bruce sang, and we sang, over and over again, and there was that word again: 'catharsis'. This time last night, I'd been in Glasgow, discussing co-parenting with Helen Flanagan in a *Weakest Link* green room. Now, I was on Thunder Road, showing a little faith in the magic of the night, before an encore of 'Born to Run', and 'Glory Days', and 'Dancing in the Dark', songs so deliciously cheesy they could have been hewn out of the cliffs of Dover itself.

There was still one more quiz to come in 2023. And it was a big one.

At any point until my mid-twenties, my *Mastermind* subject would probably have been something as agonisingly predictable as the Arctic Monkeys, or Swindon Town 1993–present. The Ritz to the Rubble: the Premier League to the brink of oblivion. But since 2014, I'd been in the sidecar of one of the great dissertations, Philip Seymour Hoffman on stage and screen, and in 2022, that dissertation had lost its designated driver. When the *Mastermind* call came the following year, there was only one thing I could choose.

However obvious many of this book's reflections on loss and legacy may be to those who have experienced something like this in their own lives, I hope that the various things Tom's friends and family have done together in the last couple of years – watching his favourite bands, watching his favourite films, cycling the country-long odyssey he'd planned to do himself – might provide food for thought for those holding onto their own friends round the river bend. Their ghosts moving through the night, their spirits filled with light. Admittedly, going on *Mastermind* with your dead friend's favourite dead actor as your specialist subject is quite a specific form of catharsis to seek, but of all the various professional environments I have stumbled into over the last two years, this was now the most important. This was the yardstick on which I was most desperate not to fail.

Mastermind wasn't just the biggest quiz of my life because of the great man, the two great men, I was doing it for. I mean, that was the main reason, plus the appearance fee (unaffected by whether I won or lost) split between the MS Society and addiction rehabilitation charity The Forward Trust, a Hoffman-adjacent cause I thought Tom would approve of. But even if representing Tom and Phil was the main motivation, this was also the quiz I had the best chance of winning. Only half of the questions would be at the mercy of my dismally unreliable general knowledge, and the other half on a specific topic I had been steered masterfully through by one of the most dedicated historians of his generation.

Tom's undergrad years had racked up just as many pints, punts and pensive 2ams of the soul as mine had, but he had always got his work done: a first in his undergrad, a first in his master's, and then, in the thirty-third and final year of his life, a new part-time postgrad in Cambridge, lending more of his wild and questing brain to the collective pot of human knowledge. There was so much in that brain. He had devised the Hoffman Project. He had written up all the film reports. Had the pair of us been subjected, at any point during the Project, to an on-the-spot quiz, he would have wiped the floor with me. He was the true Mastermind, and it should have been him in that chair. And this was not an on-the-spot quiz, where at least, like my *Taskmaster* tasks or my mid-gig shop-pops, the lack of preparation time would add a vaguely sympathetic edge to proceedings, even if they didn't work out. Here I very much could prepare. And prepare I did. In 2009, I didn't revise for my university exams because I was heading off to a TV quiz show. In 2023, I headed off to a TV quiz show having done more revision than I ever had for a university exam. The producers said they'd never seen a contestant with so many flashcards.

The *Mastermind* recording was in November, and my revision was given plenty of help in the weeks leading up to it. I watched as many of the Hoffmans again as I could, although there were plenty I was glad not to bother with: I found it hard to believe that the *Mastermind* quizmasters would have put more effort into finding an English-language version of *Szuler* than Tom did back in the day. I was also getting sent flashcards in the post: I didn't have Tom preparing me for the quiz, but I had his team, led by Jess, inviting our friends to write their own quizzes on each film in turn and passing those quizzes on to me, getting the adrenaline pumping as the big day loomed. In October 2023, I went round for a 'revision dinner' with Jess, Will, and Penelope at Tom's parents' house, and when I arrived, there was a black swivel chair waiting on the front doorstep. Jess had driven the chair there from home. Has any *Mastermind* contestant ever been provided such priceless prop-based prep?

The recording was in Belfast, and I went out a day early, to do a tour show, my first ever in Northern Ireland, at a club called the Black Box. It was a solid outing for *Organised Fun*, even if I was rather blown off the stage by Belfast-born support act, Vittorio 'the guy' Angelone, and any post-show adventures in the Cathedral Quarter were curtailed by my desire to return to my revision at the Grand Central hotel. One pint of the black stuff at the Black Box, then back to crack on for the black chair.

I had been picked up from the airport that afternoon by a driver called Martin, who surprised me by congratulating me in advance on my quiz victory, a victory apparently sealed by nothing more than the divine providence of having got in his car. 'I drive loads of people to *Mastermind*,' Martin explained, 'and they all win.' He broke this news as if he expected me to throw my flashcards out of the window then and there, to pull a Prosecco out of my bag and pop it before we'd even arrived at the hotel. Instead, I made it rather joylessly clear that I didn't believe him, and that even if his 100 per cent passenger win record was somehow the case – was there anyone who could even verify this? – it was a pressure I didn't need on top of everything else.

I explained to Martin that I was a serial quiz show failure, the many trivia questions I have got wrong on television brought up by my father every Christmas. I wasn't going to win *Mastermind*, I just wanted to get all my Philip Seymour Hoffman questions right. I asked Martin what his specialist subject would be if he was on the show, and he answered with a speed that suggested I wasn't the first to ask: his subject would be Ford cars of the 1980s. I told him that there were two Fords on my flashcards – Cortina, the place Philip Seymour Hoffman goes skiing in *Scent of a Woman*, and Capri, the island he and Jude Law point their boat towards in *The Talented Mr. Ripley*. It would certainly be a nice touch from the universe if I got a point from a Ford the following afternoon. But, I reiterated as we pulled up at the Grand Central, I wasn't going to win, and he should stop saying that to people. Thank you, Martin, and goodbye.

Back at the hotel after my gig, I had left one large chunk of first-time viewing till the very eve of battle: *Synecdoche, New York*, the one film Tom and I had never watched together, that I'd never watched at all. The film we said we'd do last: the end built into the beginning. Tom and I had laughed about how mad it would be to hire a cinema for this film, to round off the Project by forcing our friends to join us for a night of bleak Charlie Kaufman meta-drama. It was much madder, and much sadder, to watch it alone in a hotel in Belfast, broadly enjoying it but only as much as one can enjoy a film in these very specific circumstances, weeping with grief while simultaneously noting down plot points for a quiz.

I was introduced to my fellow contestants in the hotel lounge the following morning: actor and comedian John Thomson doing *Star Wars*, sports presenter Mark Pougatch doing the Men's Ashes in the 21st century, and chef Poppy O'Toole doing the history of the potato. Spaceships, spin bowlers and spuds: solid topics one and all. Everyone was making an annoyingly good show of being relaxed about the quiz during lunch, so I tried to do the same, even though I knew in my heart that these people were my enemies and I had to destroy them. I was carrying the burden of a dead friend and a history of quiz fails and a Ford-obsessed chauffeur who'd never given a lift to a loser in his life. This simply could not mean as much to the others as it did to me. My flashcards were burning a hole in my pocket, but I played it as cool as I could during a debate about our favourite Tayto crisp flavours, even if I quietly worried that Poppy might be using the conversation as revision.

Back in the solitude of my dressing room, I paced manically back and forth as the final minutes ticked down. The show's Celebrity Coordinator Tori popped her head in and asked if I'd had a nice evening after my gig, whether I'd seen much of Belfast, either from the ground, or from the stunning vantage of the Grand Central's 23rd-floor Observatory, the tallest bar in Ireland, described online as 'The Home of Sky-High Sips'. I shut this chat down immediately, with the answer that I hadn't done any sky-high sipping because I was grieving and revising. Tori winced at that conversational stink bomb as sympathetically as she could, and swapped out for her colleague Georgia, who made a marginally deeper dent into my last revision window by commenting on the shirt I'd chosen to wear on the show: a Bruce Springsteen tee that Tom's dad John had bought for me in Hyde Park that summer. I had lost my mind over my *Taskmaster* outfits the year before, but wearing this shirt on *Mastermind* had been one of the easiest decisions of my life. Georgia told me that she and her dad had been to see Springsteen together that year, and we bonded over the Boss, as everyone should, and this was a much healthier and happier use of those final minutes than any more crazed cramming would have been. And then it was time. I checked my look in the mirror and headed downstairs.

Host Clive Myrie was waiting for us in the studio. He was still relatively fresh in his *Mastermind* hosting tenure, but an old hand already, calming us before the cameras started rolling with a more twinkly-eyed version of the gravitas he's been deploying in more serious journalism his whole professional life. I have spent many a night in watching Myrie's reporting from war zones on *Newsnight*, the sharpest perspective possible for one's own domestic problems. Alas, at this point I was impervious to any perspective whatsoever. In the middle of the dark, cavernous studio, there it was. The seat on which my fate would be sealed. Jess bringing her own chair to dinner had been a highlight of the whole preparation process, something I'd told so many people about already, but all the surrogate swivels in the world can't prepare you for the real thing.

After solid but only partially successful performances from John and Poppy on their specialist subjects, I went up third.

A decade of my life had been building to this moment. Ten years since I went to the cinema to watch *The Master*, nine years since Hoffman had died, one year since Tom had, all condensed into ninety seconds of questions about these films I had watched over and over again, with and without my friend. And yet, for all of that long, long run-up, I was absolutely delighted by how many of the answers were things I had written on my flashcards in the final few days. A detail about *The Big Lebowski* that my friend Jack had texted to me after we watched it at his house in Putney. A detail about *Synecdoche, New York* that I had noted down, snivelling, in the hotel the night before. And an island in *The Talented Mr. Ripley* that I had never thought about as much as I had in the last twenty-four hours, since a chat about Ford cars with an infuriatingly optimistic chauffeur. I got all nine of my Hoffman questions right. No passes. Maximum points for my friend. Cometh the hour, cometh the man.

This was, as I had repeatedly emphasised to anyone who would listen, all that mattered to me, to do well on Hoffman, the bit of the quiz that really meant something, and the bit I could control. Full marks on Phil and no seismic blunders on the rest and I'd travel back from Belfast a happy man. But now, of course, I was dreaming bigger. I was joint leader with Mark Pougatch, who had also got nine on his specialist subject, albeit having been asked one more question than me. That was an inquest for later. We were joint top at the halfway mark, and it was going to go right to the wire, after the additional pressure point of the 'light chat with Clive'. I'd revised Clive before the show too, and was pathetically keen to show my working, to reveal I knew he was a Man City fan, via a quip about ex-City and Swindon player Kevin Horlock, a quip that of course didn't make the final edit. The chat was very short, and mostly about stand-up comedy, and then it was time for general knowledge.

Astonishingly, those gods smiled on me too. A question about Twitter, the social media platform I had been wasting my life on for a decade. A question about *Home and Away*, my second favourite soap from my days living in Australia. A question about *Frozen*, my daughter's most-watched film, my furrowed brow relaxing for a second as I thought of telling her about this one day, before scrunching itself up again as the next question saw me tumbling back to my own homesick childhood. I know dismally little about any history other than my own, but in this most important of moments I was able to answer a very specific question about Norman castles, because I could still picture the drawings I had been made to do of them as an eight-year-old at boarding school in 1999. There are whole reams of psychotherapy about how the traumatic memories of childhood abandonment can be suppressed for half a lifetime, before bursting forth to destroy their suppressors anew in middle age. On this occasion, however, a deep-buried boarding school memory was excavated at the exact moment I needed it. A history question for my friend, who loved history and studied history and made history. Sometimes life is like the movies.

I didn't get all my questions right: I said 'Nevada' and 'the Treasury' when I should have said 'California' and 'Bank of England', and I made a very silly face after the latter. But there were no howlers, and I finished with twelve points, twenty-one in total. I was some way ahead of John and Poppy, and when Mark Pougatch, after a solid start in his own general knowledge round, got four wrong answers in a row, the mantelpiece of my mind creaked in anticipation. As Mark fumbled tricky questions about puffins and the Manneken Pis, questions I would have got wrong too if I had been asked them, my fist gripped ever tighter by my side. Minutes later, that fist was clenched around the *Mastermind* trophy.

The flight back to London was only a couple of hours after the recording's end, and any more cautious traveller would have been grabbing the glass gong and galloping to the gate. I, not that it needs reiterating, am not a cautious traveller. I *had* to celebrate in some way. It was at this point that mischievous producer Tori, now dealing with a rather more buoyant guest than the shoegazing swotter of the pre-show, absolutely nailed it when it came to capping my victory, closing another regret loop, and nailing one final Hoffman callback. 'We've probably got time to stop at the Grand Central,' she said, an impish grin on her face, and ten minutes later, we were drinking White Russians, like the Dude does in *The Big Lebowski*, my trophy glinting on the table as we gazed out over the Belfast night. No drink in my life has ever been as delicious as my White Russian with Tori at the home of sky-high sips. The plane could wait. The Dude abides.

Then it really was time to go to the airport, in a cab which, guttingly, was not driven by Martin, although I did make sure to chase his number down later that week so I could pass on that his record remained intact, and apologise for my lack of faith. My return driver had less interest in my afternoon's adventures, but he was subjected to quite a lot of second-hand recounting of them regardless. I had, the day before the quiz, added Jess, Tom's parents, and Will and Penelope to a WhatsApp group entitled 'Masterminds' (I have given more inventive names to WhatsApp groups in my life, but sometimes the first draft really is best). In an experience that was always so much bigger than me, it had been so fun, and ceremonial, to update the group on my day as it progressed, and now, as the Observatory Bar's generous ratios of vodka, Kahlúa and cream collided in my stomach with a lunch consisting mainly of Taytos, I slurred the results of the quiz ecstatically into my phone. It was such a joyous thing to tell the group. Doing this for them, and for Tom, had come to assume a quite ludicrous significance in my life. It was the proudest I've probably ever been of anything.

There are caveats to this conclusion, too, of course, that it was just a day, that it was just a quiz, that as a feat of personal exertion it hardly compares to the cycle ride the others would do seven months later, and that as a moment of communal emotion it can hardly be compared to those cyclists arriving in John O'Groats, or the day a fortnight after that, in July 2024, when we went to see Bruce Springsteen *again*. This time it was at Wembley Stadium. This time we were a group of eleven, with Jess, and John and Kate, and Tom's brother James, and Will, and Tom Lambert, and several other of the finest King's men. This time I hadn't brought my sign, but someone around the river bend had pulled some strings. About halfway through the gig, Bruce played 'Racing in the Street', and I stepped into the sound, and I cried like I have never cried in my life.

Even if *Mastermind* was just one day, just one quiz, it is the only place I can end this book, a moment of pure triumph in a life still spent wallowing too much in failure. I have a lot of work to do on that front, and this is not the last we've seen of the yardstick, but I am moving forwards, surer than ever of what matters in my life, and hungrier than ever to pursue it. I am so grateful to the many people in my life who have guided me so far, and to one man who has inspired so many of us in life and in death. Tom started, so we'll finish. We miss him so much, and I'm so proud to dedicate this book to him.

Tell your family and your friends you love them as much as possible. Make as many memories as you can. Your time starts now.

Acknowledgements

Thank you to my editor, Richard Roper, for first bringing the possibility of this book into life, and for constantly buoying my confidence with praise and *Peep Show* quotes amidst firm but entirely fair notes about my more unwieldy tangents.

Thank you to my publisher, Yvonne Jacob, who has smiled patiently and with only slightly gritted teeth through every missed deadline, and with whom I am going to play a triumphant game of boules when this is done. Thank you to Raiyah and everyone else at Headline who had to navigate every tiny thing I wanted to change at the eleventh hour.

Thank you to the friends I have lived and laughed and eaten leftovers with during the last few years, in spare rooms you might really have rather used for nurseries or storage. Thank you to Elsa, the most generous of hosts, for doing everything you could to help me concentrate on this book. Thank you to Amy for the edible treats you sent to cheer me whenever I ground to a halt. Thank you to Alex for doing so much work on everything else while I spent hours microtweaking these public stories about your private life. Thank you to Matt for the writing beret: I look like such a prick in it and I love it. Thank you to Jason, Samira and Ahlam in my local Caffè Nero, for keeping me topped up with oat lattes and stroopwaffels through the many antisocial hours I spent writing this book in the bunker. The last year has taken me to a couple of rather more picturesque writers' retreats, such as doing half the *Taskmaster* chapter looking out towards the Hebrides from a cottage on Mellon Udrigle, but the vast majority of this book has been written in the Caffè Nero bunker, and I can't wait to come in and show you the book and prove I was actually doing something.

Thank you to Matt Stronge and Holly Roper-Newman, for this book's cover photos, and for taking basically every other promotional photo of me since 2016, and being so patient in a decade of me bringing nothing to a shoot beyond three overshirts and a pout into the middle distance.

Thank you to William Andrews, who has made some exquisitely elegant posters out of these photos over the last few years, and has now been a saint of patience through approximately fifty micro-revisions of the fonts and colour schemes on this book's cover. I hope you like the final version! I love it!

Thank you to everyone at Off The Kerb, the best in the business, the agency that calls itself a family and actually knows what that means. In an office of warriors with whom I hope to forever bleed Kerb, even if it takes me three nudges to reply to every email, thank you most of all to Flo, who brought me into the fold nearly fifteen years ago, only three years older than me but so much more organised and grown-up since day one. You have never given me a single piece of advice that didn't come from a place of friendship before anything else, and I hope I am always sensible enough to listen to that advice, even if at some point the advice is to slow down.

I have the best family and the best friends I could possibly hope for. I hope I've made that clear enough in the book that I don't need to go over more of them here, although there were of course a few legends lost to the final edits, and a few forgotten details I'll probably end up begging to squeeze into the paperback. But I cannot finish without saying one more very direct thanks to my parents, my sister and my brother, for being the greatest team possible, 1990–present even in the boarding school years, and for being my rocks through so many of these recent adventures, the very, very good times and the very disappointing ones. Dad always says the key to life is having things to look forward to, and I am so lucky to have so much to look forward to with you all, and with my little girl, the sweetest and funniest six-year-old you could hope to meet, who, like her mother, has brought emotions into my life that I'd never experienced before she came into it.

Finally, I'd like to thank the Masterminds WhatsApp group: Jess, John, Kate, Will and Penelope, my closest portals to Tom. Thank you for blessing and encouraging and sub-editing this delicate dance around something so devastating. I do hope you feel it's done justice to our hero.

I hope that by the time this book is published in May 2025, there will be a page of my website dedicated to pictures and playlists of things referenced in the book. Please do visit ivograham.com to see if I've delivered on this promise! And why not use the website to sign up to my mailing list, where I send an email once every few months about my upcoming professional projects/anxieties?

I would also like to steer anyone so inclined towards reading about, or supporting, any of the following organisations, which I have donated to or fundraised for over the past year.

The Tom Leece Research Fund
The Adam Brace Award
The MS Society
The Forward Trust
The Rosie Jones Foundation
Youth Music
The Trussell Trust
The Harbour Project
All Our Relations
Medical Aid for Palestinians

Some of the above are referenced in this book, and all of them have been on my mind in various ways while I've been writing it. I am greedy and self-absorbed enough to pour tens of thousands of words into my life's minor clangers for my and (hopefully) your amusement, but I hope that I never lose the sense of perspective that comes from pausing to think about the work done by the above organisations, especially the latter. These are scary times. And as Bruce himself says: nobody wins unless everybody wins.

A good historian ought to cite as many sources as possible, and while I spent a lot of time consulting Tom's family and friends in writing this book, I thought it would be special to dedicate a page of it to the ultimate group portrait of the man: a mosaic of memory. I popped a *lengthy* message on various WhatsApp groups inviting people to send me a word they would associate with Tom, either a simple descriptor, or a portal to some shared reference or in-joke to those in the know. The one-word brief was almost universally enforced, apart from one hyphenated cocktail, and one cheekily elided four-letter catchphrase from *Starsky & Hutch* (2004), courtesy of a very intimidating and permanently capitalised man called DENNO. Collating this mosaic and having some of the contributions explained was such a moving experience: my favourite, not that this exercise needs one, was from our friend Ed Cripps, a velvet-voiced linguist and legend who hit both markers with 'maremoto': both a King's Road nightclub he once tumbled into with Tom, but also the Spanish word for 'tidal wave.' 'Appropriate for Tom's thunderous intelligence and curiosity,' Ed wrote, 'and the ripples of sadness we'll feel forever.'

Remembered   Considerate Joyful
Son Modest Clarence   Husband Meganacht
Palinurus Sebulba Warthog Kind Fundemic Gossip
Reverse Compassionate Hullabalooza Astute Indelible
Snacks Oysters Boogie Dependable Eccentric Raconteur
Lido Balustrade Tall Charismatic Brigadoon Swan Punt
Piña-colada Shoes Erudite Fun Irrepressible Determined
Pal Listening Brother Bard Philomath Lexham Catan
World Thoughtful Univ FoBag Friend Oysters Limbs
Loyal Learnèd Maremoto Pétain Playful Gleeful
Do-it Admired Victoria Clever Warm Catalyst
Binding Coat Sozztronix Magnetic Leggy
Muster Bees Suit Unique Humble
Betjeman Shirley Fairfax
Excitable Costume
Drole Impact
Loved

Though a few of the answers have been covered in the book, here, for those who wish to play along at home, are my *Mastermind* questions from November 2023. Answers available upon request (or just by searching on the internet, of course). The scores to beat are (clang!) 9/9 on Hoffman, and 12/14 on general knowledge. It's not a competition. Not anymore. But those are the scores to beat.

Specialist subject: the films of Philip Seymour Hoffman

1. In which film does Hoffman play an insecure sound recordist named Scotty who has unrequited feelings for an actor named Dirk Diggler, played by Mark Wahlberg?
2. In the biographical drama *Capote*, Hoffman's title character investigates the murder of a Kansas family with what surname?
3. In *The Talented Mr. Ripley*, when Hoffman's character Freddie takes over the tiller of his friend Dickie's boat, Dickie instructs him to just point her at which island (and avoid the rocks)?
4. In *The Savages*, Hoffman's character, the drama teacher Jon Savage, is working on a book about which German playwright?
5. In *Magnolia*, Hoffman plays the nurse Phil Parma, who tracks down his dying patient's estranged son, by responding to a magazine advert for a male empowerment programme called 'Seduce and . . .' what?
6. In *The Big Lebowski*, the millionaire Jeffrey Lebowski's personal assistant Brandt, played by Hoffman, proudly tells The Dude that his boss has been awarded the key to which city?
7. In *Almost Famous*, Hoffman plays the real-life music journalist Lester Bangs, who offers the aspiring writer William Miller $35 for one thousand words on which rock band?

8. In his final film *The Hunger Games: Mockingjay Part 2*, Hoffman plays a character whose first name is also the name of which writer and philosopher of Ancient Greece?

9. In *Synecdoche New York*, what is the title of the self-help book written by the psychologist Madeleine Gravis, which Hoffman's theatre character Caden Cotard buys from her for $45?

General knowledge

1. A common expression meaning 'to achieve two objectives at once' is 'to kill two birds with one...' what?

2. In July 2023, the social media app Twitter changed its brand name and logo to which letter of the alphabet?

3. Which building in London, designed by Renzo Piano, and inaugurated in 2012, stands more than 1000 feet tall and is noted for its jagged spire?

4. What is the full title of the chart-topping 1975 song by Queen that is sometimes abbreviated to 'BoRap'?

5. Yosemite National Park is in which US state?

6. What was the first name of the British artist shortlisted for the Turner Prize in 1988, who was the grandson of Sigmund Freud?

7. In 2023, which country won the men's Rugby World Cup for a record fourth time, beating New Zealand by a single point in the final?

8. What word for a mystery was the name given to the message encryption device resembling a typewriter invented by the German engineer Arthur Scherbius and widely used by the Nazis during the Second World War?

9. From 2004 to 2007 the *Thor* actor Chris Hemsworth played a character called Kim Hyde in which Australian television soap?

10. What is the common name of the medical condition seasonal allergic rhinitis, which often causes irritation of the nose and eyes during spring and summer?

11. The mixed-breed canine known as a 'schnoodle' is a cross between a poodle and what other dog?

12. What stage musical, which opened in the West End in 2021, is adapted from a 2013 Disney film about two sisters, one of whom has magical powers?

13. What financial institution was created by an Act of Parliament in 1694, initially to raise funds for an ongoing war with France?

14. The style of castle constructed in Europe from the 10th century, consisting of a keep on top of a mound of earth, and surrounded by wooden palisades and ditches, became known as a 'motte and . . .' what?

the END Bye!